CINEMA AND SOCIETY

Its Influence and Importance in Different Spheres of Human Life

CINEMA AND SOCIETY

Its Influence and Importance in Different Spheres of Human Life

Editor

DR. DAYA NAND GAUTAM
Associate Professor
Government College, Kullu (H.P.)

Foreword by

PROF. BALWANT KUMAR
Retd. College Principal

REGAL PUBLICATIONS
New Delhi

CINEMA AND SOCIETY
Its Influence and Importance in Different Spheres of Human Life

ISBN 978-81-8484-533-4

Typeset by
RAHUL COMPOSERS
New Highway Apartments, Lakshmi Niwas
760, Pocket-D, Lok Nayak Puram, New Delhi - 110 041

Printed in India at
MAYUR ENTERPRISES
WZ Plot No. 3, Gujjar Market, Tihar Village, New Delhi - 110 018

Published by
REGAL PUBLICATIONS
F-159, Rajouri Garden, New Delhi - 110 027
Phone : 45546396, 25435369
E-mail : regalbookspub@yahoo.com, regaldeepbooks@yahoo.com

Dedicated to

DADA SAHEB FALKE

The Pioneer of Hindi Cinema

Contents

Foreword

Godard's idea—"Camera is not a technical question, but a moral one", aptly explains the Indian context of cinematic evolution. If developed countries produce developed cinema, the obvious corollary is not that an undeveloped country should produce undeveloped cinema. A developing one, like India, however is experimenting with various shades of development, both socially and cinematically. This nation has seen a dramatic shift in its social matrix since the 1990s, especially in the segment called the "Middle Class". It is, willy nilly, the middle class that directs the cinema it watches. Not only do a large number of film-makers emerge out of this undefined ocean, they know who they must sell to. The economic liberalization of the last twenty-five odd years and its impact on the lifestyle, imagination and fantasy of the expanding corpus of the middle class has influenced cinema and cinema in turn has constructed new realms of reality for its feeding audience. This relationship of give and take between the masses and their films is increasingly evident in contemporary Bollywood productions.

When we go to watch a film, we do not watch with objective distance. Aristotelian mimesis, in our cinema, however does not function at the plane of projection of reality; it functions at a more ideational plane. What we see projected on the screen, is another reality, that of our fantasies and dreams. What gets labeled as "tasteful" is determined by the economically dominant class, in this case, the great Indian middle class. According to Pierre Bourdieu, taste is part of a struggle for social recognition or status, in which lifestyle plays a key part, emphasizing cultural consumption rather than production. As a result, the aesthetic of the bourgeois sensibility acquires the status of cultural capital.

The Indian middle class, which is the primary producer and consumer of culture, contests the middle (centre) of the new Indian aesthetic and life. "Taste" of the old school middle class that centered on "art" and "parallel" cinema occupied itself with the interpretation of realism devoid of frills. Interest in cinema witnessed a surge in the 1990s with a flush of romance, music, consumeristic dreams of prosperity, and revised strategies of marketing culminating in the sanctum of the multiplex. The audience returned to the hall each Friday with a happier pocket, a more romantic dream of life, a more flexible moral kerchief and, maybe, somewhere, some remnants of nostalgia for pastoral value systems that were increasingly becoming subjects of the past. Films increasingly depicted middle class life, avoiding lower middle class realities and found eager appreciation. The lifestyle being shown and seen on screen appealed to those who had already acquired it as much as it did to those who wished to acquire it. Ashish Nandy, in his, *The Secret Politics of our Desires: innocence, culpability and popular cinema,* says,

> An average, 'normal', Bombay film has to be, to the extent possible, everything to everyone. It has to cut across the myriad ethnicities and lifestyles of India and even of the world that impinges on India. The popular film is low-brow, modernizing India in all its complexity, sophistry, naiveté and vulgarity. Studying popular film is studying Indian modernity at its rawest, its crudities laid bare by the fate of traditions in contemporary life and arts. Above all, it is studying caricatures of ourselves ... The popular cinema may be what the middle class, left to itself, might have done to itself and to India, but it is also the disowned self of modern India returning in a fantastic or monstrous form to haunt modern India.

Contemporary Bollywood cinema often comes across as escapist. But then, is not all art escapist at some level or the other? Art allows us to escape into another realm and its success lies in doing that. What differentiates one piece of art from another is the domain it allows us to escape into and the domain it offers escape from. An understanding of the dynamics of this escape offers deeper insight into personal, social and cultural realities of those who participate in it, in whatever capacity.

Our cinema today is a mirror to our economic, personal and romantic fantasies. It is a projection of the collective fantasy of a race that is moving, believing that its movement is in the only desirable direction-forward. That most films are now shot in locales outside India, are set in foreign lands, or at least have characters who simulate the Non-Resident Indian way of life, dress and language, is a manifestation of the collective dream of social and economic mobility promised by geographic mobility. This dream of mobility is reflective of the desire to move out of the present condition, irrespective of what it is. The multiplex audience has managed to reach the multiplex. Cinema takes it beyond.

A pleasant feature of new-age Bollywood cinema is its sporadic yet consistent production of crossover films like *Bhag Milkha Bhag*, *Omkara* or *Haider*. That films like *The Ship of Theseus* and *Lunch Box* found distributers as well as audience is a happy sign. If non-commercial cinema finds commercial success, we have reason to hold our heads high, for it is a symptom of the audience being educated and refined in its taste, in addition to being a part of the socio-economic boom that runs the risk of being looked down upon by the cultural elite.

Cinema has not only become a manifestation of our latent dreams, it has also become the architect of our fantasies. When something gains in importance, it is bound to attract aggressive critical engagement. So, in a technology driven age, when cinema threatens to replace traditional agencies of moral training, it is but natural that the Pandits will sit up and analyze its impact, warn us of disaster, or sing odes to its glory. It may well be worth the effort to participate in this discourse, to understand in the least, a phenomenon that is here to stay and one that we are willing participants of.

PROF. BALWANT KUMAR

Preface

The book aims to highlight the importance of cinema in human life. With the advent of advanced and sophisticated technology in the domain of mass communication the human life has become more and more dependent on and is being influenced by these technologies. The widespread diffusion of information technology has virtually led to the emergence of the concept of time space compression making this rainbow world only a global village. Cinema, as a technology of social transformation, is comparatively a new invention in the arena of information technology. The relevance of cinema as a tool towards socio-economic and political transformation of society has received global acknowledgement and recognition.

Cinema has not only offered a varied and viable alternative of livelihood and employment to millions of people around the world but has equally inspired and motivated a range of social issues including socio-economic reforms, national integration and a sense of universalism. The cinema has figured prominently in the public domain as a potent means of influence. It not only reflects the contemporary societal set-up but prompts a social change as well. Apart from soaring the people to the flights of imagination, the movies have added to the share of their happiness and have triggered the social responsibility. Many great movies and their respective legendary artists have left indomitable and ever-lasting impacts on the hearts and minds of people on the earth. Cinema has worked as a catalyst to imbibe in a spirit of rational and scientific thinking in billions of hearts and thus facilitated to structure a society with dynamic and progressive reasoning.

Similarly, the Indian cinema not only provides one of the largest markets to young and dynamic artists but is equally impressive in its socio-economic and political transformation of the society. India has the most numbers of young people in the world and cinema provides an additional source of livelihood to the aspiring youths of the nation.

The cinema candidly expresses its social role by addressing issues concerning mankind. Hindi films' subject matter and treatment have constantly evolved, reflecting changes in social and political concerns. Movies like *Mother India, Bandit Queen, Paan Singh Tomar, Udaan, Pinjar, Taare Zamin Par, Three Idiots* and many-many more left an indelible mark in the mind of people. Though, India has to measure miles more to achieve global standard in quality film making and artist building.

The book is basically an attempt to underpin the relevance of cinema in different spheres of human life. The book has vividly brought out the genesis and development of India cinema and the important role being played by a number of artists in their respective time-period. Focus has been given to the themes and technology being applied with the passage of time. The dominant role played by some of the eminent artists in transforming social values has been primarily discussed.

In nutshell, the book is an attempt to carry forward an interdisciplinary approach towards analyzing the positive and negative impacts of cinema in socio-economic and political life of the people.

DR. DAYA NAND GAUTAM

List of Contributors

Abhiyudita Gautam, Assistant Professor, Department of English, Government College, Jukhala, District Bilaspur (H.P.).

Anil Gautam, Associate Professor, Department of Chemistry, Government College Sujanpur Tihra, Hamirpur (H.P.).

Anil Kumar, Associate Professor, English, Government College, Naura, Distt. Kangra (H.P.).

Anita Rathour, Associate Professor in Sociology Government, Collage, Theog, Distt. Shimla (H.P.).

Anju R. Chauhan, Associate Professor, Government College, Kullu (H.P.).

Arati Mishra, Faculty of Performing Arts, Banaras Hindu University, Varanasi (U.P.).

Arti Pandit Dhawan, Assistant Professor (Commerce), H.P.U.C.E.S., Shimla (H.P.).

Baljeet Jamwal, Associate Professor, Economics, Government College, Nadaun (H.P.).

Balkrishan Shivram, Associate Professor, Government College Saujauli, Shimla (H.P.).

Bandana Vaidya, Associate Professor, Department of English, Government College, Kullu (H.P.).

Baninder Rahi, Research Scholar, School of Communication Studies, Panjab University, Chandigarh.

Chetan Singh, Associate Professor in English, Government P.G. College, Mandi (H.P.).

Dipali S. Bhandari, NSCBM Government P.G. College, Hamirpur (H.P.).

Gaurav Sood, Research Scholar, Department of English and Cultural Studies, Panjab University (Chandigarh).

Himani Thakur, Research Scholar, Department of Hindi, Himachal Pradesh University, Shimla (H.P.).

Janesh Kapoor, Department of English, Government College, Shimla (H.P.).

Kamayani Bisht, Assistant Professor in English, Government Degree College, Shimla (H.P.).

Krishan Lal, Assistant Professor, Government College, Hamirpur (H.P.).

Kulbhushan Sharma, Assistant Professor, Department of English, Government College, Karsog, District Mandi (H.P.).

Leena Vaidya, Assistant Professor, English Department , Govt. College, Kullu (H.P.).

M. Rabindranath, Associate Professor, Dean, School of Journalism, Mass Communication and New Media, Central University of Himachal Pradesh (H.P.).

Man Singh Manral, Assistant Professor, JNU, Jaipur (Rajasthan).

Mandeep Sharma, Associate Professor, History, Government College, Kullu (H.P.).

Manoj Kumar, Assistant Professor, G.C. Karsog, Mandi (H.P.).

Neeraj Kapoor, Associate Professor, Department of English, Government College, Kullu, (H.P.).

Nirmla Singh, Assistant Professor in Pub. Adm., Government College, Kullu (H.P.).

Nishchal Sharma, Assistant Professor, Department of Computer Science, Government College, Kullu (H.P.).

Nitika, Asst. Professor, Geography, Government Degree College, Bhoranj, Tarkwari (H.P.).

Pankaj Dodh, Assistant Professor in Political Science, National Defence Academy, Khadakwasla, Pune (Maharashtra).

Pooja Mishra, M.A., Indira Kala Sangeet Vishvavidyalaya, Khairagarh (C.G.).

Priyanka Thakur, Assistant Professor, Government Degree College, Kullu (H.P.).

Raj K. Kanwar, Centre of Excellence, Government College, Sanjauli, Shimla (H.P.).

Rajesh Kumar Singh, Associate Professor in Political Science, Government Degree College, Haripur, Manali (H.P.).

Rajneesh Kumar Sharma, Assistant Professor in Commerce, Government College, Hamirpur (H.P.).

Ramesh Kumar Rawat, HOD-Department of Journalism and Mass Communication, Manipal University, Jaipur (Rajasthan).

Ravinder Chauhan, Associate Professor in Sociology, Centre of Excellence, Government College, Sanjauli, Shimla (H.P.).

Ravindra Katyayn, Assistant Professor in Hindi, Maniben Nanavati Women's College, Mumbai (Maharashtra).

Sandeep Singh Raghav, Government College, Jukhala, Bilaspur (H.P.).

Sangeeta Singh, Assistant Professor, Government College, Hamirpur, (H.P.).

Sheetal Thakur, Assistant Professor, Government College, Bassa, Mandi (H.P.).

Shefali, Associate Professor, Department of English, Government College, Kullu (H.P.).

Sonia Hooda, Assistant Professor, DAV Centenary College, Faridabad (Haryana).

Sudesh Jamwal, Assistant Professor, Political Science Government College, Hamirpur (H.P.).

Sudhir Soni, Associate Professor, BBD Government College, Chimanpura, Jaipur (Rajasthan).

Sujay Kapil, Research Scholar, School of Journalism, Mass Communication and New Media, Central University of Himachal Pradesh (H.P.).

Sutinder Dohroo, Associate Professor, Department of English, P.S.R.G.C., Baijnath (H.P.).

Vijay Thakur, Associate Professor, Government College, Barsar, Distt. Hamirpur (H.P.).

Cinema and Society 1

ANIL KUMAR

Cinema is hundred years old today. The journey of Indian cinema began with the release of Dada Saheb Phalke's *"Raja Harishchandra"* on May 3, 1913 released as a four reel film and it was 3700 feet long. Then many film-making units came into existence, amongst them were Madan's Elphin Stone Bioscope in Calcutta, Maharashtra Film company in Kolapur and Natraja Mudaliao in Madras, etc. Throughout history, cinema has been a powerful force in Indian society's cultural and national life. Cinema has played a major role in changing our society. Patriotic films remind society remember to love our country. Good comic movies have treated many sick people through laugh therapy. In Indian society there are many traditions and practices which are based on ignorance and which have stopped the progress of our society and have done a lot of harm to our society. Cinema can also done lot of work or help to eradicate those evils which are eating our society.

Cinema can be used for promoting national integration, prohibition, inter-castes marriages, family planning, eradication of illiteracy, etc. Such themes can help the transformation of our Indian society. Cinema can be utilized as an instrument to help people get rid of social evils and also guide them to go on to the right path in our society.

It helps us to remove ignorance. Not only this, several much needed reforms can be introduced and brought about with the help of cinema. The period from 1940s to the 1960s is regarded as a golden period in Indian film industry. Some of the most important and acclaimed Hindi films were *'Pyaasa'* by Guru Dutt (1957), *'Kaagaz ke Phool'* (1959), and Raj Kapoor films *'Awaara'* (1951), and *'Shree 420'* (1955). These movies had a great effect and impact on Indian society. These films expressed social themes especially dealing with working-class urban life in India. *'Awaara'* presented the city as a dream for a youngman while *'Pyaasa'* highlights the unreality of city life. Some of the famous epic movies of Hindi cinema at that time had a great impression on the mind of society. Mehboob Khan's *'Mother India'* (1957) was nominated for the Academy Award in the best foreign language film category.

Cinema employs people from all parts of India. It attracts thousands of aspiring young actors and actresses, all hoping for a break in the Industry. Models, beauty contestants, television actors, theatre actors and even ordinary common man of society come to Mumbai with the hope and dream of becoming a Star. Since many Indian films are shot abroad, many foreign extras are employed too. There are number of jobs available for writers and other journalistically minded communicators. Writers are creative by nature and the ideas they conceive and develop are bought to the screen by actors and directors who interpret the material they are given. No doubt that the creator and as the interpreters stand the vast mass of Bollywood workers, the technicians operate the complex machinery of cameras, sound equipment, editing, stage setting, consuming and other processes essential for making film. Many young people are today involved in making documentary films, producing productions about economic and social reforms. Furthermore, there are many opportunities to work on film production for a large company. Many corporations have employed people as their staff in their public relation department in charge of audio-visual materials and film works. Most of them are involved in the work of shooting of pictures for film production companies, which work with materials provided by the staff employed by the corporation public relation department.

Film industry has also opened the door of employment to society in the field of music. In the late 1960s and early 1970s, when the promoter films started, actors like Rajesh Khanna,

Dharmendra, Sanjeev Kumar and Shasi Kapoor and actresses like Mumtaz, Asha Parekh, Sharmila Tagore appeared on silver screen of our film industry. The demand for music also increased. The film Industry has given employment to composers of film music, known as music directors, young singers are earning a lot of money through films and have become professional play back singers. Many young girls and boys are becoming dancers and getting the job of playback dancers in the film industry. Many young artists used to make their living by hand-painting, movie billboards and posters. Releasing the film music, or music videos, before the actual release of the film is a business approach and it affects the society also because a popular tune is believed to help pull gatherings into the theatres. Furthermore advertisements of products through Bollywood can boost sale business and economy of country by star endorsement.

Cinema has a tremendous power to influence the thinking of society. It has changed the society and social trends. It is creating direct impact on our social life. Cinema can go a long way towards creating national consciousness. It can also help in utilizing the energy of young generation in social reconstruction and national building programme. It teaches us the lesson of good morals and social and educative themes in cinema can also guide and inspire public opinion by introducing popular sentiments. Due to audio-visual mass appeal cinema is a powerful source of publicity and advertisements. With the arrival of television entertainment, film Industry has improved its performance and maintain a high standard among people.

Even the regional films are playing very important role in our society. These films have become second name for our film industry. These films are very popular in the society because they are rich in subject and treatment. These movies are serving action, romance and drama to the public. These films of regional level have international value also. The international film fair festivals are also accepting their values for the international film festival which was held from 20 November to 30 November 2013, the films of Tamil language, Kashmiri Language, Kannad, Malayalam, Oriya and Bengali language made their entries. Some Punjabi films such as *'Carry on Jata'* and *'Jat and Juliyat'* have earned lot of money, name and fame for India. There is special appeal for Bhojpuri films in our society. Now the society is taking seriously these regional films. These films are not like remake of south films by Bombay film industry but they are actually liked by our society.

Cinema has become a powerful instrument for culture, education and propaganda. In a 1963 report for United Nations Educational Scientific and Cultural Organization, Mr. Baldoon Dhingra quoted a speech by Prime Minister Nehru, "the influence in India of films is greater than newspapers and books combined," Watching cinema has produced a very positive effect on mental health of society. Because visual stimulation can queue a range of emotions and the collective experience of these emotions through cinema provides a safe environment. On the other hand, cinema has emerged as a highly accessible social art form. Attending the cinema provides the guarantee for the exercise of personal performance and the human need for distinction. In short, we can say that cinema attendance may be both a personally expressive experience, good tonic of laughter and therapeutic at the same time.

Cinema has become most powerful form of mass media since the day it was introduced to the world. The dawn of Indian Cinema in the year of 1886, when Indian dramatists, photographers and musicians could foresee a tremendous strength in this medium and since that day there was no looking back for the Indian Cinema. The Indian film industry has attained a respectable place and position in the Global market. No doubt that Indian film industry is changing its style and trends according to the changing tastes and preferences of the society. The art of cinema has a special position and respect in the Indian society and Indian box office has always been energetic about their every production that is being released every Friday. The Indian people are great fans of their favourite actors/actresses and they also worship them. Cinema has become a religion with an increasing fan following. The fans blindly follow their favourites in their day-to-day lives. Nobody is ready to forget Amitabh Bachan, star known for his angry young man role. Indian society copy every style of life lived by Mithun Chakraborty, Anil Kapoor, Sharukh Khan, Ranbir Kapoor, Hemamalini, Jaya Bachchan, Rekha and Priyanka Chopra, etc.

Indian films are multi-million dollar productions, with the cost production up to 100 crores rupees. We should not forget that the latest science fiction film, Raone, was made with the 135 crores budget. The latest movie Krish-3 entered into the category club of 500 crores. Our producers are winning more and more funding for big-budget films shot within India as well, such as *'Lagan'* and *'Devdas'* and other recent films. People take deep interest in the ceremonies of 'Screen Awards', 'Stardust Awards,' 'The Global Indian film and Television Honours, "International Indian film Academy Awards', (iifa) and Zee Cine Awards, etc. Due to this Indian cinema is making progress and becoming popular among the other people of the world and Hollywood actors are working in our film industry and our actors are working in the movies of the West.

But we cannot ignore the other side of the coin, cinema has become a big source of some disadvantages. No doubt that cinema is a force to influence the society but some films depict scenes of moral degradation and such scenes violate our moral ethics. Many young people have gone astray under the misleading influence of pictures. Many pictures of moral degradation and crime catch the attention of young minds very easily. Many producers produce the movies full of spin show on the western trends which produce bad effect on our younger generation. The politics kills the potential of our best-made films to get international name and fame. Film Federation of India selects so called best films for Oscar Award and controversies over the selection of best film cease to erupt year after year. Unfortunately, only one film can be sent from our country, and hence the allegations and counter-allegations of favouritism, setting political Agenda, etc. So far only three Bollywood films have made it to the nominations stage of Oscar. Mehboob Khan's *'Mother India'*, (1957), Mira Nair's *'Salaam Bombay'* (1988), and Ashutosh Gowariker's *'Lagaan'* (2001). The reason behind this reality is very simple that the Indian films which are sent as official entries for the Oscar are of poor quality.

Indian banks and other financial institutions were forbidden from lending money for movie production. This ban has been lifted now. As the finances for films are not regulated, some funding is coming from other way, i.e. Mumbai underworld. They are using money and muscle power to get their entry in film Industry. This is not good for our, Indian Society. A notable film 'Chori Chori Chupke Chupke' was found to be funded by underworld mafia. It is necessary to protect our cinema because it plays a prominent role for our society. There should be a survival plan.

To recognise Indian Cinema as an art form in the constitution of India, it should be included in both state and central lists. Cinema should come under the purview of the Ministry of Culture and not under the Ministry of Information and Broadcasting. All restored films should be screened to bring about awareness of our film heritage. There is an urgent need to protect regional cinema and it should reach the public. The film federation of India should select a film that actually stands a chance of begging any reward. There should be not politics in the selection of nominations which should be free from crimes, violence and sex. Their aim should be to produce such films of high quality of art, entertainment and a message for social reforms in the society. Funding from Mafia must be controlled strictly and illegitimate sources must be totally banned.

No doubt cinema has played a major role in changing our society. It has become a religion to our society. Through cinema we come to know about different types of people, their customs and habits. Films make society worldwise and mentally smart. Good and educative films are a boon for society. Thus, cinema can serve as a tool of imparting education. Social films can help a great deal in bringing about social change. There is need to produce a film with message like 'Taare Zameen Par'. in short, we can say that if literature is a mirror of life, cinema certainly inherits the ability to mirror society and culture. Cinema is an attempt to showcase the reality and existence of a society on the silver screen. It also conveys a strong message to society that the universal religion is that which is the love for humanity and humanness and preaches that one must never fight or shed blood in the name of religion or community. There is no place for anti-social activities such as sexual, communal violence and terrorism. A good film may be higher than any education to society and a bad film can be more injurious than poison to society.

REFERENCES

Amar Ujala, Jalandhar, Tuesday, November 12, 2013. Emery, Edwin. The Introduction to Mass communications, The Film, p. 290, Eagle Wood Cliffts, N.J., Prentice Hall, 1962.

Danik Jagran, Dharamsala, Oct. 19, 2013.

Head, W. Sydney, Broad casting in America : A Survey of Television and Radio, Boston: Houghton Mifflin, 1956.

The Tribune, Jalandhar, Saturday, Sept. 28, 2013.

The Tribune, Jalandhar, Tuesday, November 12, 2013.

Indian Cinema: Past, Present and Future 2

VIJAY THAKUR

INTRODUCTION

The ancient aspiration of representing reality which was met by photography in 1839 led to the first commercial exhibition of film on April 14, 1894 at Edison's Kinetoscope peep-show parlor. The world completed 100 years of cinema in 1995, but as it was not till 1913, that the first film was produced in India. Celebrations are being held in India this year to commemorate the first centennial of this special and widespread medium of expression, now so easily accessible to all.

Cinema is mirror of the society and society is governed by cinema. Cinema can educate the society in a country like India which is mainly illiterate and lives by orthodoxy, superstition and tradition. The Indian cinema has changed through times and has always tried to cope with the changing reality.

THE OBJECTIVE

The objective of this study is to briefly trace the growth of Cinema in India over a period of a hundred years and the various influences that have contributed to this growth to enable it to emerge as the biggest film industry in the world.

METHODOLOGY

The study makes use of both primary and secondary data. Field work has been done by conducting structured interview's and personal observation to know the view's of people. Behavioural approach has also been used to know people's perception. Information gathered through primary sources have been analysed carefully.

THE ORIGIN OF THE EARLIEST FILMS

Hindi cinema produced in Bombay, now superficially well known as Bollywood is essentially a generic cinema that pervades India. The journey of Indian cinema started with the release of the Dadasaheb Phalke film *'Raja Harish Chandra'* on May 3, 1913. It was a four reel film, 3700 feet long, later advertised by him as "a performance with 57,000 photographs. A picture 2 miles long...." It was a silent film and by the 1930s, more than 200 films were made by the Hindi film industry every year. The themes of the film were mainly Mythological or Historical.

The oldest talkie or film with sound in India was *Alam Ara* directed by Ardeshir Irani. It was made in the year 1931 and was a huge success commercially. Musicals and talkies were in demand in the 1930s and 1940s. Bollywood and all the local cinema industries in India promptly shifted to making films with sound. Unfortunately, by 1950, very few films from this period survived. Most films, including Alam Ara were victims of fire or the extraction of precious silver used in film strips, as, after the films had made their money they were done away with.

The 1930s and 1940s were disturbed times in India because of the Second World War, the Great Economic Depression, and the communal riots during the partition of the country. Indian freedom struggle was going on and majority of Bollywood cinema was brazenly escapist. Nonetheless, many film producers managed difficult socio-economic problems and utilized the movement for freedom as the setting for their storylines.

In 1937, the oldest colour film in India was made. The name of the film was *Kisan Kanya* and it was in Hindi language. Nonetheless, colour films were not so popular till the end of

1950s. During that period, generous passionate musicals and comedies were the normal features at the cinema halls. Playback singing saw the rise of such legends as Mohammed Rafi, Mukesh and Lata Mangeshkar.

THE GOLDEN AGE

The era from the end of 1940s to the 1960s is considered as the "Golden Age" of Bollywood or Hindi cinema by film history writers. Some of the most significantly applauded Hindi films ever like *Kaagaz Ke Phool* (1959), *Pyaasa* by Guru Dutt films (1957), *Shree 420* (1955) and *Awaara* (1951) by Raj Kapoor films were made in this era.

Guru Dutt is considered as one of the most famous film directors in Asia ever, together with Satyajit Ray, the notable Bengali film director of India. *Pyaasa* was rated in the "All-Time" 100 best movies list of "Time" magazine. However, both *Kaagaz Ke Phool* (1959) and *Pyaasa* had the same rank (#160) in the 2002 Sight & Sound critics' and directors' poll of the most famous films ever made. Many other movies made in Hindi language from this period also made their places in this poll like *Baiju Bawra* by Vijay Bhatt (1952), *Awaara* by Raj Kapoor (1951), *Mother India* by Mehboob Khan (1957), and *Mughal-e-Azam* by K. Asif (1960). These movies were the symbols of social issues mostly associated with the metropolitan blue-collar life in the country.

Awaara showcased the city as both a dream and a nightmare. At the same time, *Pyaasa* assessed the pointlessness of urban lifestyle. Women mainly played decorative objects in Hindi cinema for a long time. They were portrayed as victims and martyrs or victimizers of other women. Rarely have films presented women as strong women who can raise their voice against injustice, who can rebel in their own way and make their own political statement.

Mother India is a strong political statement on a woman played by Nargis who can do anything to establish that justice has been done even while remaining within the framework of marriage and motherhood. *Mother India* won the nomination in the category of Best Foreign Language Film in the Academy Award. *Mughal-e-Azam* (1960) made by K. Asif and *Madhumati* (1958) which was authored by Ritwik Ghatak and directed by Bimal Roy. Other notable and well-admired conventional and commercial Hindi movie-makers during that period were Vijay Bhatt and Kamal Amrohi. The thriving actors of that period included names like Dilip Kumar, Dev Anand, Guru Dutt, Raj Kapoor and Rajender Kumar. At the same time, acclaimed actresses like Vyjayanthimala, Nargis, Nutan, Meena Kumari, Waheeda Rehman, Madhubala, and Mala Sinha dominated the silver screen. However, storyline in majority of the films were Hero-oriented and the heroine had to take a backseat.

The ordinary woman has hardly been visible in Hindi cinema. The sati-savitri image underwent a radical make-over probably with Nutan, who, without showing skin, made a powerful presentation in strong roles such as *Seema* and *Bandini*. Geeta Bali promoted the image of a mischievious tomboy. The actresses have often indirectly dictated the terms of these portrayals such as Meena Kumari as the tragedienne, Vyjayantimala as a very good dancer, Madhubala for her beauty, and so on. Waheeda Rehman was a powerful actress who blended her dancing beautifully with roles where she could rise above the decorative quality of the characters.

Films deeply influence the audience. Scenes of *'Shaheed Bhagat Singh'*, a film by Raj Kumar Santoshi and Manoj Goswami makes people national-minded and sentimentally involved in the film show. The film dialogues occupy places in our real life. Dialogues of *Mugle Azam* found place in the normal interaction of people for a long time. People talked and walked like Prithvi Raj, the great king Akbar. Similarly, *Devdas* by Sharat Chandra and *Sholay* left a deep impact on the masses.

THE RISE OF PARALLEL CINEMA

The era also witnessed the rise of a new Parallel Cinema, primarily spearheaded by Bengali films, it started gathering momentum in Bollywood as well. The oldest instances of Hindi cinema which were part of this campaign include *Do Bigha Zameen* (1953) made by Bimal Roy and *Neecha Nagar* (1946) made by Chetan Anand. The approval of *Neecha Nagar* by columnists and the commercial achievement of *Do Bigha Zameen* heralded the era of neo realism in Indian cinema. Some of the globally celebrated film-makers of Hindi film industry include names like Mrinal Sen, Mani Kaul, Govind Nihalani, Ketan Mehta, Vijaya Mehta and Shyam Benegal.

From the time when *Neecha Nagar*, the social pragmatist cinema achieved the Grand Prize at the inaugural Cannes Film Festival, Hindi movies regularly were in contention for the Palme d'Or at the Cannes Film Festival during the 1950s and beginning of 1960s.

THE MODERN ERA

During the end of 1960s and beginning of 1970s, action movies and love stories dominated the silver screen. The heroes of these films were Dharmendra, Rajesh Khanna, Shashi Kapoor, Jeetendra, Vinod Khanna, Shatrugan Sinha, and Sanjeev Kumar. There were actresses like Mumtaz, Sharmila Tagore and Asha Parekh. Sharmila Tagore, Asha Parekh and Sadhana defined a change in fashion and style more than change in characterization. They played stereotypical roles in mainstream Hindi cinema.

Jaya Bhaduri, Smita Patil and Shabana Azmi stripped glamour off the female lead's character and played roles that were as important as that of the hero. They were not commercially successful but did very good roles in whichever commercial film they acted in such films as *Kora Kagaz, Jawani Diwani, Guddi, Rampur Ka Laxman, Sholay* (Jaya Bachchan), or *Namak Halal, Arth and Shakti* (Smita Patil), *Karm, Arth* (Shabana Azmi).

In the middle of the 1970s, love stories got out of the path for rough, aggressive cinema on mobsters (Indian mafia) and robbers. Amitabh Bachchan, famous for his "angry young man" image, was at the top of this style with other heroes like Anil Kapoor and Mithun Chakraborty. This trend continued till the beginning of the 1990s. Famous actresses from this period included names like Jaya Bachchan, Hema Malini, Jaya Prada, and Rekha. With Rekha followed by Madhuri Dixit and Karisma Kapoor, the woman in Hindi films became louder in every sense—voice, articulation and delivery of dialogue, sexual aggressiveness and terms of character.

Mrinal Sen made *Bhuvan Shome*, a powerful satire in 1969. A number of Hindi movie directors like Shyam Benegal kept on making practical parallel films during the 1970s like *Ankur* 1974 and *Bhumika* 1977. Other prominent directors of this era are

Kumar Shahani, Mani Kaul, Govind Nihalani, Ketan Mehta, and Vijaya Mehta. A new concept of Hindi film named as the 'art film' was introduced. It faced disapproval and censure of the Film Finance Corporation at the time of a Committee on Public Undertakings probe which took place in 1976. The commission made allegations that the Film Finance Corporation was not taking sufficient measures to promote commercial films. As a result, the decade of the 1970s witnessed the emergence of commercial films that were box office successes like *Anand* (1971) which catapulted Rajesh Khanna to superstardom and *Sholay* (1975) by Ramesh Sippy, which helped Amitabh Bachchan carve his niche as an action hero.

There were spiritual films like *Jai Santoshi Ma* which was first screened in 1975 and became famous for its pious music. One more popular film in the 1970s was *Deewar* directed by Yash Chopra which was released in 1975. *Deewar* was a thriller and the story was founded on Haji Mastan, the real world gangster which was depicted by Amitabh Bachchan. *Salaam Bombay*, directed by Mira Nair, released in 1988, was the most globally applauded Hindi movie in the 1980s. It bagged the Camera d'Or award at the Cannes Film Festival held in 1988. The film also achieved the nomination for the Academy Award in the Best Foreign Language Film category.

Throughout the end of 1980s and the beginning of 1990s, the tendency went back to family dramas, love stories, and musicals with films grossing huge revenues like *Maine PyarKiya* (1989), *Qayamat Se Qayamat Tak* (1988), *Dilwale Dulhania Le Jayenge* (1995), and *Hum Aapke Hain Kaun* (1994). This gave rise to a new generation of stars like Salman Khan, Aamir Khan, and Shahrukh Khan and actresses like Madhuri Dixit, Sridevi, Kajol, and Juhi Chawla. During this era, melodramatic films and action films were commercially successful and stars like Govinda and Akshay Kumar and actresses like Karishma Kapoor and Raveena Tandon played roles in a number of melodramas. Movies like *Babul* raising topic of widow-remarriage or those like *Kabhi Khushi Kabhi Gham* reasserting Indian customs of respect for parents' views tend to make us wonder if movies are merely about entertainment.

In addition, the 1990s saw the debut of a series of new actors in both mainstream films and art films. Some of these films were successful in terms of revenue. The most prominent instance of these films was *Satya* which was released in 1998. The story was written by Anurag Kashyap and the director of the film was Ram Gopal Varma. Satya was decisively successful in terms of box office and resulted in the surfacing of a different variety of films that are collectively called as Mumbai noir. These films acted as a mirror of the city life and the socio-economic issues that affected Mumbai. By the late 1990s, there was a renaissance of parallel cinema. These cinemas frequently used actors like Manoj Bajpai, Tabu, Manisha Koirala, Nana Patekar, and Urmila Matondkar.

THE 21ST CENTURY

The 2000s witnessed a prolific rise in the fame of Bollywood among all the film industries across the globe and it is still there. This helped the Hindi film industry reach new pinnacle in terms of motion picture photography, ground-breaking plots and technological progresses in domains like computer graphics and special effects. Some of the biggest cinema production houses like Dharma Productions and Yash Raj Films were the financiers of neo noir Hindi movies. A new generation of actors like Abhishek Bachchan, Hrithik Roshan, Preity Zinta, Rani Mukherjee, Aishwarya Rai, Priyanka Chopra, Rani Mukherjee, Kajol, Kareena Kapoor, and Vidya Balan ruled the 2000s and some of them still have a strong screen presence carrying forward the legacy of emancipation of women in a much more aggressive way Actresses like Vidya Balan, Tabu have struck a balance between glamour and convention helped by their looks and the image they present.

In the mainstream cinema category, *Lagaan* achieved the nomination for the Best Foreign Language Film at the 74th Academy Awards and also won the Audience Award at the Locarno International Film Festival. At the same time, *Rang De Basanti* and *Devdas* both achieved nominations for the BAFTA (British Academy of Film and Television Arts) Award in the Best Foreign Language Film category *Rang De Basanti* brought light to the hushed topic of MIG crashes which was kept under wraps by political wings. It was only after the movie that public started demanding accountability. There are many medium budget movies, particularly from the new age directors like Madhur

Bhandarkar and Prakash Mehra that induce us to question lives around us. These movies inspire us to consider the social institutions and develop knowledge about the rights and duties of people about which awareness could not be generated even by government initiatives. Some films such as *Corporate, Gulaal* and *Rann* even bring light to several social and political problems and act as instruments for public opinion.

THE FUTURE

The industry is currently focusing on making films that attract all tiers of the audience. This would also help in maximizing box office revenues. There is a thought of broadly categorizing the films into cinema that is popular among the countryside people and cinema that suits the metropolitan psyche.

The newest trend in Bollywood involves bold experimentation in the story line dealing with day to day lives of common man. Therefore, you can realize the extent to which Bollywood impacts your life when your child decides against doing engineering after they watch the movie *3-Idiots*. Films taking up unusual themes like Black by Sanjay Leela Bhansali and *Pa* have been critically acclaimed. Films based on lives of forgotten heros like *Chak De India* and *Paan Singh Tomar* have also achieved great success. Children's films like *Makdee* and *Stanley Ka Dabba* have made their presence felt.

The woman is stronger, almost equal to a man in current films such as *Dhoom, Dhoom II, Shaurya, Aitraaz* where there is almost no difference between the heroine and the vamp because all the female stars are willing to step into negative roles if they are strong and can make a lasting impression on the audience Thus, the portrayal of the woman is greatly distanced from the Indian woman on the street, urban or rural, educated or not educated, working or non-working and so on. Ethical values have changed to a large extent too because premarital sex, adultery, sexual overtures where the woman takes the initiative are quite common and have also got audience's acceptance. Otherwise films like *Astitva* and *Gangster* and *Jism* and actresses like Bipasha Basu and Kangna Ranaut would never have clicked the way they have.The stereoscopic era of motion pictures began in the late 1890s when British film pioneer William Friese-Greene filed a patent for a 3D movie process. In his patent, two films were projected side by side on screen. The viewer looked through a stereoscope to converge the two images. Because of the obtrusive mechanics behind this method, theatrical use was not practical. Animation films, whether 2D or 3D animation caters to the interest of all age groups. The first animation picture *The Banyan Deer* in 1957 was followed by *Ek, Anek aur Ekta* in 1974, a documentary film based on the values of unity. Because of the superior technology available today outstanding Animation films and 3D films have flooded the international market with unprecedented popularity. Indian cinema too is following suit and plans to convert popular classics like *Mughal e azam* and *Sholay* to the 3D format. Another off shoot of the technological advance is films like *Ra One* and the *Krissh* series where amazing stunts of the Super heroes based on the hugely popular Hollywood film Superman are depicted to the delight of the younger audience.

CONCLUSION

Cinema is an art form which can entertain and educate as well. Its utility is great in India as a big portion of its population is illiterate. Producers and financers consider it as a tempting and lucrative business. For actors and actresses, it is a means to earn money and popularity. The director, story-writer, song-writer and cinematographer take it as an art work. To some, it is an audio-visual translation of literature and has its own message.

The question confronting us today is not any longer whether the man in the street can grasp the message but how to employ the communications media so as to let him have the full impact of the message.

The cinema, having the power of contributing to the cultural and human growth of the individual, can oppress freedom when it distorts the truth and presents itself as the mirror of negative types of behavior, using scenes of violence and sex tending to excite violent emotions to stimulate the attention of the viewer. Eve-teasing, physical assault and many other crimes are depicted glamorously which encourages the viewers to commit such crimes and leads to an increase in violence against women. It is not in accordance with the most authentic and deep demands and expectations of the human beings to produce films which are devoid of content and which are aimed exclusively at entertainment, or have the sole motive of increasing the size of the audience.

The urgency of such a problem in our society needs to be addressed by those who are responsible for the industry—so that they may commit themselves to working with professionalism and responsibility—as well as to the viewers—so that they may know how to react in a critical way in the face of the ever more demanding proposals offered by the world of cinema.

References

Tejaswini Ganti (2004), Bollywood: A Guidebook to Popular Hindi Cinema Routledge Publications.

Rajiv Vijayakar (2009), The History of Indian Film MUSIC, Time group books.

Ram Avtar Agnihotri (1990), Social and Political Study of Modern Hindi Cinema: Past, Present and Future Perspectives. Commonwealth Publishers.

Bhaichand Patel (2012), Bollywood's Top 20: Superstars of Indian Cinema, Penguin Books India Pvt. Ltd.

Film and Television Institute of India (FTII), Pune Center for Research in art of Film and Television (CRAFT), Delhi.

Role and Responsibility of Cinema Towards Society 3

MAN SINGH MANRAL

Since its beginning with the film 'Raja Harish Chandra' (1913), the cinema has remained the most powerful media for mass communication in India. Cinema has the ability to combine entertainment with communication of ideas. It has the potential appeal for its audience. It certainly leaves other media far behind in making such an appeal. Cinema presents an image of the society in which it is born and the hopes, aspirations, frustration and contradictions present in any given social order. Cinema has a great responsibility to give proper direction to the society. Unfortunately, in recent years it has deviated from its social obligation. It is causing great harm to social responsibility. The need of the hour is that it should be exploited as a powerful tool to educate, inform and aware the masses apart from entertaining them.

The first two decades saw the making of black and white mute pictures in which there were no dialogues—the actors communicated through gestures and actions—and the audiences were entertained by the antics of actors and actresses. The period of black and white movies continued well into the 20th century, but the beginning of films with dialogues—in which the actors properly and effectively communicated with one another was made with 'Alam Ara' in the year 1914. With the advancement of technology came the coloured movies with vast improvements in sound, stunts and outdoor shooting. All along this journey, cinema remained an integral part of Indian society.

Cinema has been the biggest source of entertainment for people in the entire length and breadth of the country. All sections of society—rich or poor, young or old, literate or illiterate—are crazy about watching movies. For poor sections of society, cinema is the only source of entertainment. The poor people have no access to other sources of entertainment except watching a movie. They cannot go to a hill station to enjoy some days away from work; they cannot go on sight-seeing to other cities-forget other countries; they cannot go on a long drive, on a bike or a car, or for dinner in an expansive hotel. These entire ventures are beyond them. People remember and repeat the dialogues of their favorite actors, and hum the tunes of the songs they like, long after watching a particular movie. Rich or poor, in terms of entertainment, movies are matchless for everybody.

Cinema plays a very important role in society. As we all know, the country is a melting pot of different regions, religious faiths, communities, castes and creeds. People speaking different languages and following different customs and traditions are all fond of Hindi movies. There are movies in other languages which are watched by people knowing and speaking those languages, like Punjabi, Marathi, Gujarati, Assamese, Tamil, Kannada and Malayalam. But people prefer Hindi movies. In this way, cinema binds the people of different regions and communities together. They serve the most important cause of national integration.

As a matter of fact our Mumbai filmdom called Bollywood is a unique example of secularism. Actors, singers, music directors, composers, producers, directors and other artists hailing from different parts of India work together while making a movie. As a matter of fact, Bollywood is like a mini secular India where people of different faiths live together and work together to achieve excellence in cinema. They regard one another for their act. Indian cinema not only plays a significant role in integrating society but also imparts human values on people such as honesty, hard work, sympathy, charity, brotherhood. Almost all movies have stories in which goodness is rewarded and wickedness is punished...

The hero is an incarnation of good qualities. He is respectful towards elders, adores his parents, helps others, stays away from drinking and gambling and is strong enough to beat a gang of bad guys. It is the hero who is admired by everybody and loved by the beautiful heroine.

There is justice and hope in every story in Indian cinema. This has great influence on people especially the young boys who want to become like heroes. There are films on religious themes like Samporna Ramayan, Jai Santoshi Ma, Shiv Shakti, Nanak Nam Jahaz, and Veer Hanuman which touch the religious sentiments of people and give the message of truth and religious faith. Society owes a lot to cinema for inculcating such feelings among the people.

Every Hindi movie has on an average six to ten songs sung by versatile male or female singers. The lyrics of these songs are written by well-established poets and lyricists. Famous music directors prepare tunes and background music of these songs. Band of expert instrumentalists play different instruments like sitar, tabla, bango, harmonium, flute, etc. as per requirement of the song before the song is finalised. These songs become very popular among people. They like to listen to these songs again and again on radio, TV, CD player, etc. Millions of cassettes/CDs are sold every month. Cinema, thus, is rendering a great service to the cause of music. India has a great tradition of classical, folk and popular music. All these types of music are promoted by films. Cinema, therefore, serves our tradition of music.

Film-making is an art. In this sense, cinema encourages various arts-acting, singing, dialogue-writing, story-writing, directing, lyrics-writing, composing and music directing. Bollywood is an industry and film-making is a business. Cinema provides employment to millions of people across the country. Apart from the actors, actresses, story-writers, lyricists, singers, musicians, there are distributors, CD-making companies, recording companies, instrument-makers, cinema-houses and their staff, shopkeepers selling CDs, etc. designers of dresses, dress-makers, cameramen and several others related directly or indirectly with film-making who earn their livelihood through cinemas.

Cinema is the true reflector of the society we live in. What does Cinema stand for? Well, in my language, cinema is something that stands for humanism, ideas, tolerance, for reason, for progress, for adventures and sometimes also for the search of communal truth and reflects social aspects. Since time immemorial, cinema has been acting as the mirror of our society and tends to simulate the incidents that take place in our lives. Indian Cinema has always been a pure source of recreation. Not just entertainment, but it also create awareness, educate people and enthrals millions of lives throughout the Country. It has been successful in bringing out many hidden aspects of the society and many social prospects too.

An era with which we can relate modern cinema seems to have flourished in the 70s, starting with providing complete entertainment to the masses. Though directors like Shyam Benegal, Govind Nihilani and others kept the flame of art cinema alive, the commercial cinema surpassed the artistic cinema by leaps and bounds. Now the times are changing and hence the trends when it comes to modern cinema. It was then during the 80s-90s when Indian cinema witnessed huge commercialisation. We saw movies like Kayamat se Kayamat Tak, Chandni, Tezaab and Maine Pyaar Kiya in 1980's and Darr, Baazigar and Dilwale Dulhania Le Jayenge in 1990's which brought in romance. The kind of love stories with happy couple and happier endings.

This trend continued until the late 90s and early 2000's with the release of super romantics like Kuch Kuch Hota Hai, Hum Dil De Chuke Sanam and Kabhi Khushi Kabhi Gham. Late 90s also witnessed these kind of films like Satya, Chandni Bar and Traffic Signal that got a lot of critical acclaim. These movies left a lasting impression in the minds and heart of Indian audience.We saw movies like Lagaan and Rang de Basanti that earned huge appreciation from people all around the world. The sole reason behind the success of "Rang de Basanti", "Gadar" and "Lagaan" was the element of patriotism. Movies like '3 Idiots' and 'My Name is Khan' experimented with new subjects and saw huge success and became famous with larger groups of Indian audience.

The entertainment tax charged by the government runs into several crores of rupees for one day. Cinema is thus a great source of capital for the government which is spent on various projects of development. Cinema thus participates in the country's development. Cinema also promotes fashion. The latest designs in clothes, hair style and even bikes and cars are promoted by the heroes and heroines. This not only brings freshness and change in traditional designs but also sustains what is called the fashion boom. Many businesses like readymade garments, jewelers and saloons thrive on the fashion sustained by cinema. Cinema has also made negative contribution to society. The nudity and violence shown on the silver screen has an adverse effect on many young minds. Various tricks and methods to deceive people shown in some movies tend to mislead young people. Moreover, movies invariably advocate western culture and way of life which is an encroachment on Indian tradition and customs. People blindly follow what is shown in films. This creates various types of problems in society. It is also said that films give people false dreams and take away their will to fight against the problems of life. In films the problems are solved quickly, but it does not happen like that in real life.

There are variable views about the effects of cinema. Producers and financiers consider it as a tempting and lucrative business. For actors and actresses, it is a means to earn money and popularity among masses. The director, story-writer, song-writer and cinematographer take it as an art work. To some, it is an audio-visual translation of literatures and has its own message. As for government, it is a potential source of revenue and employment. For majority of cinema-goers, it is nothing but a cheap and interesting form of entertainment and pastime. Whatever may be the reason, cinema has occupied a major share of market for its cine lovers.

Man has instincts, different thoughts flow which leaves an effect on the minds. The person laughs with the films and tears with them. Scenes of 'Shaheed Bhagat Singh', a film by Raj Kumar Santoshi and Manoj Goswami makes people national-minded and sentimentally involved in the film show. The film dialogues are occupying places in our real life. Dialogues of 'Mugle Azam' found place in the normal interaction of people for a long time. People talked and walked like Prithvi Raj, the great king Akbar. In the same way, plays by Agha Hashat and Devdas by Sharat Chandra left a deep impact on the masses. In the same way, film 'Sholey' created an impending effect on so many.

Cinema has wider mass appeal. It has great potential to influence society. Hence, certain social responsibility is attached to it. Cinema should not depict such stories which may lead to erosion of social morals and values. Cinema is said to be the reflection of society but at the same time society is influenced by cinema. Being an audio-visual medium, it is all the more powerful. It has the power to mould and shape the society. It is a form of visual education. Its utility is great in India as a big portion of its population is illiterate.

Cinema is evolving as a popular subject. Cinema is one of the significant factor, that generates, promotes and visualizes smoother national feeling, is based on national societal endurance. Cinemas can accelerate the economy, the increase of efficiency and promotion of welfare in modern society. With changing times, the trends of Indian cinema are also changing. Earlier, the trend was more specific to Indian audience but now, it inclines more towards a global concept. We now find Indian actors who are willing to explore their skills in experimenting with bold and untouched subjects with reflect the society and culture at large. The type of films that are coming up have that Indian feel in terms of family bonding and virtues. Modern parallel cinema is bold, comedy is original, cult films are being conceptualized and there is a constant passion to improve Indian cinema, now marking its centenary, is not synonymous with "Bollywood", the term applied to Hindi-language popular cinema from Mumbai (formerly Bombay).

However, cinema over the years has lost its educative and social aspect. It has become only a commercial object. It has ignored its educative values. Now films are produced just to earn more and more money. The producers and financiers are merely concerned about the commercial value of the films. Driven by this desire, they pack the films with the ingredients of sex, violence, etc. It poses a challenge to the social fabric. It leads to the decline of moral values of society. This tendency is not good in the larger interests of society, and nations as well. It is always good and well groomed to see good subjects on cinema. They have a very positive and long-lasting effect on the minds whereas cheap and shabby movies affect the tender minds of audience very badly.

There is general feeling that present day crimes are all due to effects of cinema. Besides open and demonstrative subjects throw tarnished messages. They spoil our culture, and society. Cinema and TV badly affect the health of the youngsters. They neglect studies and physical games to spend more time on this entertainment. School-going children and society children fail to make use of good impacts and are influenced by the bad part of the programmes on the air. The portrayal of women in cinema is a cause of great concern. She is presented merely an object of entertainment. She is required to merely dance, sing, expose and vanish. There is a little film in which she is depicted in influential role. This gives a message to society that women are weak and unimportant. Eve-teasing, physical assault and many other crimes have become an integral part of cinema.

The depiction of such scenes is so glamorous that it produces in the viewers a tendency to commit such crimes. Such irrational portrayal of various scenes leads to the increase in violence against women. The recent case of the brutal rape of a medical student in Delhi has highlighted the sad state of affairs in India. Infant foeticide, domestic violence against women, dowry death's, etc. are part of the same malaise that has afflicted the system, where women are looked down upon, objectified and treated as second rate citizens. Certainly yes, the government needs to enact tougher laws to punish the guilty. However, what is the film industry (which is largely responsible for influencing the way young minds think) doing to help (or not help) the cause of women? Particularly but not exclusively in south Indian movies the hero is often depicted treating the heroine with disrespect, engaging in eve teasing, and this is considered machismo. The woman is expected to just live with it. Even when rape scenes are shown, the plight of the woman is shown but the rapist does not suffer any consequences. Is this not sending the wrong message?

Often movies have 'item songs' where women are objectified as objects of sex, dressed in skimpy clothes. The recent song 'Dreamum Wakemum' from the movie 'Aiyaa', is a case in point, where the lyrics leave no room for doubt as to the intent of the song. Have you ever seen/ heard such crass song lyrics from the west, especially in a family movie? Is it not time that Bollywood behaves more responsibly and maturely?

In the olden days we used to talk about movies having double-meaning dialogues. However directors and writers have become much bold and have done away with the need to be less-brazen about the import of their dialogues. The majority of film-goers are young, vulnerable adults, whose minds can be moulded either to become rapists and eve-teasers, or to become responsible and respectful young men and women.

A number of film stars in recent days have come forward to condemn the rape of the young girl. But has anyone owned up responsibility for showing women in bad light in cinemas? Can't an established actress, not refuse to act in an item number? Do actresses not have a responsibitlity to avoid scenes that might influence men to abuse/disrespect women.

There have been many movies in Bollywood since then. Some figures estimate that there are about 1,500 movies released in Bollywood annually. They are filled with raunchy songs, "item" numbers – a gratuitous song which features a scantily-clad woman often dancing for the pleasure of a room full of men– and very minor decorative roles from the 'heroine'. The hero often harasses the heroine, who is somehow charmed by his behaviour and falls madly in love with him. The portrayal of women in Bollywood, and their larger effect on Indian society has been called into question following the brutal gang rape of a young girl in the capital, New Delhi.

Many argue that Indian popular culture is full of misogyny, and Bollywood too needs to own up to its role in fuelling this culture. As Ritupurna Chatterjee writes, "it will be highly presumptuous to assume that Hindi cinema is the root cause of a spike in sexual assaults. But Bollywood and regional cinema in equal parts, because of their reach, scope and influence, have a larger role to play in assuming responsibility for the message it sends out to millions of audience—some highly impressionable." India's population has now exceeded 1.2 billion, and even though literacy has increased quickly in the past years, a little over 25 per cent of the country's population is still illiterate. Is it fair to blame Bollywood, or even expect it to produce movies that adhere to a higher standard? As Bollywood mega star and bad boy Salman Khan argued in an interview—each movie has a good guy and a bad guy. It isn't Bollywood's fault that people choose to follow the villain.

The superstar also added that if not the death penalty, rapists should be sentenced to life. Others, like director Anurag

Kashyap, agree with the general sentiment that Bollywood, being such a huge influence for Indian society, has a responsibility to produce movies that show women in progressive light, but hold that censorship is not a viable way to achieve this goal, tweeting that moralising censorship would create "another kind of Taliban". By the time I was 18, a movie called Dil Chahta Hai exploded onto the scene and instantly became a cult classic. It is a story of three boys, Akash, Sameer and Siddharth, who have a last road trip to Goa before their "adult" lives begin. Fancy cars, beaches, no parental supervision and even a romance with an American girl made every Indian teenager want to go to Goa instantly. The second half of the movie sees the boys struggling with 'adult' issues. Unsurprisingly, one of the plots revolves around Akash needing to crash a wedding to convince his love interest not to go ahead with an arranged marriage, while his friend falls in love with a divorcee who dies in the course of the movie. While the stories bring up different aspects of Indian society, and how women are victims to its ways, they are mainly served up as plot devices to show how the boys grow into men.

One of the biggest blockbusters of 2009—I was 26 then—was a movie called '3 Idiots'. It dealt with the intense premium Indian parents and education institutions put on rote learning as opposed to creativity. The formula, using three boys to tell the story of education in India, again used women only as accessories in the story.

The larger point being made here is that even when a female movie character's role is more than decorative, the heavy emphasis on men's problems makes it appear as though it is the Indian man who is complex with real problems and the woman only serves as a support system. Movies have found new cities, settings and even broader societal issues to tackle, yet, seem to be in a state of arrested development when it comes to the power dynamic in gender relationships. There are a few movies that have broken the mould and present women as strong independent characters. Women with not only professional lives and the confidence to stand up to a man, but also the independence to make a decision for herself and not be punished for it in the course of the movie.

Bollywood is correct to say that it is free to express what it wants and tell the stories it wants. They have rejected censorship as a tool to "elevate" the kind of content they generate. Some writers have argued that only blaming the producers of pop culture is dangerous, and that the audience needs to introspect as well—Shougat Dasgupta pleads with audiences to "question the invariably sexist, xenophobic, homophobic, plain stupid assumptions of the pop culture we consume".

It is interesting then that many were shocked by the message sent by one of 2012's most highly anticipated movies, Cocktail, the story of three young people sharing a flat in London. Ditching his club hopping, alcohol drinking girlfriend, the leading man, a womanizer, falls in love with the god fearing docile "good" girl. What happens? His former paramour, played by leading actress Deepika Padukone, then ditches *her* short skirts for *salwar kameezes* and the neighbourhood bar for the kitchen to win him back. If this doesn't send the wrong signal about female.

There have been several definitions of cinema till date. While to some schools of thought it happens to be the greatest medium of entertainment, others do opine that it is a medium that disseminates moving pictures. It would have been better (perhaps) if all had ended here. There is another definition of cinema - it is a medium that does reflect the true mood of the society and also the changing reality. In accordance with several pundits, the Indian cinema does fit in the last definition and in the best manner. Without a doubt Indian cinema has played a major role hitherto and through decades it has also been the most appreciated medium of entertainment. Now the question remains whether it has been the medium of entrainment only or of something else.

Surely you're interested to know the definition of this word- else. If truth be told, the Indian cinema has changed through times and has always tried to cope with the changing reality. If we take the mainstream cinema or simply Bollywood into consideration, it will be found that lots of changes have occurred. Gone are the days of 50s (termed as the Golden Age of Hindi Cinema) when a good number of classics like 'Madhumati', 'Sujata', 'Do Aankhen Bara Haath' and lots of others did dominate.

Even if the regional cinema industry has struck back exceptionally well, they have remained out of the main scenario.

And who doesn't know that exceptions are always exceptions. What can be deduced here then? The influence has never been unidirectional, Indian society and cinema has been influencing each other altogether.

References

Encyclopaedia Britannica (India) Pvt. Ltd.; Gulzar; Nihalani, Govind (2003). Encyclopaedia of Hindi Cinema. Popular Prakashan, ISBN 978-81-7991-066-5.

Asif, K.; Kabir, Nasreen Munni; Ak_h_tar, Suhail (2007). The immortal dialogue of K. Asif's Mughal-e-azam. Oxford University Press. ISBN 978-0-19-568496-4.

Saari, Anil; Ca??opâdhyâ?a, Pârtha (2009). Hindi Cinema: An insider's view. Oxford University Press. ISBN 978-0-19-569584-7.

Mazzarella William, Censorium: Cinema and the Open Edge of Mass Publicity, Mazzarella, 2013.

Singh, Jai Arjun, Jaane Do Bhi Yaroo (2010). Wadhwani Sangeeta, Bollywood on the Bend, 2010.

Mulay, Vijaya, From Rajahs and Yogis to Gandhi and Beyond : Images of India in International Films of the Twentieth Century, 2010.

4

Social Relevance of Kalpana Lajmi's Rudaali : The Professional Mourner

SHEFALI AND NEERAJ KAPOOR

Indian cinema reflects and represents the society from which it originates, the society with its myriad customs, traditions, conventions and ways of living. Particularly, the parallel cinema not only presents a kaleidoscopic view of the hierarchical social system through the gendered identity of every individual but also holds the power to redefine it. On one hand, the social constructs used as tools to sustain inequality in the society are highlighted by the serious cinema, and on the other, it also points to the ways how the same can be or are being redefined by the exploited class. Thus, it shows not only the reality but also points to possible solutions to the problems faced by the marginalized class.

In keeping with the hardships and problems of the woman protagonist of *Rudaali*, a novella by Mahasweta Devi, on which Kalpana Lajmi's *Rudaali* is based, abounds in the issues of oppression and double exploitation of the marginalized low caste women by men of their own caste and those of the upper caste on different levels—emotional, social and economical on account of social hierarchy and patriarchal system which give men a higher status than their counterparts in social stratification.

The Film depicts the story of a woman Shanichari, named so as she was born on Saturday and so considered as "accursed" or "unlucky" and her life is represented as the embodiment of her misfortunes with her birth into a low-caste, her father dying soon after her birth, her mother abandoning her and running away with the owner of a touring drama company, her husband being a drunkard and dying of cholera, her son marrying a prostitute and then running off never to be seen again, her love for a high-class man she can never be with and finally her discovery that the rudaali she befriended is actually her mother and has died. She herself time and again calls herself, *"Dried Shanichari, withered Shanichari wretched Shanichari unlucky Shanichari........"*

The film runs in a series of flashbacks telling the sad story of Shanichari as she narrates it to Bhikni, a Rudaali who has been called by the dying landlord Ram Avtar to mourn his death as he is sure that not even his son, Laxman Singh would shed a single tear on his death. While waiting for his death, Bhikani spends a few days with Shanichari and the bond between the two women gets stronger and Shanichari gives vent to her feelings before her. In her tale of sorrows, she also tells Bhikni about some moments of motherly joy in the company of little Budhua, her son and about her fascination for Laxman Singh, the son of Ram Avtar. It is Bhikni who advises Shanichari to take up the profession of Rudaali as a survival tool as by exploiting this custom, she would not only gain financial security but also some respect. Shanichari is hesitant to accept the suggestion as she feels that she would not be able to shed artificial tears on the death of strangers when she could not weep on the series of misfortunes in her family. After Bhikni has left her for two days, as she has been called by dying Bhishamdatta, the man with whom she had eloped after her husband's death, that Shanichari visits Laxman Singh, perhaps for the last time, she receives the sad news of Bhikni's death and her message to her that she was Peewli, her mother. At this moment it is also reported that Ram Avtar, the landlord is no more. This incidence leads to the final scene of the film when Shanichari unleashes her dried up tears, the real ones and let them flow, though on the mourning of Ram Avtar and hence becomes a professional Rudaali.

The film presents a satire on a custom practised by the high class landlords and noblemen of hiring Rudaalis (the female professional mourners from low castes and classes) to mourn over the death of their family members for raising their prestige besides having a means of entertainment through the gendering of death rituals. Anjum Katyal in her essay "Metamorphosis of Rudaali" writes, "Grief is turned into a commodity, and mourning is labour.... In fact, this commodification of grief is shown first as a characterstic of the malik mahajan's social class.... and even grief is distorted in the desperate struggle for survival." . Irony as a powerful tool has also been used in the film to highlight the love for wealth of the landlords when the landlord, Ram Avtar, on the verge of his death, is concerned about the expenses and asks for a cheaper Rudaali and instead of feeding eleven brahmins on his death, directs to feed five as it is only a question of following religious compulsions. On the other hand, Shanichari has to carry out the cremation of her mother-in-law at night in order to avoid the fine for keeping the corpse overnight inside the hut. In an emphatic manner the film highlights the politicized religious communities enjoying privileged positions in society though having biased practices. Shanichari is reprimanded by the village priest Mohan Lal for not performing proper cremation of her mother-in-law and holding proper Kriya-ceremonies of her mother-in-law and husband. The religious obligations force her into indebtedness to the landlord.

Even the delineation of the minor characters like Moti, Phoolbano and Mungri brings forth the exploitation of kept women and prostitutes by high class people for their sexual gratification. The moral bankruptcy and hypocrisy of so called high class people become quite apparent in the film when they would not allow these women to shed tears on their deaths as it would lower their status and in accusing Shanichari for turning her home into a whore house by keeping Mungri in her home after her marriage to her son though they still look at Mungri with lustful eyes.

The subjugated status of low caste women is also highlighted by the representational system of the film by showing them veiled, in shadow, lowered gaze, facial expressions, body language and dark clothing. The background scores also throw a light on the mental and emotional agony of the protagonist. Even the words spoken by the lower classes like "Hukum" for the landlords signify the absolute power enjoyed by the latter.

The film, while depicting the exploitative system also foregrounds the issue of survival. As Mahaswata Devi in her interview said, "Rudaali is about .... how to survive". Shanichari's tale is a tale of a woman who has to stay functional despite the prevalent patriarchal practices, the grind of which crushes her emotionally, psychologically, socially as well as economically. Instead of shedding tears she has to move on for survival. The film shows her resistance and self-affirmation in her anger for unfairness of her situation highlighted in her arguments with her mother-in-law, when her wayward and drunkard husband is praised and considered to be the breadwinner, while it is she who struggles to make both ends meet and has to attend to the requirements of the house, her defying the religious tradition by performing the funerals rites of her mother-in-low, her verbal defence of herself and that of her son in marrying a prostitute and giving her a home, though in the latter case she has her own fears again rooted in the social system when she says to her son," **"Hukka Paani Band Kar Denge..."** Inspite of deprivation at various levels and her total loss, Shanichari shows endurance and fortitude in facing the trials and tribulation of her life. The film delineates beautifully how her humanistic core is intact despite a series of misfortunes which also keeps her going and is represented in her relationship with her son Budhua, her love for Laxman Singh and her bonding with Bhikni and her concern for her unborn grandchild for whom she allows Mungri to stay in her home. Her devotion towards her family can be seen in her rejection of Laxman Singh's offer to stay in the *Haveli* on the condition of leaving her family, although she loves him. She is both caste and class conscious and does not intend to bring bad name to Laxman Singh by being associated with him. When Laxman Singh asks for some water, she says, *"It will pollute your caste"* and again when asked to sing on the occasion of the birth of Laxman's child, she reiterates *"If my shadow falls on your son on this* *auspicious day....*" Another survival strategy the film brings to fore is the "Woman-woman boding" which implies that women can help women in their struggle for existence and survival as Bhikni does by giving emotional support as well as by sparking-off the possibility of economic self-reliance in Shanichari by suggesting her to be a Rudaali and exploit the custom for her survival.

So, we can conclude that the film by Kalpana Lajmi is a powerful presentation of a subaltern perspective, and survival of Shanichari in the face of innumerable odds is the triumph of the deprived, the oppressed and the exploited.

References

Lajmi, Kalpana (Dir.), *Rudaali: the Professional Mourner*, A Motion Film, 1993. Cast: Dimple Kapadia, Rakhi Gulzar, Amjad Khan, Raj Babbar.

Devi, Mahasweta and Ganguli, Usha, *Rudaali, From Fiction to Performance,* translated with an introductory essay by Anjum Katyal. Publisher Seagull Books, Calcutta 1999.

Representation of Kashmir in Santosh Sivan's *Tahaan*: A Boy with a Grenade

5

Priyanka Thakur

Cinema is a technologico-cultural product which can be studied as a "representation", as described by the cultural theorist Stuart Hall, of a society. According to Stuart Hall, representation is a process through which 'meanings' are assigned to people, objects and events by "the words we use about them, the stories we tell about them, the images of them we produce, the emotions we associate with them, the way we classify and conceptualise them [and] the values we place on them" (3). The meanings are neither inherent in things as fixed entity nor the world is exactly reflected in the system of representations; rather meanings are constructed and produced.

As a cultural product, cinema has the capacity to produce meanings and therefore circulate these "constructed" meanings in the society. Various discourses, in Foucauldian sense, are created through this audio-visual cultural product, which add to a certain kind of knowledge.

Ananya Jahanara Kabir in her book *Territory of Desire: Representing the Valley of Kashmir* brings out the relationship between the camera and the Kashmir valley with the starting point in 1860s when the adventurer-photographers Samuel Bourne and John Burke first entered the valley with their tools of photographic endeavor. In the next century, these photographers, along with surveyors and archaeologists, were transformed into the tourists. In the postcolonial India, this tourism was enhanced by a series of 1960s "Kashmir" films, like *Kashmir ki Kali* (Dir. Shakti Samanta) and *Jab Jab Phool Khile* (Dir. Suraj Prakash), with a blend of technicolour. There are very few black and white films, which had been shot earlier in Kashmir, but colour gave the film makers a chance to set their films in the scenic valley of Kashmir as compared to the dusty plains of India. These technological colours made the valley an ideal locale for falling in love and hence making the valley a landscape of desire for modern India. The general rule was that Kashmiri characters in these films were more or less limited to a tourist vision of Kashmiris. The Kashmiri was more often either a houseboat owner or a tourist guide. The pastoral valley these films offered for the modern nation's cinematic consumption completely diverged from the actual political situation then prevalent in Jammu and Kashmir, like the situation after the arrest of Sheikh Abdullah in 1953 and the massive popular demonstrations of 1963.

This rendezvous of the youth, love and the beautiful landscape was interrupted by the political violence of the 1990s. Bollywood's romance with Kashmir came to an abrupt end in 1989, when filmmaker Muzzafar Ali's "*Zoonie*" was stopped abruptly mid-way through shooting. Now, during this period, a new kind of "Kashmir" films emerged on the celluloid. It was a kind of "cinepatriotism", as called by Amit Rai in "Patriotism and the Muslim Citizen in Hindi Films", that reconstructed the valley as a cinematic battleground, criss-crossed by lovers, militants, the military and mujahideen. For instance, in 1994, *Roja*, directed by Mani Ratnam, indicated the loss of the landscape of the valley and sent a message that the tourists can no longer visit Kashmir, a place of natural beauty as it has been made inaccessible by the activity of the anti-nationals and "terrorists". It is important to note that the political violence had made filming in the valley impossible, and Mani Ratnam used Manali as its imitation. Besides being chauvinistic, the filmmakers mixed the attire and culture of Kashmir with Himachal Pradesh and twisted the soul of real Kashmiri characters. As observed by various film critics, films based on

Kashmir are unqualified and mocking the life of people caught in the conflict. Film critics and academicians agree that Kashmir is being wrongfully depicted on the screen.

This "loss of Kashmir", as depicted in *Roja,* was time and again served to the Indian audience with films like *Mission Kashmir* (2001) by Vidhu Vinod Chopra and *Yahaan* (2004) by Shoojit Sircar. The thriller genre made the world outside the valley believe in the Kashmir shown on the big screen.

From *Kashmir ki Kali to Mission Kashmir,* the changes in the titles indicate the loss of the idyllic Kashmir and formation of the "terrorist infested" Kashmir. Post-1989 films are example of how films can feed on the fears and ignorance audience. Such is the political complexity of the issue of Kashmir that very few film makers have successfully demonstrated a degree of impartiality that does not simply denigrate all Kashmiri Muslims as cross border terrorists with an undying allegiance to Pakistan.

Cinema is a powerful cultural discourse. It has circulated images about Kashmir amongst the people whose only source of any kind of knowledge about the valley is the visual medium. The mediation of camera always brings in selection and manipulation of what is seen and therefore what is finally served to the audience is a discourse which includes and excludes certain statements about the subject. These films about Kashmir "stand for" Kashmir and finally Kashmir gets a signification or a meaning through them.

Different filmmakers have found different ways of telling stories about Kashmir that have become a part of national experience. My paper is an analysis of a much recent film, *Tahaan: A Boy With a Grenade* (2008) by Santosh Sivan who is well known for his cinematography. It is a representation of Kashmir with the main focus on the eponymous protagonist and his search for his donkey named Birbal. The focus of the film is the ordinary lives caught in conflict. How successfully has the director represented the fractured lives of the people of Kashmir is the main aim of this paper.

Tahaan (Purav Bhandare) lives with his grandfather (Victor Banerjee), mother Haba (Sarika) and elder sister Zoya (Sana Sheikh) in Kashmir. The family lives with the hope that the boy's father, who has been missing for over three years, will return home.

The death of the grandfather pushes them into financial crisis. The local moneylender and his manager (Rahul Khanna) take away the family's assets, including Tahaan's pet donkey, Birbal, in lieu of an unpaid loan. While the rest of the family seeks redemption from the crises, Tahaan is determined to bring Birbal back home. After securing money using various means, Tahaan reaches the moneylender to reclaim Birbal. He is told that an old man Subhan Dar (Anupam Kher) bought the donkey and went across the mountains.

The irony being that his father went missing behind the same mountains. Gathering courage, Tahaan goes in search of the old man. He finds him and Tahaan is hired to help guiding Birbal; he is promised Birbal as his payment. However, after completing his work, Tahaan does not get the donkey. Subhan gifts the donkey to his eight-year-old nephew. On his way back home, Tahaan encounters Idrees, a teenager who discourages him, saying that his efforts will not be sufficient to get Birbal back. He agrees to help him get Birbal back, but instead he asks him to do a favour.

Tahaan is asked to take a package across the mountains in his onward journey. Idrees also hands him over a grenade and says that when the time is right, he will be told what needs to be done. At a checkpoint the package and grenade are not discovered due to the fact that the soldiers know and trust Subhan Dar. Tahaan is about to use the grenade on an army detention camp and has already removed the pin, when he changes his mind and throws it safely into a river. On the other hand, Subhan's nephew learns that Tahaan is fond of Birbal, and at his request Subhan gives it back to Tahaan.

The film *'Tahaan'* is set against the picturesque backdrop of Kashmir, shot in real Kashmir and not in Manali, and is told from the point of view of Tahaan who is too innocent to comprehend the situation around him because all he wants is his donkey. For him, bringing his favorite donkey Birbal back home is the sole purpose of his life. Now the director has tried to touch upon almost all the aspects of the lives in a conflict zone. Kashmir which is represented in the films is a land which has sufi music on one side and guns, explosions and army raids on the other. Frisking and identity parades which Kashmiris face as a routine are also incorporated in the film.

Apart from the beautiful landscape, the films also shows that part of the valley which has concerting wires and curfews to make the valley as the biggest militarised area of the world. Throughout the movie, the director has kept a balance approach to the depiction of the conflict in the valley. After watching the film, the audience will know the fact that the Kashmiri men are detained in the detention camps by the Indian army but will remain unaware of the darkness and brutalities of these camps. Even the representation of the army raids proves their existence in the valley but hides their reality.

Similarly, the manipulation and the indoctrination of the Kashmiri youth by the extremists is only touched upon superficially and nowhere in the film are shown reasons for the vulnerability of the youth.

Santosh Sivan's representation has tried to bring out the old desire for Kashmir amongst the Indians when Tahaan meets a couple of tourists outside the house where her sister works. And one of them says, *"Arre Kashmiri Bacha Kitna Pyara Hai.. Ek Tasveer Kheechte Hain Iss Ki"*, that is, let's take a picture of this Kashmiri kid. And they ask Tahaan to smile. It shows how the valley is desired throughout India, either as a scenic beauty or as something which is too inaccessible. The photograph of a Kashmiri child becomes a souvenir for the Indian tourists.

Other area which is represented in the film is the culture of ammunition in the valley. The militant, Idrees, takes Tahaan to a hideout, where other militants are shown cleaning their guns when suddenly Tahaan asks them, *"Kya Main Isse Chala Sakta Hoon?"* which means if he can use the gun. And a militant replies, *"Ye Bachon Ka Kaam Nahin, Magar Mard Chala Sakta Hai."* It means it is not made for kids to play, only a brave man can use it. The director tries to portray that it is normal for people in Kashmir to use guns.

The image shows half reality as nothing is shown about the reason for the armed insurgency and why the youth got involved in the uprising. It is also shown that Tahaan is asked by the mysterious Baba, a militant leader, *"Ye Pahaad, Yeh Jungle Kis Ke Hain?"* – who owns these mountains, jungle and waterfalls? He would ask the same to all he would meet and they would reply, 'These belong to God,' but Idress, the local militant, tells Tahaan, *"Ye Sab Hamare Thhe, Ab Nahin Rahen, Ab Sab Ghulam Hain, Sab*

Karza Hai Hum Pe." Although a lot of historical facts are hidden in these dialogues but the orator of this dialogue is militant; this will convey the message that only militants are disseminating these thoughts about Kashmiri Nationalism. A common reaction could be that the director is trying to tell that how an idea of evil is cultivated among the children of Kashmir.

Continuing with his balanced representation, the director also brings in mass exodus Kashmiri Pandits in his narrative. There is a heart-breaking shot, where the houses of Kashmiri Pandits are shown burnt with no inhabitant living in them. It depicts the pain of Kashmiri Pandits, who lost their ancestral houses. The invisible Kashmiri Pandit in a burnt house is symbolic of the absence of the voices of Kashmiri Pandits in the discourse of Kashmiri Nationalism. This invisible Kashmiri Pandit is an old friend of Subhan Dar which points towards the bond of friendship between Pandits and Muslims in the valley before 1989.

The effects of the Kashmiri conflict are most readily felt in the plot line of Tahaan's father. Tahaan's father acts as an invisible symbol of the continuing repression and persecution faced by Muslim families in an Indian controlled Kashmir.

The figure of the child is crucial in acting as an obvious symbol of innocence but also as a contrast between the casual brutality of the adult world and the sensitivity of the one occupied by children. With Tahaan at the centre of the film, the valley is represented as an innocent entity caught between two sides—militants and military.

One of the more direct political comments is offered through the relationship between Tahaan and Idrees, underlining how children in such extreme political contexts are susceptible to exploitation for sinister purposes. But by suggesting that the Indian military are in truth responsible for the illegal detention of his missing father, the final moments of the film seems to blame both the militants and the army for failing the people of Kashmir. When Tahaan lies on his back in the dingy confines of his home and tries to grab a handful of sunlight, the visual is beautiful because the boy is trying to claim for himself a piece of a golden dream, a little slice of the magical story that his grandfather narrated earlier. Is the dream that of a strife-free Kashmir? Is it that of a goal in life, represented so movingly by a pigeon washed up on ice in the beginning of the film? Is it that his missing father will return? Is it that he will soon become an adult, one of the *mard log*? Or is it that he will get back his beloved donkey, Birbal.

Apart from all the faults in the representations, the film manages to bring out some crucial aspects about the ordinary lives in the conflict. Tahaan's mother is shown without a literal voice in the film but this literal voicelessness can be a sign of metaphorical voicelessness of the Kashmiris, especially Kashmiri women who have lost their men in this protracted conflict. The concern of Tahaan's mother for him is representative of the anxiety of all Kashmiri mothers. She is also represents the Half widows of Kashmir, women whose husbands have disappeared but not declared deceased. Although, in the end, her husband is shown alive in the detention camp, yet in a scene many Kashmiri women are shown standing with the photographs of their disappeared men outside the army camp. This absence of Tahaan's mother's voice also brings out the fact of post-traumatic disorders due to which many Kashmiri women have lost their voices.

Families losing their men is a common scene in Kashmir and it had been represented in the film in a scene where during combing of the village by the army, all the men (*mard*) of the families are asked to come out into the open. As Tahan has no other men in his house, he comes out as a *mard* of his house. It shows how the childhood gets lost under responsibilities in the conflict. Throughout the film Tahaan wants to be the man of his family and he even trains his donkey so that through him he can earn some money.

Tahaan is a film that has moved away from idyllic beauty and cinepatriotism and has brought, at least in some ways, Kashmiris back to the focus in true sense. It does not reinforce the image of the valley as a land of militants but rather try to give to its audience some slices from the everyday life of a Kashmiri. The film in the end gives out a humanistic message through two children of the film. The donkey which is so dear to Tahaan and which is gifted to his nephew by Subhan Dar, can be become a symbolic apple of discord between these two little boys. But the nephew after realizing that Tahaan is so attached to the donkey, gives it back. Subhan Dar is happy to see such a gesture by the little boy and says that it is more important to be a good human being than anything else.

References

Hall, Stuart, ed. Representation: Cultural Representations and Signifying Practices. 1997. London: Sage, 2003.

Kabir, Ananya Jahangir. *Territory of Desire: Representing the Valley of Kashmir.*

Minnepolis: University of Minnesota Press, 2009. Print.

Freedom of Expression and Indian Cinema 6

SUDESH JAMWAL AND BALJEET JAMWAL

INTRODUCTION

As the first and only universal entertainment in the whole world, the movies absorbed more and more people of all walks of life. 'Freedom of expression' has been guaranteed under Article 19(1) of the Indian Constitution and granted to all citizens of the country but 'freedom' has not to be mistaken as a 'license' to say anything or do anything which may even adversely go against the susceptibilities and sensibilities of people.

Freedom of expression implies freedom of speech, freedom of writing and freedom of exhibiting. One can express one's thoughts through all means and full freedom has been granted to do so. While movies are the pandemic medium, even though more and more people and communities started to oppose its negative effects on society. More and more organizations or groups increasingly opposed the movies for degrading values of society through depicting or speaking of sex, violence, drugs or disrespecting religion.

This made people of the industry to think of an internal administration of the issue. The exhibition of movies is a business, pure and simple, originated and conducted for profit like other spectacles, and not to be regarded as part of the press of the country or as organs of public opinion within the meaning of freedom of speech and publication.

If we go through the historical background we came to know that in 1927, Hays and a group of major Hollywood producers introduced a guideline of 36 specific issues for producers which became known as "Don'ts and Be Careful." Under the modern Indian Constitution, freedom of speech is highly qualified, subject to what the government deems "reasonable" restrictions. The state can silence its citizens for any number of reasons, including "public order," "decency or morality" and "friendly relations with foreign states."

RESEARCH POINTS

1. whether film industry follows the production code;
2. whether freedom of expression be permitted unlicensed;
3. whether there is a need of Board of Censor or not.

METHODOLOGY

The study is based on secondary data which has been taken from different magazines, journals and newspapers. The qualitative data only be used in this study

Production Code

Production Code is in two parts first of which covered general principles and the second included particular applications of general principles:

1. No picture shall be produced that will lower the moral standards of those who see it.
2. Hence, the sympathy of the audience should never be thrown to the side of crime, wrongdoing, evil or sin.
3. Correct standards of life, subject only to the requirements of drama and entertainment shall be presented.
4. Law, natural or human, shall not be ridiculed, nor shall sympathy be created for its violation.

Production Code aimed at forming a "correct entertainment" based on its strong emphasis on the morals of the movies and implications of sex and violence in film productions.

The policy not only influenced depiction of sex and violence, but also representation of religion, politics (domestic and foreign), corporate capitalism, ethnic minorities, the conduct of lawyers, doctors and other professionals, and a host of other issues was considered in the Code. Film, is an artistic medium, not just a business, whose expression is protected—if film is expression that does not infringe on the constitutional rights of others, than its content is guaranteed protection. The term sacrilege is vague and could be used as an umbrella term for further free speech restriction. Movies are "a significant medium for communication of ideas," and are, therefore, to be protected. In the 1952 ruling by the Supreme Court in USA made the biggest change to the world of film industry by granting them freedom of expression. This helped producers and directors to make movies with all their so-called artistic desires, while still groups oppose their influence on morals of the society.

WHETHER FREEDOM OF EXPRESSION BE PERMITTED UNLICENSED?

In the matter of exhibition of films there is a Board of Censors which issues the certificate for the exhibition of a film. The Board does apply its scissors in cutting out certain parts which to them appear to go against any social dictum or any religious sentiment or any national issue. Too much openness in sex; too much goriness in violence, physical or vocal have been cut down by this Board of Censors on so many occasions and in so many cases. There have been controversies raised on such cuts in many cases. Recent examples are Shekhar Kapoor's *'Elizabeth'*, Deepa Mehta's *'Water'*, Kamal Hassan's *'Hey Ram'* and *'Vishwaroopam'*.

The freedom granted under Article 19(1) of the Constitution has to be rightly understood. The social psyche and the social perspective of India has to be taken due note of. India has a conglomeration of creeds, religions, and ethos and this aspect of the Indian society cannot be ignored by film-makers, artists and writers and the 'freedom of expression' has to be used with caution and with due regard to the social sensibilities of the variegated Indian society. Freedom should not be misjudged as license to do or say anything with impunity. This 'freedom' shall have to take an account of other people's freedom of thought and belief. To quote the English essayist, A.G. Gardiner, 'Liberty is not a personal affair but a social contract.'

Censoring movies in the name of maintaining public peace, respecting emotions of people and similar other reasons are too naïve and simplistic arguments in front of the issue of freedom of expression. It may give wrong message to the public and likely to be misused in the future. The best course would be to let the viewers watch the movie and form their own opinion about it.

THE NEED OF A CENSOR BOARD

In the prevailing circumstances, it is better to have a rating body than a Censor Board of the very nature we have at present. The most important criteria regarding such body should be that the Government can forward its suggestions/recommendations but the decision must be taken by it independently. The rating system uses five classifications for films :

1. Proper for general audiences.
2. Parental guidance suggested for children under seventeen.
3. Parental guidance suggested for children under thirteen.
4. Restricted to persons seventeen or older unless accompanied by an adult.
5. No children under seventeen admitted.

The power of censorship delegated to the States has to be narrowed down drastically. They must satisfy the Central authority as to why the ban in their territory is indispensable and that there is no alternative left. In India while we enthusiastically profess right to information, we cannot sit back and ban films and censor information. Banning motion pictures is equivalent to banning the right of freedom of speech and expression. The test for allowing restrictions upon free speech should be more stringent. Legal restraints upon individual freedom of speech should only be tolerated where they are absolutely necessary to prevent infliction of actual harm. If at all, any limiting line is to be drawn in the extreme cases, it shall be left to the judiciary on which the country has enormous faith.

CONCLUSION

If democracy has to evolve, screening of films and

documentaries can never be denied for reasons based on mere speculation. Some developments regarding such subject are encouraging; but others are depressing. Needless to say we still have greater heights to scale in this direction. India's courts, meanwhile, do little to rein in government authorities. The country's Supreme Court, in the end, did stay Mr. Nandy's arrest, but it also reinforced the state's position that he had "no license" to make such statements: "An idea can always hurt people," the chief justice opined. "An idea can certainly be punished under the law. But India cannot hope to be a true cultural capital of the world – let alone a truly free society – until it firmly protects the right to speech. Without an unqualified constitutional amendment that guarantees this freedom, as the American Constitution's First Amendment does, the country cannot fairly claim to be the "world's largest democracy."

Cinema and Freedom of Expression 7

NITIKA

INTRODUCTION

Cinema is a means of communication as well as entertainment. The themes are expressed in cinema within the social, cultural, political, religious and economic constraints. All these are further guided by central board of film certification. This paper is about the freedom of expression in cinema within the above mentioned constraints. Freedom of expression is any act of seeking, receiving and imparting information or ideas, regardless of the medium used. There is no absolute freedom of expression as it is limited by so many issues in the society. With the acculturation, globalisation and technological advancement the freedom of expression has also changed over the period of time.

Freedom of Expression is also dependent on the education level of the audience, technological feasibility of expressing particular ideas, e.g. Science fiction etc, Cultural beliefs and customs, need of social reforms in the society and political environment of the country. Over the decades these factors have influenced the freedom of expression in films and films have emerged as an effective means of entertainment as well as communication while adapting to the changes in the various factors influencing freedom of expression. Indian Cinema began with mythological themes as the audience was already familiar with such subjects so the transition from stage performance to film medium was rather easily accepted. Moreover during the early years of film production the film produced did not have the advantage of sound so the ideas had to be conveyed without sound. With such limitations the themes revolved around mythological stories.

During the same period the literacy rate in India was about 7 to 12% with almost negligible literacy rates among women. This factor also probably limited the themes of films to mythological, social, cultural and popular historical themes with which the majority of audience was familiar. Later with the independence of India and increase in literacy rates, per capita income and technological advancement the themes of Indian films changed according to the needs of the time. The film production also increased significantly which led to the regulation of films by the Cinematograph Act & Rules 1952. This act made it mandatory for certification of all the films according to the content and the target audience before the release. All the films are reviewed by the central board of film certification and if necessary the board consults the advisory panel to ascertain if the film is fit for public viewing. Any shortcomings are removed before certification and release of films. Despite these constraints there are examples of films which were released only to be withdrawn later after the public outcry. Over the next decades with change in political, economic, social and cultural scenario the Ministry of Information and Broadcasting, Government of India made Cinematographic Rules, 1983 replacing the Cinematographic Rule, 1952 to keep up with the changing requirements of regulating the films released in our country.

EVOLUTION OF CINEMA AND FREEDOM OF EXPRESSION

Indian Cinema began with Father of Indian Cinema Dadasaheb Phalke who was born on 30th April 1870. He was producer, director, and screenwriter. He produced the very first full length feature film "Raja Harish Chandra" in 1913. He produced 95 films and 25 short films till 1937. Government of India instituted "Dada Saheb Phalke Award" in his honour in 1969.

The films produced by Dada Saheb Phalke had mythological themes. Since the medium of films as a means of communication and entertainment was nascent at that time, the mythological themes were preferred as the mythological storytelling was already prevalent in pre-cinema period and the people readily accepted the themes that they were already familiar with. More over the literacy rates in India during this period ranged from 7 to 12 percent and female literacy was close to zero. With these literacy rates probably such themes were the best option for the films.

Similarly, the first film in Southern India was made in 1916 by R. Nataraja Mudaliar—*Keechaka Vadham*. And the subject was again a mythological one from the Mahabharata. As the public became familiar with the cinema a satire about the English way of life and their imitation by some Indians was humorously brought out by Dhiren Ganguly in his comedy named *England Returned* in 1921 and slowly the cinema strarted depicting social issues also. In 1925 Baburao Painter produced a film named-*Savkari Pash,* this film depicted the exploitation of the Indian peasant by the greedy moneylender.

In 1919 Baburao K. Mistry formed the Maharashtra Film Co. and produced a film called *Sairandhari* (1920) depicting maratha history in the film. This theme also became relevant in the era of Indian freedom struggle as these films aroused sense of patriotism among the audience. Formation of corporation was followed by more funding for the film production and more freedom in choosing different themes which were socially relevant during that period.

In the early thirties, with the technological advancement sound could be incorporated into the films making expression of ideas and themes more emphatic and easy. *Alam Ara* produced by Ardeshir Irani (Imperial Film Company), released on March 14, 1931 was the first Indian cinema with a sound track.

Slowly over the next decades as the cinema developed as a film industry the freedom of expression probably got diluted with the need of making money and sustainability of industry.

With the improvement in literacy rate and purchasing power of the consumers the films are being produced keeping up with the demands of the consumers. The film as a product is required to respect the moral values of consumers in India and overseas. Most of the films are produced with more and more entertainment value rather than as a means of expression of opinions or facts. This has led to the films with common social themes like corruption being produced with lots of entertainment to enhance returns on investment.

Censorship

The Central Board of Film Certification, the regulatory body for public exhibition of films, is entrusted with removal of any content in films which it deems offensive, including sex, nudity, violence or subjects considered politically subversive. All the films are certified by the board before they are released for public viewing.

The objectives of film certification ensure that :

(a) the medium of film remains responsible and sensitive to the values and standards of society;
(b) artistic expression and creative freedom are not unduly curbed;
(c) certification is responsive to social change;
(d) the medium of film provides clean and healthy entertainment; and
(e) as far as possible, the film is of aesthetic value and cinematically of a good standard.

Rule 11 of Cinematograph (Certification) Rules, 1983 regarding assessment of public reactions to films—states "with a view to determining the principles to be observed in certifying films, the Board may take such steps as it thinks fit to assess public reactions to films, and for that purpose, the Board may hold symposia or seminars of film critics, film writers, community leaders and persons engaged in the film industry, or such other persons and also undertake local or national surveys to study the impact of various kinds of films on the public mind".

In Cinematograph Act, 1952, Section 5 A deals with certification of films as under:

Certificate U/UA is granted to the films suitable for unrestricted public exhibition, or as the case may be, for unrestricted public exhibition with an endorsement of the nature mentioned in the proviso to clause (i) of sub-section (1) of section 4.

Certificate A is granted to the film is not suitable for unrestricted public exhibition, but is suitable for public exhibition restricted to adults.

Certificate S is granted to film which is not suitable for unrestricted public exhibition, but is suitable for public exhibition restricted to members of any profession or any class of persons.

Section 5B. of this Act states (1) A film shall not be certified for public exhibition if, in the opinion of the authority competent to grant the certificate, the film or any part of it is against the interests of the sovereignty and integrity of India, the security of the State, friendly relations with foreign States, public order, decency or morality, or involves defamation or contempt of court or is likely to incite the commission of any offence.

(2) Subject to the provisions contained in sub-section (1), the Central Government may issue such directions as it may think fit setting out the principles which shall guide the authority competent to grant certificates under this Act in sanctioning films for public exhibition.

In spite of the regulation of contents of films certain films certified by central board of film certification were later banned due to communal, religious or political reasons. Tamil film Vishwaroopam was banned after certain Muslim groups protested about some offensive content in the film. Similarly, films Dam 99, Jodha Akbar, Aasrakshan, Fire, Water, and The Da Vinci Code were banned for similar reasons in different states of India.

No doubt, Indian Cinema has very unique identity in which we moved from black & white silent films to 3D films over the decades. India enjoys the privilege of being one of the best film industries in the world. Indian films are an important source of entertainment as well as a means of expressing social, political, cultural & religious issues of the people.

References

http://www.civilserviceindia.com/current-affairs/articles/freedom-of-expression-and-indian-films.htm

http://www.equalityhumanrights.com/human-rights/what-are-human-rights/the-human-rights-act/freedom-of-expression/

http://infochangeindia.org/agenda/freedom-of-expression/the-secret-life-of-film-censorship.html

http://www.academia.edu/3087216/American_Cinema_in_Light_of_Freedom_of_Expression_Censorship_and_the_US_Constitution

http://www.taipeitimes.com/News/editorials/archives/2009/08/06/2003450485/2.

http://www.cinemaofmalayalam.net/his_indian_cinema3.html

Cinematograph Act, 1952.

Cinematogarh Certification Rules, 1983.

http://en.wikipedia.org/wiki/Censorship_in_India

Cinema as Trans-active Representation of Literature 8

Janesh Kapoor

Reading a literary text partakes of a subtle engagement with a system of word-images formed in our mind in the process of reading. In other words, the written word/text signifies image(s) which in turn signifies spatiality. It is the spatial character of the word/text which lies at the core of its dramatic or cinematic representation. The representation of a literary text on the celluloid is an intricate process of transformation from a somewhat linear linguistic space to a multidimensional, hybrid space of the silver screen. This process may involve a number of stages as the *modus* of trans-representation across virtually divergent media. The first obvious step is the translation of a text first into a script and then screen play which has an interlinear linguistic dimension. This is followed by the dynamics of representation on the screen necessitating an involution of the linguistic syntagm into an active, paradigmatic mode. Hence, I have ventured to designate cinema as a "trans-active" mode of representing literature.

That the above is not a far-fetched notion is invested in the very notion of a story in the domain of narratology, which describes a story as a series of events enchained and embedded in each other to form a sequence. The term 'event' is a verb which denotes action or an active mode of representation. Moreover, in cognitive narratology, telling stories forms a part of our basic response to understating and explaining the phenomenal world around us. Thus, stories lend themselves to interpretation and translation, whether linguistic or into another mode of representation, including theatre and cinema. Filmic representation of a text is therefore a form of translation in the active mode in the temporal and spatial matrix furnished by the celluloid. While the term 'transaction' is not a new one in the theory of translation, I propose to build upon the hyphenated form of the term as 'trans-action' to emphasize that filmic representation is a form of translation involving an active or dynamic/graphic mode of representation. The theoretical framework for my thesis is provided by Walter Benjamin's concept of translation according a kind of 'afterlife' or extended life to a text, albeit in a modified form.

Of course, as with Benjamin also, the first criterion for translating a text is its "translatability". "The question whether a work is translatable has a dual meaning. Either: Will an adequate translation will ever be found....? Or, more pertinently: Does its nature lend itself to translation and, therefore in view of the significance of the mode, call for it?". The translatability of a text is directly related to the notion of its transformability into a different mode of representation. Benjamin is also of the view that "the higher the level of a work, the more ... its translatability". Further, even if a work does not prove to be amenable for translation, it still represents an unfulfilled "claim", as every literary work worth its name contains something "unfathomable" in addition to its surface structure and apparent meaning. Thus, Benjamin looks upon translation as a "mode", which implies that "a specific significance inherent in the original [work] manifests itself in its translatability".

As such, in Benjamin's theoretical matrix, translatability of a work represents a claim on humanity to undertake an excavation into the deep structure of a work to arrive at some vestige of its otherwise "unfathomable" meaning and fulfill its claim at translatability/transformability to some extent at least. Thus, in his view, "all translation is... somewhat provisional". As Tejaswani Niranjana points out in her perceptive reading of Benjamin, "Every translation, in taking the text further from its origins, raises it spiritually into a new realm....". Niranjana's notion is derived from Julian Robert's comparison of Benjamin's notion of translation to the Romantic concept of *Kritik*, "which was supposed to 'raise the power' of a work by creating a fuller universe of meanings through intense contemplation. For Benjamin, suggests Roberts, *Kritik* could be a paradigm for intellectual [or artistic] activity other than that which is purely poetic".

The above arguments offer an adequate logic and pretext for viewing stage and filmic representations of literary texts as valid forms of translation in an active-representational mode. While nowhere has Benjamin talked about a trans-formal (involving a trans-representation of a text from one form/mode of representation into another), his concept of a "central reciprocal relationship" between the two languages involved in linguistic translation may be reformulated as a formative and reciprocal relationship between the two forms of representation: text and its filmic version.

A few words more of theory before I attempt to illustrate my concept of cinema as a trans-active representation of literature. Since Benjamin's theoretical foundations are grounded in historiography and historical materialism, his views on translation are an attack on essentialism and empirical historicism, to borrow another phrase from Niranjana's reading thereof. While Benjamin envisions historicism as presenting "an eternal image" of the past, historical materialism partakes of a "specific" and "unique" engagement with it, "since it has recourse to of a consciousness of the present that shatters the continuum of history". It is characterized by a discontinuity with the past and which is subsumed into an "allegorical" image in which "the past and the now flash into a constellation".

Hence the inter-formal translation of a text into the virtual space of the celluloid may be viewed as an engagement between the text and its filmic version seeking its representation in a fresh mode just as a historian's engagement with the past seeks to conflate the past with the present, the "now". This engagement or inter-readability, accords an "afterlife" of sorts to the text through the process of translation. Thus, the original text becomes an allegorical or an archetypal image which must be re-interpreted and re-represented to give it a fresh lease of life. This is evident from the various representations of the *Mahabharata* in its folk, tribal, literary, dramatic as well as filmic representations: Peter Brook's cinematic adaptation of the epic has, as a case in point, accorded to it an international status in essence. Similarly, Shakespeare's Prospero also acquires a new perspective and life as it were in *Last Lear*, which deals with the life of a stage artist famed for enacting Shakespeare's character.

Cinema has been designated as a trans-active mode of representing literature partly on the basis of my experience of amateur theatre. Oft times, in the process of directing a play, I have had to search for new paradigms and metaphors to translate and represent a play for the stage. On several occasions metaphors have simply *happened* to me and I have had to look for a mode to represent them in the active mode on the stage. It is perhaps pertinent for a translator following any mode of translation to take recourse to one's repertoire of experience of other texts, inter and intra-texts including oral and folk literature permeating his psyche like archetypal images warranting interpretation and fresh representation of the text which forms the subject of his immediate or temporal engagement.

Thus, the process of representation is simultaneously a dual process of deconstruction and reconstruction to impregnate the text being represented to induce its fresh birth, or a new *avatar* as it were, new, yet forming a continuum with all its past translations or trans-representations. Thus, the translator, irrespective of the mode, has to undergo a period of gestation, while grappling with the issues of fidelity to the original or to step beyond the original in the process of delivering a twin of the original. Of course, the symbiotic ties between the two remain intact in either case.

While it is possible to sustain a contextual fidelity with the original in interlinear linguistic translations in general, a new context must be sought in order to trans-represent a text into another mode as the context or the frame of reference which is essential for expressing and determining meaning is a different one. I will now try to substantiate the arguments for my thesis with a comparative evaluation of U.R. Anantha Murthy's story "Ghatashradha" and its filmic version "Diksha" directed by Arun Kaul.

Ghatashradha implies a funeral rite performed for a person in one's lifetime. It is the worst form of excommunication imposed on a community member, particularly among the Brahmins, in which a person is denied the right to live (cf. 'death-in-life') for a serious breach of community norms, customs and traditions sanctioned by religion. In Anantha Murthy's story, Sheshagiri Udupa, the high priest of the Brahmin community in a South Indian village, performs *Ghatashradha* for his widowed daughter, Yamunakka, who has not only become pregnant through an illicit relationship with a school teacher hailing from other community in the former's absence, but has also committed the heinous sin of aborting the fetus. The film based on Anantha Murthy's story adheres to the theme of the original in essence. However, Arun Kaul, the translator-director, makes a labour of love to expand and re-contextualize the thematic concerns of the story and to reinvigorate the stereotypical image of orthodox brahminhood.

That he is going to recast the thematic matrix of the original and seek to add fresh temporal and spatial dimensions to it is evident from the very title that he assigns to his film. 'Diksha', according to *Oxford English-Hindi Dictionary* means "preparation or consecration for a religious ceremony; instruction (especially in disciple hood to a teacher by reception from him a particular mantra); initiation...; self-dedication (to a purpose, a person)...", which is a far cry from the title of the original story. In the film, it implies not merely initiation but dedication to and continuation of the principles dear to the teacher by the disciple. Udupa is transformed into a brahmin who follows the tenets of his religion with great care and concern, but has the imagination to interpret those tenets in a humanistic context. Thus, when his widowed daughter returns home, she is not forced to shave her head to great consternation of other community members. Udupa is also instrumental in performing the funeral rites for Kateera's aunt, a low-caste woman who did not deserve such rites at the hands of a Brahmin. This episode does not find any mention in Anantha Murthy's story. However, Arun Kaul uses this as a pretext for delineating the contradictions and conflicts inherent in a brahmanical society. This expanded context also allows for a graphic portrays of the tension between tradition and modernity which Kaul too might have experienced as a Brahmin in the contemporary context.

To continue with a description of the film version, Upadhaya, Udupa's disciple, is sent to confront him on both the issues and to elicit an explanation and possibly an apology from him for the satisfaction of other Brahmins. However, as Udupa explains to Upadhaya, he performed the funeral rites to sustain Kateera's faith in him and in the meaning and purpose of life. Otherwise, Kateera's humaneness would have been annihilated. In the same vein, he upholds Yamunakka's right to live a normal life even after her husband's death. Upon this Upadhya alleges that why should Udupa expect him to be his mouth piece when he was quite capable of maintaining his independent view point. To this Udupa replies that this is precisely the kind of *diksha* which he has imparted Upadhaya and he would be happy to be questioned and contradicted by his pupil if he fails to discharge his duty. This *diksha* or initiation is consummated in the form of Upadhya's protest against and rejection of Udupa's decision to perform *Ghatashradha* for Yamunakka orchestrated by Kateera's vehement and hostile rejection of the same earlier on. Thus, Udupa's decision, which is more on account of his inability to redefine and reformulate the norms of his community in a context which is amenable to individual and community existence, is represented as a flawed vision both on the conceptual as well as pragmatic planes.

It is possible to work out several points of departure as well as conflation between the original story as well as its filmic representation. For instance, Kaul makes use of the wider canvas accorded by the virtual space of the film version to develop and delineate certain strands of character and characterization which have been hinted upon in the story. The peculiar relationship between Kateera and Nani, Udupa's young and naïve disciple, who is also the narrator in the original story, is delineated in a beautiful way. When Nani insists upon touching Kateera, as he does not understand why he should not touch him, Kateera climbs upon and jumps across trees teasing Nani to come and touch him if he can, is a feast to the eyes. Nani's fondness for Kateera and his consternation upon not being able to reach out to him is a fine rendering of the innocent but subtle relationship between the two.

The filmic representation thus transcends the telling mode of the story to its graphic, pictorial representation involving sound, sight, landscape/geography and habitat rendered in the active experiential mode. The attitude of the community towards Yamunakka, particularly the characteristic widow, Godavaramma, the immateriality of Yamunakka's relationship with the school teacher through his equation with the 'Brahamrakshasha' in Nani's imagination, Yaminakka' s disgust and helplessness about her illicit relationship, her anguish over her situation which she must hide from others, the elemental urge of the motherly instinct in her as she draws Nani's ears to her womb to experience the magic and the miracle of the phenomenon of life taking form inside her, the scene of the ruined temple invaded by a cobra, where Yamunakka goes to meet her lover, the atmosphere of the settlement of low people where Yamunakka is taken for aborting the fetus—all add new experiential, life-like dimensions to Anantha Murthy's story in the virtual space without losing its semblance to the original to become its allegorical representation in a trans-active mode.

That Kaul has transcended/transgressed the original story in his filmic representation of it finds sanction in Anantha Murthy's own artistic vision and practice. The view point proffered by Murthy in his stories is empirical, open-ended. The decision to perform *Ghatashradha* for Yamunakka followed by Udupa's marriage to a young girl is rejected by Nani, who in spite of his naiveté has a simple but productive faith in life and human relationships.

The atmosphere in and around the village, the austerity of the brahmanical fold as contrasted with the liquor and tobacco-ridden atmosphere of the people on the margins where people fighting and cursing each other is synonymous with cock-fights, a favourite past time is rooted not only in the immediate context of the story but also in other works by Murthy, including *Samskara,* his magnum-opus. The journey through the demonic and the ghastly most often serves as a foil to the restrictive, life-denying ritualistic existence. Chandri in *Samskara,* who is a prostitute steps beyond the atmosphere saddled with the burdened of sin, indecision and taboos to bring to fruition the seed of her relationship with Praneshacharya, the scholar burdened with the wisdom of scriptures, who might follow suit if he is to live a fuller and freer life. The resolution of the tension between tradition and modernity, which Kaul has tried to work out in his film, also finds a natural corollary in Murthy's later work, *Bhava,* in which the issues raised in *Samskara* are reviewed in a fresh social and temporal context.

It might then be stated by way of conclusion that while stepping beyond the immediate context of Murthy's story in his filmic adaptation of it, Kaul has made an imaginative digression to give expression not only to the innate conflicts of a society to which he belongs, but has also approximated the artistic and social concerns of Murthy as expressed in his extant and subsequent works in a cumulative way. He has taken Murthy's work further by raising it to a hybrid plane of inclusive representation through in a trans-active mode. In fact, in de-contextualizing and re-contextualizing Murthy's story for filmic representation, Kaul does not merely transmit the information contained in it (which would have been a bad translation or representation), he imaginatively and skillfully projects the sub-text embedded in the surface narrative to comprehend and trancreate the complexity of the original.

References

Benjamin, Walter, "The Task of the Translator", in *Illuminations*. Ed. Hannah Arendt. Trans. Harry Zohn. New York: Schocken Books, 1969.

Niranjana, Tejaswani, *Siting Translation.* Hyderabad: Orient Longman Ltd., 1995.

Anantha Murthy, U.R., "Ghatashradha" in *Stallion of the Sun and Other Stories.* Trans. Narayan Hegde. New Delhi: Penguin Books, 1999.

Diksha, Dir, Arun Kaul, Rashtriya Film Vikas Nigam & Doordarshan, 1991.

Cinema, Literature and Education 9

CHETAN SINGH

Cinema, like literature, is an art of narration. Though these two art forms work with entirely different mediums, the end goal of both is same i.e. to represent life. Apart from the differences in their modes and mediums the rest of their worlds are the same—both entertain, both educate, both are loved, both are praised but then both are doubted and questions on their role in society have also been raised. As far as criticism is concerned cinema has to suffer a double attack in society it is also severely challenged by the literary artists as well. For example, in the 1950s the literary writers became too upset with the adaptations of literature. But it remains a fact that many literary works have reached the zenith of fame only because of cinema. Today, the world of cinema is replete with movies based on literary works. No doubt, at times both of them have been used to serve the function of sheer propaganda or pure pleasure only but then there is much more awaiting in them. For centuries literature has been used as a powerful medium of educating the masses.

And in the contemporary world of information technology, and in the light of recent developments in the pedagogy, cinema too has evolved as a powerful medium of imparting education. Today, cinema is not just meant for entertainment or passing away leisurely hours only; it is a very powerful means of mass communication. It entertains as well as an educates. It combines instruction with delight. It draws its material from society, literature, folklore, day-to-day incidents, history and many other sources and presents it artistically in real or unreal way catering to the taste of the viewers. It not only throws light on various aspects of human life but also condemns disinterestedly the abuses and malpractices in the society. Browsing any movie site on the net reveals the real potential of cinema— history, biography, adventure, documentary, sci-fi, sports etc. i.e. every aspect of life is there. With all this in hand, the educative value of cinema cannot be ignored.

The present paper is an attempt to discuss the role of cinema in promoting literature across the cultural and linguistic lines *vis-à-vis* its informative and educative contents. Many masterpieces of world literature, written in different languages, can be seen on the screen which further inspires the audience to read the texts, whether original or translated. Many concepts which a student or a general reader fails to comprehend from the books or from the teacher are understood within a second when seen on the screen. Though nothing can replace a teacher in imparting education, yet information technology and audio-visual aids including cinema can serve as a powerful tool of learning.

The first and foremost aim of the world cinema in general and the Indian cinema in particular in its initial stages was to give some positive message to the society *vis-à-vis* providing entertainment. It was because of this that from the very first time of its appearance, cinema had an important feature—the mass character. Cinema has a great influence on the attitudes and beliefs, aesthetic tastes and feelings, mass consciousness of people. The spiritual education of youth, their aesthetic sense, and formation of their moral value system is influenced by the cinema with a power no less than that of literature. Movies based on literary texts as *Guide, Chitralekha, Tamas, Rudaali, Samskara, Parineeta, A Passage to India, Pride and Prejudice, The Mayor of Casterbridge, Suraj Ka Satvan Ghoda,* Shakespeare's plays and other classics, etc. not only help students in appreciating the aesthetic and contextual appeal of the works but also develop a better understanding of life.

History of cinema is, in fact, history of adaptation of literature. There is no beginning and end of the amalgamation of literature and cinema, still this journey can be traced roughly from the BBC series on the complete works of

Shakespeare. Even Indian Film Industry is not untouched by this fast emerging genre. The movies like Satyajit Ray's *Pather Panchali* **(1955) was based on** Bibhutibhushan Bandyopadhyay's **novel,** Bimal Roy's Devdass (1955) **based on** Sarat Chandra Chatterjee's **novel of the same name (1917),** Anurag Kashyap's Black Friday (2004) **based on** *Black Friday – The True Story of the Bombay Bomb Blasts*, **a book by** S. Hussain Zaidi, Vijay Anand's Guide (1965) **based on** R.K Narayan's **novel of the same name,** Aparna Sen's The Japanese Wife (2010) **was based on** Kunal Basu's **short story of the same name,** Purnendu Patri's Letter From The Wife (1972) was **based on** Tagore's **short story** *Stree Patra*. **A long list can be added from the adaptations and appropriation of literature in the world cinema. But to transpose a character into a film is a difficult task as it requires faithfulness and originality. That is why Virginia Woolf objected the transformation of a literary text into a film.**

Not only does cinema represent and represent literature and life in a new medium, it also lends a voice to the social issues, e.g. *Chitralekha, Pinjar* and *Chokher Bali* give substance to the stature of women while *Chithariyavar*, a Malayalam movie, gives voice to the voiceless Dalits.

The collaboration of literature with cinema increases its far-reaching appeal which now encompasses various socio-economic issues which were marginalized so far. Though both literature and cinema are arts of narration, their ways of representation are completely different. There are multifarious effects of this symbiosis which are positive as well as negative. Our texts reach out to local audiences only when they are modified in order to make them relevant to the cultural and ideological concerns of the new audiences that were far removed from the writer's vision. On one hand it provides a larger audience to literary texts, while on the other, we observe an acute decline in the readership of these texts in the presence of their audio-visual counterparts. But on the one hand these adaptations and appropriations of literary texts are really doing some good to literature and on the other hand, in the pursuit of entertainment and popularity they are reducing our canonical texts to mere adulterations. It is true that films are produced for profit only. Profit always involves the creation of the benefit to the consumer. That's why early Hollywood attracted much more attention among the mass audience than the outstanding German expressionists and the French avant-garde of that time.

Today, Hollywood is a major producer of blockbusters and high-budget films. Next to the cinematic blockbusters, the mass appeal of literature is seen on Television also. For instance, Sharat Chandra's *Chanderkanta* got a huge applaud only when it was shown on the Indian television. And with the advent of animation technology, both in cinema and T.V., not only the mythologies have become common household stories but the children have an easy access to the world of science, history, geography and all other disciplines of learning. Children learn as easily with a good film as with a good educator. They can be a very good medium of education.

Different studies draw attention to the fact that students can identify with the characters and share their emotions and actions showed in an audio-visual setting. Experiences come from an interaction with a learning environment and personal construction of knowledge occurs through the interaction between the individual's knowledge schemes and his or her experiences with the environment. In this way, movies are analysed by considering the potential of audiovisual, scientific and common languages to be used as a tool to mediating science teaching and learning. Audio-visual medium shows itself as a valuable possibility to facilitate knowledge construction. This occurs because of the integration of an individual's reality with the surrounding environment, which develops, in the student, the sensitivity and perception of the setting.

Cinema also plays role as a tool for science education. Science fiction combines science and pseudoscience for entertainment. It allows an opportunity to compare and contrast two drastically different eras of life on this planet. It also addresses the ethics of technological advancement (Rose, 2003). It is believed that with the appropriate supporting material the science teachers be trained in using this new technique. Audio-visual can help reverse the negative attitudes that many students have toward real science by moving them from familiar experiences they enjoy to unfamiliar experiences they expect to be dull and difficult like learning physics, biology and chemistry (Dubcek *et al.*, 2003).

Movies can provide contexts which focus on social issues that should engage students. Where movies catch student's attention they provide different point of view, providing the teacher with an interesting possibility to discuss the issues. This environment provides a kind way of talking about the social context and the scientific content related. The movie shows that learning science involves social interactions, discussing about socio-scientific issues supported by audio-visual context seem to be an important possibility to mediate process of making-meaning on the science classroom.

A good film serves better than strong prohibitions. But, then, one bad film can be worse than ten thousand bad educators. It destroys at once a long established morality. We need not condemn cinema and TV. The programme makers are rather to blame. They are responsible for the kind of behaviour they offer to people. Violence is served to anybody on TV as if everybody advocates it. It is here that the role of a teacher really becomes important. We all have to agree that neither the classroom is the only source of learning today nor are the other sources harmless, especially cinema. In this situation it is obligatory for the teachers to provide the students with the much needed analytical skills for appreciating the cinematic art and make it really useful as a handy tool of learning. It is only in the hands of real smart teachers that cinema becomes a great treasure of learning, which it really is.

REFRENCES

Hena Naquabi, *Patrakarita Avam Jansanchar*, Upkar Publisher, New Delhi, 2007.

Carsten Strathausen. *The Relationship Between Literature and Film: Patrick Suskind's Das Parfun.* http://www.googlesearch.com.

Stephen, J.Ferenga and Daneil Ness (Ed.), *Encyclopaedia of Education and Human Development*. Pentagon Press, New Delhi, 2006.

B.M. Sharma (Ed.), *Distance Education.* Commonwealth Publishers, New Delhi, 2007.

Dully Andrew, *Concepts in Film Theory,* Oxford: Oxford University Press, London, 1984.

Cinema with a Purpose : Women Empowerment Through Films 10

NIRMLA SINGH AND RAJESH KUMAR SINGH

Cinema is a chief source of entertainment, to take the viewer to a world of fantasy. However, cinema has also shaped the cultural and social values of people of this country. Acknowledging this impact of cinema on society, this paper argues that cinema can be socially relevant by empowering women in cultural domain. With a theoretical understanding of recent cultural studies, this paper traces the representation of women in popular Hindi cinema over the years. A section is devoted to the analysis of contemporary women-centric movies with specific theme of women empowerment. In conclusion, it has been argued that cinema should strive for social change through entertainment.

Indian cinema is almost 100 years old. From the 1960s onwards, India became the largest producer of films in the world, replacing Hong Kong. Sadly, however, quality films represent a minority of the large number of films produced. All these years cinema is meant as the chief source of entertainment. Films are believed to be the opium of the Indian masses as people rely on this medium to help them escape to a world of fantasy.[1] In a very explicit way, cinema has shaped the cultural, social and political values of people of this country. If such is the impact of cinema on society, should it confine itself to entertainment only? Can cinema be socially relevant? With this question and keeping the theme of this national seminar in mind, this paper argues that cinema can have a purpose – a cinema that is uncompromising in its attitude and aims to change the existing power structure in society. Power and patriarchy in any society does not simply operate from top to bottom through state apparatuses, but articulated in and through the culture of daily life. Theories like poststructuralism, postmodernism and thinkers like Foucault and Bourdieu view the cultural order as a realm of ideas and symbols that are the medium by which power is organized in society.

It is here, the role of cinema in women's empowerment becomes important. We generally believe that women's empowerment can be achieved through governmental initiatives and policies. But this is half truth because the real empowerment will happen only when the established cultural norms and patriarchal order are challenged in which women have been accorded a subordinate role, primarily confined to home and excluded from public affairs of society. In this paper, there has been an attempt to examine the relationship between women empowerment and popular Hindi cinema. While cinema in India is a diverse strand of expression incorporating mainstream cinema, art/parallel cinema, middle cinema and regional cinema. The analysis of women empowerment in this paper is limited to mainstream/popular Hindi films better known as *"Bollywood"* [2]

MEANING OF WOMEN EMPOWERMENT

Before analysing the films aimed at women empowerment, it would be pertinent here to define this key concept. Empowerment essentially means decentralization of authority and power. It describes a process which helps people to assert their control over the factors which affect their lives. In brief, it can be said that empowerment is the expansion of individuals' choices and actions, primarily in relation to others, and being able to act on those choices in a number of domains. Thus, women's empowerment is an active multidimensional process, which should enable to realize their full identity and power in all sphere of life. It consists of their greater access to knowledge and resource, greater ability to plan their lives, greater control over their circumstances and power to free themselves from the shackles of customs, belief and practice.[3]

REPRESENTATION OF WOMEN IN MAINSTREAM HINDI CINEMA

If we look at how women's issues are treated in cinema and how they have been represented in Hindi films, we will find that leading lady of Hindi Films has more or less played defined roles which conform to the values upheld by Indian society. The image of woman as *'Sita'* has been repeatedly evoked in many films after independence. Through the idea of loyalty and obedience to the husband, Hindi cinema successfully institutionalized patriarchal values. Films like *Dahej* (1950), *Gauri* (1968 *Devi* (1970), *Biwi Ho To Aisi* (1988), *Pati Parmeshwar* (1988), depicted women as passive, submissive wives as perfect figures and martyrs for their own families. This can be said even for more recent and popular films like *Kuch Kuch Hota Hai, Hum Aapke Hain Kaun, Dil To Pagal Hai, Kabhi Khushi Kabhi Gham.*

While women had very much important roles in these films, their identities were absent from the film's text. Their roles were defined in relation to their family, especially the male characters in the family. Most of these films also laid down the conditions for idol womanhood.

Thus, the narratives of Hindi cinema have undoubtly been male dominated and male centric. Themes have been explored from the male audience's point of view. Film scholar and critic Shoma Chatterji observes, "Women in Hindi cinema have been decorative objects with rarely any sense of agency being imparted to them. Each phase of Hindi cinema had its own representation of women, but they were confined largely to the traditional patriarchal framework of the Indian society. The ordinary women have hardly been visible in Hindi cinema".[4]

WOMEN CENTRIC MOVIES

On the positive side, there are film-makers who have reacted against the streotypes set by mainstream cinema and have tried to explore subjects from women's perspective.

Contemporary films like *No One Killed Jessica* (2011), *CheeniKum* (2007), *Chameli* (2003), *Lajja, Ishqiya* (2010), *Paa* (2009) and *Dirty Picture* (2011), have extraordinary themes and portrayed women as central to film's story. These films are different from early heroine-oriented films like *Mother India, Aradhana,* and *Guide,* etc. where women ultimately are upholders of traditions, family bonding, thus depriving them of any sense of power and agency.

If one has to name films with specific objective of women empowerment, we can mention the name of *Lajja, Dor, Chak De India, English Vinglish, Astitva,* etc.

Lajja: In Rajkumar Santoshi's *Lajja,* Madhuri Dixit played the role of Janki, a theatre artist who can't tolerate the double standards adopted by men. Rekha who plays the role of a village lady who believes in women empowerment. *Lajja* brings out the fact that though our society talks and preach gender equality but when it comes to implement, it fails.

Dor: The movie *Dor* is about the plight of widows in India. Ayesha Takia who played the role of a young widow has the zest to lead her life despite losing her partner at an early age. She takes a bold step and runs away from this slavery life of a widow to find freedom.

Chak De India: The movie *Chak De India* talks about the conflicts that women face when they decide to excel in the field chosen by them. Sports is always a male dominated area, but in this film a team of girls bring home the Hockey World Cup. This movie surely inspired more girls to step into the world of sports and make their mark.

English Vinglish: The movie *English Vinglish* is a story of a common housewife who is weak in English and therefore always becomes a joke in front of her husband and children. But this woman not only learns English but also makes her family realise her importance, for more than her knowing English.

CONCLUSION

In a bid to reach the masses, popular Indian cinema has become melodramatic and rhetorical. Thus, over the years cinema with a purpose and based on socially relevant theme are looked upon as "art cinema" which meant unfortunately that it was not meant for public. This reflects a situation in which these well known lines of William Blake become relevant:

"When the nations grow old the
Arts grow cold;
And commerce sits on every tree"

Probably, we all would agree that this situation must change. Cinema can play an important role in bringing a change in attitude in society for empowering women. It has to create a separate and independent space for Indian women to help them realise their dreams. Consequently, cinema must begin a quest for social change through entertainment.

Notes and References

1. Gokul Singh, K.M. and Dissanayake, W. (1998), Indian Popular Cinema: A Narrative of cultural change (p. 88), U.K., Trentham Books Limited.
2. Bollywood is the informal term popularly used for the Hindi-language film industry based in Mumbai, Maharastra.The term is often incorrectly used to refer to the whole of Indian cinema; it is only a part of the total Indian film industry.
3. Manish Gangwar, Nita Kandekar, M.K. Mandal, Prakash Kandekar (March 2004), Empowerment Status of Rural Women: Insight from Dairy Co-operatives, *Social Change* (p. 113).
4. Nidhi Shendurnikar Tere (2012), Gender Reflections in Mainstream Hindi Cinema, *Global Media Journal*—Indian Edition, Vol. 3, No. 1 (pp. 2-3).

Portrayal of Women in Mainstream Hindi Cinema : An Analysis 11

ARTI PANDIT DHAWAN

INTRODUCTION

Cinema is one of the most powerful modes of creative expression. It is a popular media of mass consumption. Cinema plays a key role in forming opinions, constructing images and reinforcing values. But it is used largely to sell mindless entertainment. Even when questions are raised about the distorted ways in which popular Hindi cinema tends to project reality, serious discourse is encouraged. Senior members of Indian film industry prefer to take an ambiguous stand on the matter and indirectly, defend the working of market forces. The film industry has preferred films that appeal to all segments of the audience. Cinema no doubt is meant and believed to entertain but its impact on the society is significant.

The third of May 1913 The Coronation Cinematographer Theatre, packed to the hilt, watches bevy of 'women' in wet saris cavorting around a fountain. The film is *Raja Harishchandra*, and the director is Dhundiraj Govind Phalke. He had hoped to find 'real' women to play the role of queen Taramati and the other female characters in the film but had failed. He had advertised in the newspapers and even visited women in red-light area. But the women there didn't fit into Phalke's vision. Queen Taramati's role was reluctantly given to a young man, Anna Salunke, who became quite well known for his female impersonations, playing both Sita and Ram in Phalke's *Lanka Dahan*.

Sometime later when Phalke heard that a travelling drama company was going to pull up its tents for six months, he requested the director to lend him two of his female actors for his next film, Mohini Bhasmasur Kalabai and her mother Durga thus became the first women to act in Indian feature film, one of the many testaments to the pioneering spirit of Phalke. He was also the first to set up studio—Phalke films. The company later became the Hindustan Film company. The stories told were the ones audience were familiar with—mythology, folklore and stories they grew up on.

The world changed radically for film industries across the globe in 1927, with the release of The Jazz Singer, which starred A.L. Jolson which had the memorable tag line: 'See him and hear him sing'. It was only a matter of time before the talkies came to India. In 1931 on the first day of India's first talkie—Imperial Film Company and Ardeshir Irani's Alam Ara, starring Master Vithal and Zubeida and featuring ten songs. Majestic theatre was surrounded by huge mobs fighting to buy tickets. Black market vendors did brisk business, selling the tickets at twenty times their price. Sound also gave birth to film music. Sound technicians, musicians, music directors and singing actors were added to the roster. In 1937 Ardeshir Irani made first colour film in Hindi, *Kisan Kanya*.

NEED OF THE STUDY

Hindi Cinema has been a major point of reference for Indian culture in this century. Over the years Indian cinema has seen a clear shift in the role of women in Indian society. Time has changed and so has the perception of women in society. Various movies started from 'Raja Harish Chandra' to 'Kahani' reflects this trend. Issues of gender, social and economic justice, secular nationhood are nowhere more explored in the Indian cultural mainstream than in Hindi cinema. The discussions in this paper are mainly related to the mainstream Hindi cinema but where ever need was felt parallel cinema is also mentioned.

Hindi cinema, which can be considered as the biggest source of entertainment in India, does need to ensure a fair and cohesive image of women in Indian society. Hindi cinema has shaped and expressed the changing scenarios of modern India to an extent that no preceding art form could ever achieve. A deeper insight into the complex processes of modernization, colonization, nationalism and freedom for women can be acquired through the Indian cinema. Hindi film industry is the largest film industry in India. In this paper an endeavour has been made to make general analyses of the shift through six decades of history, bringing to life the women who peopled the cinema and popular imagination, and shaped fashion and culture. For filmmakers, the modern independent Indian woman cannot fit within the confining frames of box office hits.

Mainstream cinema has restricted itself to defined sketches of womanhood and gender stereotypes. The need of the study was felt as the impact of cinema on the society is significant. The portrayal of women on screen is crucial in furtherance of sterotypes already existing in the society.

EARLY DAYS OF WOMEN IN HINDI CINEMA

One aspect of women in the early days of Indian cinema needs to be highlighted. It was white skinned female actor (mostly referred to as Anglo Indians) who were more popular and in demand, with advertisements of plays often highlighting the presence of 'Gouri Miss' (white lady) or 'houris' (fairies) from paradise. Films were considered a disreputable business and women from traditional Indian households would not have anything to do with them. In contrast, women of Baghdadi Jewish origins and Anglo-Indians were willing to step into films. In her paper, Kethyrn Hensen attributes the audience acceptance desire for these female actors to the face that the male Indian spectator could posses the 'English' beauty, and in so doing enact a reversal of the power relations that prevailed in British dominated colonial society. Ruby Meyers, Aka Pramilla, Iris Gasper, aka Sabita Devi, Susan Soloman aka Indira Devi, Winnie Slewart aka Manorama were few Anglo-Indian female actors.

A significant event for the film industry in India was the arrival of Durga Khote in *Ayodheycha Raja* (1932). A highly educated, English speaking Brahmin girl made film an acceptable proposition for women from 'respectable' families. Her contemporary Devika Rani, the daughter of Indian Surgeon

General M.N. Choudhary, was not just an accomplished actress but also well versed and trained in cinematography and film making. By the mid 1930's Indian actresses were beginning to make inroads into Hindi films.

The era of studios offered an eclectic fare—social melodramas, costume films (quasi-historic and fantasy) and stunt films (adventure stories and revenge sagas). The early films from silent era up to the 1930's—use these plot points to uphold patriarchy. These films showed the dangers of exposing women to the capitalist 'modern' system. However, there were an equal number of films where the female protagonists were used to dissect patriarchal norms, show the corruption of the feudal hegemonic practices in villages and the newly created capitalist culture in the cities. Bombay talkies headed by Devika Rani had unusual films, e.g. *Achhut Kanya* (1936), *Jeevan Naiya* (1936). Another studio that re-wrote the rules as far as women on screen were concerned was Wadia Movie Tone. The Wadia brothers are best known for giving Indian cinema its first action women, fearless Nadia.

The progressive writers association (PWA) established in 1935 had a deep impact on films. Mohan Bhavnani's Mazdoor (1934), scripted by Prem Chand, is credited with the first realistic portrayal of workers in Bombay. The Indian's People Theatre Association (IPTA) also produced films—like K.A. Abbas's *Dharti Ke Lal* and Chitan Anands *Neecha Nagar* and supported V. Shantaram's *D.R. Kotnis Ki Amar Kahani* which addressed progressive themes.

ENTRY OF PROFITEERS AND OF MALE CENTRIC THEMES

With change in the profile of the financers, came a change in the way women began to be represented in cinema. The idealism and progressive outlook of the PWA and of studios like Prabhat, New Theatres and Bombay Talkies gave way to more commercial considerations and increasingly male centric themes. There seem to be fewer women-oriented family socials in the 1940s, the trend towards the traditional' 50s already rearing its head. There were a few notable exceptions such as Kamal Amrohi's *Mahal* in 1949 and the films made by IPTA, but

Mehboob Khan's *Aurat* (1940) and *Andaz* (1949) that see women begin and end the decade in traditional mores.

WOMEN IN HINDI CINEMA : A JOURNEY

1950s: The fifties witnessed actresses who commanded space in every film they were cast in due to their charismatic presence and historian talents. It wasn't surprising that many films were heroine-oriented to utilize the appeal of these actresses. One of the icons of the decade was Nargis, introduced to films at age of five by her actor, singer and film maker mother Jaddanbai. The improvement in cinematic technology led to major changes in the industry in this decade.

1960s: Forties to sixties was the Golden Era of the Hindi Film Industry. Sixties was dominated by musical romances and saw the women protagonists' enter the narrative as sweethearts. There were rare glimpses of vibrant, individual women in the romances, where the protagonist was giveen a well sketched identity. The sweethearts soon settled into domestic roles. This, however, did not take away from the strong characterizations of the protagonists featured here since one could see glimpses of the modern woman of the future.

1970s: This was the decade when angry young man established himself as the voice of the cinema and the masses. 'Amitabh Bachchan' was largely responsible for this phenomenon. The anger seeped into characters played by Dharmendra, Vinod Khanna and Shatrughan Sinha too. Then there were the multi starrer masala films which had two or more actors as lead. Be it Dewar, KalaPathar, Naseeb or Trishul, the actresses had to share whatever little space was left to them in the commercial format. Those who made a mark in this decade despite of the dominance of the action genre were Hema Malini, Rakhi, Zeenat Amaan, Neetu Singh, Jaya Bachchan.

1980s: A significant number of notable characters in the eighties were wives who crossed the laxman rekha either by choice or because of circumstances. Either way, it was a marked departure from the stereotype, since most of these women did not suffer the same fate or had to make compromises like their Sita clone predecessors. For the urban educated women in the country, the eighties was the period of self awareness. The women's liberation movement that had begun study classes and launched organisations was consolidating and growing, reacting to the events across the country and making its voice felt in protest or in appreciation. Films like *Biwi ho to Aisi* (1988), *Pati Parmeshwar* (1988) portrayed women as domestic, honourable and noble.

1990s: The expansion of television in the 1990s became the most competitive challenge facing the Hindi film industry, replacing a scenario that has invigorated many a national cinema in the postwar period. As in other context, however managed to maintain its century-old allure and retain its audience despite the challenge to its central role in Indian popular culture. Throughout the 1990s, a combination of new media forces impacted India most powerfully under the rubric of "globalization", simultaneously opening India to international markets and Indian middle class homes to international commodities and cultural programming. Cognizant of these changes and in competition with it, the Hindi film industry was forced to systematically tap into its overseas market of NRIs (Non-Resident Indians) by reinventing itself. Patriarchy continued to reign supreme even in a tasteful lollypop wrapped in a designer wear Working women were hardly visible in Hindi films. In *Hum Sath Sath Hai* (1999) Sonali Bandre is a doctor in the film but hardly shown in professional ambience. In *Kuch Kuch Hota hai* (1998) Kajol who is boyish has to turn girlish to woo the hero. In *Biwi No. 1* (1999) Karishma Kapoor is successful in bringing her husband back to domestic arena signifying the victory of traditional wife over modern mistress.

The 1990s therefore is a watershed decade marked by an economic and cultural sensibility distinct from that of preceding era. The nineties saw the emergence of an unlikely but iconic group of heroines in Indian society. The much hated word 'stereotype' denotes the description of women characters in this decade, there indeed were protagonists who could be placed in sharp contrast to the norm. In the mire of subdued, suppressed and tamed female protagonists, there are the few who choose to break the mould. These were women who refused to conform—be it shackles put upon their sexual, social or political identity.

THE MILLENNIUM: A NEW AGE

The actresses in this decade got the opportunity to work in both commercial and off-beat cinema, gaining them both critical appreciation and commercial recognition. These included Aishwarya Rai, Kareena Kapoor, Rani Mukherji and Priyanka Chopra. Then there were those like Konkana Sen Sharma who came in through off-beat films and then stepped into commercial cinema. This decade also witnessed a stream of starlets who across as a part of ensemble movies. The multiplex phenomenon created the need for actors who have some star value attached to them to pull in the crowds or for the films to get noticed.

In *Agneepath* (2012) Priyanka Chopra's and in *Dhoom 3* (2014) Katrina Kaif's roles are not substantial. As far as the protagonists are concerned most of Hindi film protagonists can find their inspiration in Indian mythology. Even if there were rule breakers in every decade, many of the noteworthy characters featured in this section through the decades have been regressive. The millennium decade, however seems to have achieved a certain breakthrough by subverting mythology and in some cases, turning myth driven stereotypes on their heads. There are some leading ladies like Vidyha Balan (Paa, Kahani, Ishquiya) and Konkna Sen Sharma (Page 3, Mr. and Mrs Iyer and Life in Metro) who have appeared in strong and independent roles and with box office hits too.

There are some contemporary films like *Paa* (2009), *Salaam Namaste* (2005), *No One Killed Jessica* (2011), *Dedh Ishiquiya* (2014) which explore bold themes like sexuality, divorce and live in relations. This paper mainly relates to mainstream popular cinema but it is important to mention Madhur Bhandarkar's films as women in his films are portrayed as bold and empowered. His films like *Chandani Bar* (2001), *Satta* (2003), *Page 3* (2005), *Corporate* (2006), *Fashion* (2008), *Heroine* (2012) depict women in realistic and strong characters.

Hindi cinema can help the society to break the perceptions and can give power to the women while simultaneously forcing society to sit up and think very hard. The films certainly do reflect the desire, the hope, values and traditions. In Hindi cinema subject matter and treatment have constantly evolved reflecting changes in political and social concern. It is often said that Hindi cinema reflect Indian society because masses can identify with them.

CONCLUSION

The role of cinema as a catalyst or an agent of social change has to be well recognised as Hindi cinema has a large audience. The increased visibility of women in power seems to have let to defining changes in the character of protagonist in the new millennium. The women's space in the most issue-based films on terror and gangsters are still paper-thin. They were either victims or the love interest and as usual, bearing the burden and the pain of human condition remained the prerogative of the male protagonist. Women characters hardly had a shot at heroism.

Women character in Hindi cinema is still regarded as 'entertainment'. Though it has to be said that in popular or mainstream cinema, the malaise is not limited to women characters. If one finds women's characters insubstantial, the men are overdone, with larger than life machismo in plots that are fantastical and often mediocre. When it is difficult to find a subtext to male protagonists, who dictate the box office, looking for an evolved and honest representation of a female protagonist can well be an exercise in futility.

Women in India have always played a significant role, along with men in contributing to the material and spiritual well-being of the people and also in the progressive renewal of the society. Hence, it may be suggested that Hindi cinema gives due recognition to the women's important dual role. Cinema can effectively emphasise the need for education of women, health care of women, equal status in the family and the right to be treated with respect and dignity in all walks of life Hindi cinema can play an important role in restoring women voices in the new millennium.

There is a need to ensure more significant roles for women in Hindi Cinema and just not limit the role to provide glamour, relief and respite. No doubt, box office collection is very important but it has been proven by the success of *Mother India, Kahani, Ishquiya, Dedh Ishquika, Paa, Fashion* and numerous other films that films which portray women as substance can also be commercially successful. There is a need for the camera to shift its focus from women's body to her identity as a strong individual.

References

Chakravarty, Sumita (1993), National Identity in Indian Popular Cinema (1947-87) Austin, University of Texas Press.

Chatterjee Saibal (2008), Hollywood Bollywood: The Politics of Crossover Films, Anwar Jamal Vant Prakashan, 21A Daryaganj, New Delhi.

Ganti Tejaswini (2004), Bollywood: A Guide Book to Popular Hindi Cinema, Routledge, New York.

Hansan Kathryn (1998), Stri Bhumika—Female impersonators and Actresses on Parsee Stage, EPW, 29.

http:mediaindiagroup.wordpress.com/tag/women-in-100-years-of-indian-cinema.

http:www.c.s.jhu.edu/baghi/women.html Amithabha Baghi—Women in Indian Cinema

Mohan Reena (1992), Kalabai Video Documentary.

Prabhu Uma (2003), Encyclopaedia of Hindi Cinema, Harsha Bhatkal.

Tere Nidhi Shendurnikar (2012), Gender reflection in Mainstream Hindi Cinema, *Students Journal, Global Media Journal*, ISSN 2249-5835 Sponsered by University of Calcutta.

Usharao N.J. (1985), Women in a Developing Society, Ashish Publishing House, Punjabi Bag, New Delhi.

Virdi Jyotika and Creekmur, K. Corey (2006), Contemporary Asian Cinema Edited by Tereska Anne Circko, Berg Publishers, New York, U.S.A.

Cinema : It's Social Impacts 12

RAJ K. KANWAR

INTRODUCTION

Cinema is a powerful medium. It speaks with the language of universality. Cinema in the course of story-telling, documentary, realism or fiction through its very nature demands a universal language. By accessing and understanding what makes a universal issue, the audiences can better engage with the world around them. Cinema has a unique charisma and is different from other art forms. Cinema communicates ideas and emotionally moves us. Films remix the real, the unreal, the present, real life memory and dreams on the same shared mental level. However, other than being a very important means of entertainment and delight cinema has played a significant role to bring about social changes. Cinema as an effective media can raise the awareness level and can also bring about sustainable behavioural change thereby reducing vulnerability to the various current social issues and problems. It helps channelize communication and discussion and also acts as a vehicle for creating a supportive and enabling environment.

Cinema provides education through entertainment as a tool to create a knowledge base and helps in removing stigma and discrimination attached at the hands of the society as in case of various serious social problems like HIV/AIDS virus. The messages in such cases need to be informative, educative as well as entertaining as these are all mutually exclusive. The big cinema banners should take the lead in making serious films with attention-grabbing social themes meant for all classes of the society. Cinema renders a yeoman's service in providing accurate and correct news coverage and facilating, dringing forta and generating social impact is the effect in totality that an activity has on a community. Also, Social Impact refers to the social organization that works on a global scale and is dedicated to aiding civil societies, international agencies and governments steering them to positive economic, social and political change. It is a collective process whereby the values, attitudes or institutions of society, such as learning, family, religion, and business expand into customized. It includes both the ordinary procedure and deed programs initiated by members of the community. Cinema can raise the awareness level and can also bring about sustainable behavioural change thereby reducing vulnerability to the various social problems viz. HIV/AIDS, dowry, child labour, corruption, communal violence, gender discrimination, religious bigotry, subaltern/subordinate issues, women trade and so on.

It acts as a channel for communication and discussion creating a supportive and enabling environment. Cinema has proved itself as a powerful tool for the social change particular in the context of Indian Society where things described in Manu Sanhita still rule the roost. Movies have become such an inseparable part of our lives, that it is tough to imagine a world without this form of entertainment. Of course, with the advent of newer technology, the number of theater goers has reduced drastically, but the number of movie viewers have sky rocketed. The movie industry is booming and shows no signs of relenting. The reason why movies are so ardently revered is because; they open a window of innumerable possibilities for it's viewers. It lets you escape into a world which is far from the daily realities and hassles of life.

CINEMA AS A TOOL FOR SOCIAL CHANGE

Cinema is a reflection of the society, both present and past. It is a powerful medium for social change. Other than being a very important means of entertainment and regaling the audience, it has played a significant role to bring about social changes. Indian cinema has seen a great transformation since the early nineteen-thirties. The decade saw the emergence of big banners in the Indian cinemas. These big banners took the lead in making serious films with gripping social themes meant for all classes of the cinema. The film and it's innovations sometimes has to catch up to society but sometimes it leads society too. Movies are stories; movies are people who come out with ideas about something they want to say, something they want to tell someone. Movies are a form of communication and those communication stories come out from societies—not just where society is presently and what it's doing now—but where society has been.

It's been that way for as long as movies have been around! Movies are different things to different people, that's what is so incredible about them for some movies are about escapism. Movies are about sitting in a theatre watching something—watching a story unfold with people watching that happen and emoting an emotion knowing that for those two hours, when people walk into that theatre, they don't have to worry about what is going on outside.

Movies can educate too. These tell us things we never could have known. These tell us things we might not know, and give us a way to explore the past, the present and the future. Every country has stories to tell, about their past, their culture now, and views of what the future will look like through their eyes. Cinema has become a powerful vehicle for culture, education, leisure and propaganda. In a 1963 report for the *United Nations Educational Scientific and Cultural Organization* looking at Indian Cinema and Culture, the author (*Baldoon Dhingra*) quoted a speech by Prime Minister Nehru who stated, "*... the influence in India of films is greater than newspapers and books combined.*" Even at that early stage in cinema, the Indian film-market catered for over 25 million people a week- considered to be just a 'fringe' of the population. In a nutshell, cinema attendance can be both a personally expressive experience, good fun and therapeutic at the same time.

In a rather groundbreaking study, Konlaan, Bygren and Johansson found that frequent cinema attendees have particularly low mortality risks—those who never attended the cinema had mortality rates nearly 4 times higher than those who visit the cinema at least occasionally (Konlaan, Bygren, and

Johansson 2000). Their finding holds even when other forms of social engagement are controlled, suggesting that social engagement specifically in an artistic background is important for human survival."

Contemporary research has also revealed more profound aspects to film's impact on society. In a 2005 paper by S.C. Noah Uhrig (*University of Essex, UK*) entitled, "*Cinema is Good for You: The Effects of Cinema Attendance on Self-Reported Anxiety or Depression and Happiness*" the author describes how, "*The narrative and representational aspects of film make it a wholly unique form of art*". Moreover, the collective experience of film as art renders it a wholly distinct leisure activity. The unique properties of attending the cinema can have decisively **positive effects on mental health**.

Cinema attendance can have independent and healthy effects on mental well-being because visual stimulation can queue a range of emotions and the collective experience of these emotions through the cinema provides a safe environment in which to experience roles and emotions we might not otherwise be free to experience. The collective nature of the narrative and visual stimulation makes the experience enjoyable and controlled, thereby offering benefits beyond mere visual stimulation. Moreover, the cinema is *unique in that it is a highly accessible social art form, the participation in which generally cuts across economic lines.* At the same time, attending the cinema allows for the exercise of personal preferences and the human need for distinction. As the frames move and tell a story, it is that movement which emotionally connects you. This is fundamental about why movies have become global. What hadn't happened for many years, and what started to happen relatively recently was a couple of things. Firstly, movie theatres began to be built all over the world, the phenomenon of movie theatres is only a few decades old. These theatres give people a place to go, to escape and to learn.

Spurred by the communal upheavals in Gujarat, as a social activist Nandita Das addressed the issues of social and human rights in her first debut direction in "Firaaq" based on post-Godhara Hindu-Muslim riots in 2002. The film impressed the international audiences at the London, Toronto, Pusan and New York film festivals. The British Film Institute (BFI) hailed the film as *"the elegant document of human traumas"*. Firaaq means both 'separation' and 'quest'. The film highlights the tolerance and basic humanism necessary for preserving the secular and democratic fabric of India.

ECONOMIC IMPACT OF CINEMA

Film has a uniquely powerful global presence within human culture. In 2009, across major territories, there were over 6.8 billion cinema admissions (*compared against a world population of roughly the same number*) creating global box office revenues of over US$30 billion. The convergent nature of film creates consumption across a number of channels. In the same year combined DVD and Blu-Ray sales in the United States, Canada and European Union alone were US$32.5 billion (*amounting to over 1.1 billion units sold*). When we consider revenues and audience figures from those who consume digitally, via television, repeat view content they already own and view through the highly illegal but vast black-market in films, the figures become truly staggering. The direct economic impact of film is clear, but the effect to the wider economy is also significant. The UK House of Commons Culture, Media and Sport Committee-in a 2002 report on The British Film Industry stated, *"...Of the 23 million people who visited the UK in 2001 – spending approximately £11.3billion – Visit Britain (formerly the British Tourist Authority) estimates that approximately 20% visited the UK because of the way it is portrayed in films or on television. The flow-on effect from film (i.e. the use of services and purchase of goods by the industry) is thought to be that for every £1 spent on film, there is a £1.50 benefit to the economy."* India, for example, wasn't making six hundred films a year fifteen years ago.

All of a sudden, the business part of film allowed people to invest and make movies- and also have somewhere to make their money back, in theatres! Movies do well, and make money, by word of mouth. Advertising is a big part, and of course having the right movie to start with, but word of mouth is powerful. Bad word of mouth can kill you, we all know that. Movies have the shortest marketable life of any marketable product. One can make a movie for $65 million, spend another $50 million on marketing internationally and that movie could be gone within two weeks? No other commercial product has such a short life, with that kind of investment required. With a movie, you have one chance.

That's why the movie business is such a dangerous game to get involved in. Still, with 1,000 films produced annually (about double Hollywood's output), Bollywood is the world's most prolific cinema factory. According to the DI International Business Development (DIBD), a consulting unit of the Confederation of Danish Industry, Bollywood generated revenues of $3-billion in 2011 – this figure has been growing by 10 percent a year. By 2016, revenue is expected to reach $4.5 billion. Bollywood gross receipts have almost tripled since 2004. But since ticket prices are so much lower in India than in the US, Hollywood generates much higher revenue – as much as $51 billion annually, according to Bollywoodcountry.com. On the other hand, it might be easier to turn a profit in Mumbai than in Los Angeles – the average Bollywood film costs only about $1.5 million to make, versus $47.7 million for Hollywood.

Marketing costs are also significantly lower in India. The film industry has played a massive role in generating employment for people, the world over. Since there are so many people involved in making and producing a movie, it naturally has a wide range of job openings. More the people, the better it is. However, it requires specialized training and knowledge, in order to work for a movie. The below mentioned table shows the Top Bollywood Movies in terms of Domestic Collection.

Film	*Net Collection in Cr.*	*Year*	*Film*	*Net Collection in Cr.*	*Year*
Jab Tak Hai Jaan	102	2012	Agneepath	123	2012
Singham	102	2011	Rowdy Rathore	134	2012
Golmaal 3	103	2010	Dabang	140	2010
Bol Bachan	104	2012	BodyGuard	148	2011
Housefull 2	114	2012	Yeh Jawaani Hai Deewani	188	
Ghajni	115	2008	Ek Tha Tiger	199	2012
Barfi	115	2012	3 Idiots	202	2009
Ra One	116	2011	Chennai Express	227	
Ready	120	2011	Krish 3	230	
Don 2	120	2011			

POLITICAL IMPACT OF CINEMA

A film is not just about songs and dance but a medium that can be used for social interest and awareness. Cinema can be a medium of education and change. It is by the filming of movies like these that cinema can be termed as transformative. Cinema, with its powerful tools of fiction and non-fiction can please, transform, and deceive shapes in the audiences. During the Second World War movies in the USA created a feeling of valour and heroism in what we were doing and you saw this in films that came out at the time such as the Purple Heart. The period during the 1960's became prominent for a more assertive Indian nationalism. *Mughal-e-Azam* carved a niche for itself because of its panache. It was not only because of the extravagant sets or the soulful music that the audience was left enthralled. The thrilling war scenes, the captivating Mughal romance, the stunning actress and striking actor too left an indelible mark on the audience. Mehboob Khan's *Mother India* dealt with several social issues. It was one of the earliest films that were women centric. It became a landmark in Hindi cinema. Released in 1957, it brought the character of mother at the centre-stage in Hindi films. It was also nominated as an Oscar for the best foreign language film. Bimal Roy's *Do Bigha Zameen* dealt with common man and exploitation. It was this film that bagged first filmfare award for the best film in 1953. Through their film Nayak released in 2001, the filmmakers posed queries on the way our democratic system functions. It asked the audience "Are we really a democracy?"

The famous movie *3 Idiots* changed the way students looked at marks. The concept of "run after knowledge, marks and success will follow" spread like wildfire throughout the world. So much so that this highly acclaimed movie was shown at the UN for both the message and stellar performance by each of the actors. The film *Aarakshan* too sparked off debates. The tagline for this film was "*India* vs. *India*". It gave the audience a chance to question the education system followed in our country. Based on the social issue of reservation, it became the centre of arguments and disputes. The recently released movie I am Singh puts into limelight the atrocities that Sikhs had to face after the 9/11 attack. Infact the 9/11 tragedy became the base of other movies as well including *New York* and *My Name is Khan*. From

Mrityudand to Satyagraha, Prakash Jha has made movies that voice the anguish of common people.

Satyagraha was more of a documentation of Anna Hazare's movement. The youth of our country has been facing the brunt of corruption for a long time. We saw worldwide movements like the one at Tahrir Square (Egypt) through video filming. But though cinema is popular all over India, it is only in southern India that movie stars have had the most success as popular politicians. Movies and politics have the strongest links there. Recently one of the national parties has bought the rights to "Jai Ho", the Oscar-winning song from "Slumdog Millionaire", to use for its election campaign.

Going by the number of patriotic films which have been made in Bollywood, the story of India's freedom struggle has always been a hit with the filmmakers. A few examples:

Anand Math: This 1952 Hindi patriotic-historical film was based on the popular Bengali novel by the same name written by Bankim Chandra Chatterjee in 1882. The film's story revolves around the events of the Sannyasi Rebellion, which happened in the late 18th century in eastern India, especially Bengal.

The movie '**Shaheed**', starring Manoj Kumar was released in 1965. A hit back then, it also narrated the story of freedom fighter Bhagat Singh Azad.

Haqeeqat: Set against the backdrop of China-Indian War of 1962.

Lakshya: The movie inspires one to join the army, or at least snap out of a passive state.

Upkar: With this film, director-actor Manoj Kumar garnered popularity as Bharat. The film was made because Prime Minister Lal Bahadur Shastri had appreciated Manoj's earlier film 'Shaheed' and encouraged him to make another based on the Jai Jawaan, Jai Kissan slogan. Manoj essayed dual roles, both a jawan and a kisan in the film. Manoj become an authority on screen patriotism with this film.

"Mangal Pandey: **The Rising"**: The Aamir Khan starrer film revolved around the life and struggle of Mangal Pandey. Pandey was popular for attacking the British officers in an incident that was the first act of what came to be known as the Sepoy Mutiny of 1857 or the First War of Indian Independence.

Border: The film was an anti-war film which revolved around the Indo-Pakistani War of 1971. It was an adaptation from real life events that took place at the Battle of Longewala fought in Rajasthan (Western Theatre) during the Indo-Pakistan War of 1971 and Bangladesh Liberation War.

Some other films produced at different times like 1857 (film); 1942: A Love Story; Kranti; Netaji Subhas Chandra Bose: The Forgotten Hero; Shaheed Uddham Singh (film); Veer Savarkar (film) highlighted the roles of our heroes of Indian Independence Movement.

CONCLUSION

Cinema has great responsibility to give proper direction to the society. Society and cinema are replicate of each other. Unfortunately, in recent years it has deviated from its social obligation where films are produced just to earn more and more money. The producers and financiers are merely concerned for the commercial value of the films. Driven by this desires, they pack the films with the ingredients of sex, violence, etc. It poses a challenge to the social fabric. It leads to the decline of moral values of society. It is causing great harm to social responsibility. This needs to be checked without any delay. Cinema has a major role to play in a country like India. The need of the hour is that cinema should be exploited as a power tool to educate, inform and aware the masses apart from entertaining them producing films with themes that generate awareness against greed, power, and the downward spiral that they can cause.

References

Palash Ghosh : Bollywood At 100: How Big Is India's Mammoth Film Industry?

Vikas Shah : Thought Economics, June 2011; An interview with Tom Sherak, President of the Academy of Motion Picture Arts and Sciences.

Politics and films : An Indian Affair; blogs.reuters.com/india.

Ruchismita : Essay on the role and performance of cinema in spreading awareness.

Pradip Biswas : Excerpts from the interview with Nandita Das during recently concluded Kolkata Film Festival, Nov. 10-17, 2013.

S.C. Noah Uhrig (*University of Essex, UK*) 2005, "Cinema is Good for You: The Effects of Cinema Attendance on Self-Reported Anxiety or Depression and Happiness".

Impact of Cinema on Children 13

KRISHAN LAL

INTRODUCTION

Cinema is an important means of information, entertainment, education, etc. Before the existence of cinema folk media was playing this role. Cinema has taken the role of folk media to some extent. Cinema is projecting many things in unreal way. Cinema has great influence on the developing brain of the children. Children are the future of any nation. Children should be taught the constructive ideas so that they can lead nation in a good way. Cinema is a good source of entertainment, information and education. It has positive as well as negative impact on the thinking and behaviour of children. Children consider actors and actresses as role models in their life. If these role models are doing something wrong even then children consider this act, good to be followed in their life. Children try to imitate the acts and behaviour of their role models. According to the United States department of justice, law enforcement agencies arrested approximately 2.8 million juveniles in 1997. Out of them juveniles account for 14 % of murder arrests and 17 % of all violent crime arrests (Senate committee on the Judiciary, 1999). More generally, increased television viewing is associated with higher level of depression and anxiety.

Television and other media represent one of most under recognized and important influences on the health and behaviour of children and adolescents in 1990. Cinema increases academic learning of the children and broaden their thinking as well as creating problems in the life of children. Research should be conducted regularly to know the impact of cinema (media) on the public in general and children in particular.

DATA COLLECTION AND METHODS

The information incorporated in this paper is based on day-to-day media reports, information and content related to films, experience and informal interaction with children. Both positive and negative impact of cinema on the life of children was discussed.

DISCUSSION

Cinema has both positive and negative impact on the life of public. It is a means of creating national integration, bringing the social issues in the forefront. For actors, directors, writers, artists, producers, etc. it is also a means of gaining popularity and money. Cinema is a media. Media is the fourth pillar of democracy. It can make or spoil future of a country by its role and responsibility. Children are most important human resource of a country. They are the future of a country. Youth will govern the country according to the education, experience, information and values they got during their childhood. Today is the age of information technology.

Media is providing more and more information to the public including children. Due to speedy spreading of information, life of public (especially children) is getting influenced very easily and quickly. It is becoming difficult to sort the good information from bad information. Same information is good in one circumstance and bad in other circumstance. Same information can have good impact on the life of one individual and bad impact on the life of other individual. Sometimes people are being projected in a bad way in films and children become biased about the life of such people.

In old times old peoples like grandparents were inculcating values in the children by telling some stories. Now-a-days such stories are losing their existence and grandparents, parents are becoming unable to spare more time for their children. So children are not getting value education informally. Films, games and cartoons are becoming an important part of entertainment. Films are the reflections of the different happenings in the society but different happenings in the society are also the reflections of different films. In fact, media and public are influencing each other. Content and way of presenting the things in cinema/media result in different ways.

Content of cinema should be prepared in such a manner so that it cannot have bad impact on the children and ultimately on the society. Most of the films are stereotyped. Love affairs, rash driving, eve teasing, luxurious life, wining the dangers situations and unrealistic situations are very common in the films. Some films pose the heroes and heroines adopting wrong practices to achieve their goal in life (in unreal life). Children got spoiled because they consider unreal life (as in cinema) as real life and try to live their life as shown in films.

Many times heroes and heroines are being projected as naughty students and their teachers and parents are projected as being befooled by them. In many films youngsters use narcotics etc. and misbehave with their elders, seniors, and teachers. Films also show homicides and suicides committed by different persons after unsuccessful love affair or some other failure. Dangerous, vulgar, brutal, obscene scenes should not be incorporated in films such scenes may be represented through writing, saying or minimizing their duration. Value education should be imparted to the children. Life safety and security is becoming a challenge now-a-days. Censorship of the content, being presented by the media should be done strictly considering its long term effects on the society. Children should not be exposed to violence, kidnapping, human trafficking beyond certain limit. Modern day children are more vulnerable to learn such bad acts because they spend more time watching films, games, cartoons and advertisements etc. Media has more influence on the life of public in general and children in particular.

Due to the influence of media children are getting irritating habit. Human values are getting deteriorated. Children are getting involved in killings. In some cases kidnapping of children by fellow children have occurred. Children are getting inspired to get involved in sexual activities because of films related to these activities. Advertisements are showing only positive things about these products though such products may be harmful also. Children want to have things they are inspired to have by the advertisers. Rash driving is becoming very common as children and youngsters are being inspired for it after seeing the stunts and advertisements which inspire them for doing so. Many accidents are resulting due to rash driving.

Children want to earn money by easy means only, illegal these may be. Children want to dress like their role models, eat the things being eaten by their role models, even to speak like them. Many children are spending less time for their home work but more time viewing the things being telecasted. Good things should be telecasted more and more. Feature films regarding the real story of great leaders, saints, scientists, etc. should be prepared and telecasted. Materialism should not be encouraged.

Children should be given more knowledge about their culture, flora, fauna and other scientific facts. Media personnel should have social responsibility. Parents should keep a close watch on the activities of children. Advertisements should be presented truthfully. Cinema should show through the films, how life security and safety can be increased. Good family life should be shown in the films so that people can follow good films and can live life full of happiness and social values. Social reformers should be given more importance in the films. Eradication of superstitions should be shown through films. Sentiments of any community should not be hated through the films. If sentiments of some community are hated then such things can instigate the public and it can lead to sabotage and violence, etc.

In India more films regarding the life of Dr. B.R. Ambedkar, Saint Kabir, Saint Ravidas, Raja Ram Mohan Roy, Ravinder Nath Tagore, A.P.J. Abdul Kalam, C.V. Raman and other great personalities should be prepared and telecasted. Difficulties of the children in real life should be highlighted so that their difficulties can be eradicated by the concerned authority. Films should show and encourage the public to take care of children if children are in some danger. Different agencies which can help the children in danger should be highlighted by media. If some product is not good for the health of children then it should be compulsory for the concerned producers to communicate the same to the viewers. Wrong food habits are making the children unhealthy leading to obesity and other disorders. For seeing the films, news, serials etc. children are remaining exposed to harmful radiations for more time. This is resulting into insomnia, irritating behavior, adverse effect on eyes and change in food habits, etc.

CONCLUSION

Some quota should be fixed for preparing different types of the films with different themes every year. Films should be prepared by considering the children also as viewers. Fixed percentage of films should be related to life of children, women, and marginalized sections of the society, scientific events, peace and harmony, sanitation and environment and social reformers. If good films are produced considering a goal then such film producers should be encouraged through relaxation in tax liability and in some other way. Great importance should be given in films to inculcating ideas in the mind of children about equality, eradicating of untouchability, poverty, boded labor and superstitions, etc. Content of the material being telecasted should be framed in such a way so that it cannot have adverse impact on the tender mind of children. Scenes related to violence, human trafficking, kidnapping, quarrel etc should be minimized in the films and whenever such scenes are essential to be incorporated in the films presented in such a way that these cannot have adverse effect on the mind of children. Human values should be given more importance in real and unreal life situations so that children can learn and follow the same.

Children should be made aware of the real and unreal life situations. Children should be encouraged to see the better content of the cinema, etc. Mutual respect should also be shown in the films also. Quarrel should be shown to very less extent only if it is very necessary to justify the story of a film. Hitting someone brutally or with some sharp edged weapon should be banned in the films. One who is representing bad character in the films should not be highlighted in films. Poor people should also be shown as heroes and heroines. Children should be prepared for real life situations through media. Affection towards each other should be given due weight age in films as well as in real life. Children should be encouraged to work hard to achieve their goal so that they can form a healthy society.

Good films should be telecasted many times especially on special occasions. Children should be encouraged to differentiate between saying and doing which is becoming very common now-a-days. Unhealthy customs should not be highlighted through the scenes in films or serials but children should be given the required knowledge by telling the story verbally only. Different life situations should be dealt in an appropriate manner both in real and unreal life. National integration, safety and security, eradication of poverty, eradication of superstitions, and prevention of diseases, corruption and hatred among each other should be considered along with entertainment.

References

Senator Orrin G. Hatch, Utah, Chairman. Senate Committee on the judiciary September 15, 1999. Children, Violence and the Media. A report for parents and policy makers. Retrieved from the website - http://www.indiana.edu/~cspc/ressenate.htm

Strasburger, V.C. and Donnerstein, E. (1999). Children adolescents and the media : issues and solutions. *Pediatrics,* Vol. 103 (1) 129-39.

Susan Pitman (2008). The impact of media technologies on child development and well-being. On Child retrieved from the website http://www.ozchild.org.au/userfiles/docs/ozchild/research-papers/ImpactOfElectronicMedia.pdf

Actor, Acting and Activism : A Cinematic Kaleidoscope 14

KULBHUSHAN SHARMA

INTRODUCTION

Cinema, in literal sense, means the process of making a film. Cinema is the reflection of the past and the present. It has its roots in drama. *Vachik* and *Angik* forms of theatre were very popular among the masses. Even in Himachal, we have a strong source of entertainment, *Karyala,* a form of theatre. Besides providing entertainment, it is a form of communication—a powerful vehicle for carrying forward the culture, education, leisure and vital information to reform the society. The cinema has figured prominently in the public domain as a potent means of influence. It not only reflects the contemporary societal set-up but prompts a social change as well. Apart from soaring the people to the flights of imagination-a momentary escape from reality, the movies have added to the share of their happiness and have triggered the social responsibility. Films have become an effective way to spark debate on a variety of social issues.

The basic purpose of cinema is to entertain and a dialogue from a recent movie justifies it—"*Film sirf teen cheezon se chalti hai-entertainment, entertainment and entertainment*" and then, of course, to educate because movies are also taken as a form of literature. It is the depiction of reality on a very big canvas. Movies are created with recreation as its base. No doubt, it has social and political implications. It is a potent means of changing the system and it moulds the opinions of the people. The film industry has grown into an educative industry. Hindi films' subject matter and treatment have constantly evolved, reflecting changes in social and political concerns. Movies have left an indelible mark in the mind of people. The cinema, candidly, expresses its social role by addressing issues concerning mankind.

OBJECTIVES

Present paper will explore the intersection of films and social change by investigating the history of contemporary cinema. In brief, the paper will take up some concrete examples of what impact the cinema has on Indian society and how the humanistic and hermeneutic qualities of actors turn and inspire them into activism.

ROLE OF CINEMA IN SOCIAL TRANSFORMATION

Cinema can provide audiences a vibrant, vivid experience. From overwhelming scenes and dramatic revelations to sharp one-liners, they augment an emotional outburst. Exploring the range of cinema, V.T. Usha avers: "Cinema is unarguably the most powerful medium of the present with tremendous affective and performative potential. In terms of performance art-forms evolving from myth to modernity, from ritual to theatre, cinema has grabbed the space within and outside the human mind." The cinema is a unique form of art as it renders a completely distinct leisure activity. It does have a purgative, soothing and positive effect on mental health. Moreover, the cinema is unique in that it is a highly accessible social art form and people find it not heavy on their pockets. The cinema goers not only have a good personal experience, good fun, but, it acts as a therapeutic experience.

Cinema has truly played a major role in changing our society. Cinema has come a long way towards arousing national consciousness and also in channelizing the energies of the youth in social rejuvenation and nation-building by a skilful adaption of good moral, social and educative themes. Patriotic movies make us remember our love for nation. Movies like—*Haqeeqat* (1962), *Upkaar* (1967), *Border* (1997), *Lagaan* (2001), *LoC* (2003)—

made on Kargil, *Rang De Basanti* (2006), etc. are imbued with the nationalistic spirit.

Cinema is a reflection of society, both present and past. It gives us a way to explore the past, the present and the future. Movies are stories, movies are people who come out with ideas about something they want to say, something they want to tell someone. Acting makes for a good activist. Some actors act for the sake of acting (*Art for Art's sake*) but some are able to transform their acting to a different level altogether. An actor has a very strong imagination which raises in him the empathy towards the pain and pleasure of the people. The actor is deeply connected with the process and his active involvement within the movie transcends his role to a different level-his contribution and active involvement in society. These two inherent connected qualities in him make for an activist.

The manner in which the film-maker conceptualizes the film, the content, his intention and commitments, primarily qualifies him for the being an "activist". It is not enough for a film to be activist; it must help in creating the space for activism, thus, fashioning the social change. There lies the real purpose of cinema where the reel is converted in real sense into reality. The synergy and *syzegy* of actor, acting and activism has to be amalgamated and fused to the benefit of the society. Using all the available means of persuasion and coercion at their disposal, the film-makers take their raw-material from real-life situations and present it with a diverse set of tactics and strategies to prompt social change.

The Cinema has successfully recaptured the past in movies like—*Mother India, Anand Math, Do Beegha Zameen, Pinjar.* There are many bio-pics made to immortalize the endeavours of popular figures—*Gandhi, The Legend of Bhagat Singh, Shaeed-e-Azam, Mangal Pandey, Bandit Queen, Paan Singh Tomar, Bhag Milkha Bhag,* etc. are some of them.

The cinema exercises a great influence on the mind of the people. It has a great educative value and the utility of films is treated as a means of education. Cinema films have the power to influence the thinking of the people. They have changed the society and social trends. They have introduced new fashions in society. Aamir Khan's *Taare Zameen Par,* Sanjay Leela Bansali's *Black,* Prakash Jha's *Gangajal, Peepli Live, Udaan, A Wednesday* are some movies that changed the opinion of the people. They may be described as trend-setters as they create a direct impact on our social life.

Cinema has become a powerful vehicle for culture, education, leisure and propaganda. The Hindi cinema has a vast range—Bollywood to Mollywood to Tollywood, the Hindi cinema is also considered as an "all-India formula film" by the critic Chidananda Das Gupta. Unarguably, India produces an enormous number of feature films in many different languages, including several dialects. The social impact of the cinema in India is also seen in the nationwide popularity of film-based programmes, talk-shows, reality shows like—*Randezvous with Simi Grewal, Koffie with Karan, DID, Nach Baliye, Big Boss,* etc. on various television channels. It's the young generation that is attracted by the film programmes and they keep the headphones plugged to their ears while travelling or walking. The people have liked the songs in all generations-ranging from K.L. Sehgal's desperate cry of the heart *"Jab dil hi toot gya"* to Mukesh's innocent rendition *"Sab Kuch Seekha Hamne"* to Rafi's soulful saunter to heart *"Khoya Khoya Chand"* to Kishore's frantic search *"Mere Sapno Ki Rani"* to YoYo Honey Singh's rap tune *"Ek Glassy"*. The songs have seeped very deep into the Indian collective memory and conscience.

Talking about the great therapeutic quality of the movies, the comic movies have treated many patients through laugh therapy. Sometimes, movies are about escapism. Movies take us away for a while from the harsh, stark realities of life and emote our emotions for three hours that makes us forget what's happening outside. They move us with the moving images and we get emotionally connected to them. The popular hilarious comedies like *Padosan, Golmaal, Angoor, Chupke Chupke, Jaane Bhi Do Yaaro, Three Idiots, Munna Bhai MBBS, Hera Pheri, Andaz Apna Apna,* etc. have left the viewers in splits.

The Indian Film Industry is celebrating the 100 years of its glorious past. It has showcased all the vagaries of Indian culture and tradition. Critic, Irfan Ajeeb pays a tribute to the Indian Cinema: "One hundred years on Indian cinema is a global commodity and appeals to every culture and country around the world. Labelled 'Bollywood' by the West in the 1990s—a term that has helped to globalize an industry that churns out in excess of 300 films a year—Bollywood is today not only an industry but also a tradition and culture. Its influential stars are fervently followed by their idolizing fans and there are certain celebrities such as Bachchan who are regarded as God-like figures."

Film, therefore holds a truly unique place in the story of our civilization. It is an art, a language, a medium for education, inspiration, and much more. It provides employment for hundreds of thousands of people around the world, and enjoyment for the countless more. However, we must not forget that more than anything—film is a hugely entertaining medium and takes us into the throes of imagination to escape our lives for a brief period. That's where lays its true essence and fascination.

The actor and acting are inseparable from each other. A lot of hard work goes into the making of a film. Starting with a good story, a writer floats the idea, the director, actors, cinematographer, make-up artists, visual effects specialists, and the entire crew put their effort into it. The movies are not as simple as they appear to be on the silver screen. The actors get emotionally involved, not only, with the film also with the idea itself. The next stage is to transcend it to a higher plane-into society. Aamir Khan's *Satyamev Jayate*, *Being Human* by Salman Khan, a special programme on *Girl Child* by Priyanka Chopra are the finest examples of actor's activism in real life and their sincere engagement with the society.

Simply speaking, the power of movies and how, through the synergistic impact of moving-image, sound, narrative and other elements—they can create a powerful sense of emotion and engagement. Movies can communicate concepts, ideas and stories. They allow us to be cognitively transported to a different time or a place, and experience life through different eyes-gaining new perspectives, inspiration and understanding. The ancient Greeks, for example, used drama as a method of dealing with emotions. There is a healing property of storytelling that allows us to access areas of human experience which otherwise cannot be accessed through rationality of thought. The acting on the screen and the activism on the larger canvas-life must get harmonized to build a sound society. Only then would it be possible for the cinema to play a pivotal role in society when it gets transcended onto a higher plane.

"The Show must go on 'n' on..."

References

Ajeeb, Irfan. (2007). *100 years of Indian cinema – The Bradford connection: The Guardian.*

Gill, Aastha. (May 30, 2013). *Bollywood turns 100 – a long journey for Indian Cinema .The Upcoming.* http://www.mea.gov.in/articles-in-foreign.

V.T., Usha, *Exploring cinema, censorship and its impact: The Hindu*. December 3, 2013.

Bollywood Songs and Youth 15

Anju R. Chauhan

INTRODUCTION

This chapter focuses on filmy songs and singers in the first half and the second half tries to investigate and explore the effects on youth. Filmy songs are the heart beat and throb of every individual. One of the distinctive characteristic of Hindi cinema is the use of songs. Songs mirror the times in which they were made. Bollywood songs reflect India and India reflects them. The year 1931 is marked as the starting point for movie singers. De de khuda ke naam pe; rootha hai asman gum ho gaya mahatab; teri katil nigahon ne mara; De dil ko aaram aye sari gulfom; bhar bhar ke jam pila ja sager ke chlane bale; Badla dilwae gay a rab and Dras bina more hai tarse naina pyare were the seven songs that paved a way for hindi songs. Main ban ki chidiya (Achhute Kanyaa 1936) was sung by Saraswati Devi and Babul mora chhote bi jaye (Street Singer 1938); Ek bangla bana nyara (President 1937) was sung by K.L. Saigal. It was a time when the British exiled Saigal from Awadh to Calcutta.

Saigal imbued it with all the pain and longing of a man in exile. This was a period of frenetic activity almost as if Hindi Cinema was making up for its 20 years of enforced silence. The average film featured nine songs, many had more. The first songs to hit the nation as a whole may have been from Achhute Kanyaa. 30s belong to Saigal and he is the pioneer of all the singers. Do naina matwale (Saigal; My Sister in 1944) Pancholi created Gul-e-Bakaarti (1939)and made baby Noorjahen (Awaaz de khan ho) known to the world at large and again it is a chance happening that pancholi hired Haider Ali to do Khazanchi in 1941.

Hindi movie song would not have been there without the pioneering framework provided by Khazaanchi. Haider Ali hailed the age of hindi songs in bollywood. At the emergence of cinema, it was purely a source of entertainment and pleasure. Some of the movies reflected the pulse of the society. Unemployment, diseases, epidemics, freedom struggle etc.were the themes in movies.

In the early 1940s, Indian scene had its own domestic perturbations. Politically, Quit India Movement was significant as were the down and dirty war profiteers.The youngsters working in industry held a tough regime for stable employment was coming to an end. World War II and freedom movement followed by Independence, partition led to migration of some of the greatest talents to Pakistan. The greatest singers of the age were Shamshad Begam, K.C. Dey, Pankaj Mullik, Santa Apte, Govindrao Tempe, Ashok Kumar, Devika Rani, Surender Wahidan bai and sister jyoti Bibbo, Manjo and a few more. Suraiya, Jamaal Sheikh spent a career singing mainly for songs filmed on themselves. Ghulam Haider Ali, a legendary music composer is said to be Lata Mangeshker's Godfather. It is he who had contributed the name of 12 year old Lata to a National Level Talent Contest and this provided our best composers with the motivation to produce the very best of melodies and the northwest frontier shuddered as the typhoon hit home. Lata became dominant playback singer of the 1950s.

Lata said of Shamshad Begam in an interview, "I could never achieve the kind of popularity, stardom, respect she enjoyed". Lata and Asha are one of the best known and most prolific playback singers in India. 50s is full of idealism and disappointment. Manna Dey, Rafi, Geeta Dutt, Shamshad Begam, Lata, Asha, Suraiya, Talat Mukesh, Hemant, Kishore Kumar dominated the singing zone in Bollywood. These singers rendered their voices for the favourite actors like Raj Kapoor, Devanand, Dalip Kumar. 50s was also a period of nation building; saathi haath badhaana and mehnatkash insaan jag utha; but along the way, perhaps a sense of illusionment had begun to creep in Yeh duniya ... is an unforgettable and uncomfortable reminder of all that was rotten in the still fledgling republic 60s.

In the 1960s, age bhi (Asha) Waqt, became a hit. Asha's voice brought alto than soprano, more suited to quintessential 60s club crooner. In 60s, Pyar kiya to darna kya song (Mughle-e-Azam) was picturised in colours for the first time on the screen. Rock type of songs started in 60s ; most of the songs were sung by Mohammad Rafi for actors like Shammi Kapoor, Joy Mukharji, Biswajeet. Kishore Kumar is the song hero of Bharat Rattan Awardee Sachin Tendulker. In 1965, after Indo China War, patriotic songs like Ae mere watan ke logo sung by Lata became a hit and is admired till today. In 70s, it was first the age of Rajesh, the lover and then an angry young man Amitabh; then Rishi Kapoor. The music was peppy, westernized, the aural equivalent of the fashion then in vogue.

The youth imitated the hair styles and fashions of their heroes and heroines. Rafi's and Kishore's popularity increased. Kishore achieved popularity with songs like Mere samne wali khidki (Padosan 68) Zindagi ka safar (Safar); Wo sham (Khamoshi); Phoolon ke rang se (Prem Puja); O mere raja (with Asha in Johny mera naam); jaane ja dhoondta (with Asha in Jawani Diwani); Aap ki kasam; Zindagi ke safer (74); Musafir hoon (Parichay); Dil kya kare jab kisi se (Julie) etc. 70s resulted in drainage and degradation in economy; hence resulting in frustration among youth. Corruption started cropping up (Roti Kapra Aur Makaan).

Tuneful version of the disco songs became the hallmark of 80s. I would like to remember with Gujral song, mera kuchh saman ...... 90s belong to Yash Chopra with najaane mere dil ko kya ho gaya; Dil to pagal hai, etc. Ram Gopal Verma's 'saiya' had a song goli maar bhejo mein about Bombay underworld and the nature of these men's lives. This song is an unpretty example of the gritty, realistic, violence that took roots in songs in 90s. 2000 saw many things going retro and love for ethnic rose and also the carvings for remix. (Saas gaali dewe—from Delhi-6), 2000s (the first decade) Maula mere le le meri jaan from the movie Chak De India, in 2007, plays in the background as the central character falls from grace and years later, jostles its way into story.

While 'Babul mora ... was the lament of a man in exile; 'maula mere' is a song that helps Bollywood express itself. The

2010s will belong to Ranbir Kapoor—songs from 'Barfi' 'Aashiyan, itni si khushi, itni si hasi, chal manayen aashian' is liked by youth.... Evergreen Songs like Kahin door jab (Mukesh), Biti na bitai raina (Lata & Bhupender); Jis gali mein (Mukesh); Dil he ke manta nahi (Kr Sanu & Anuradha Paudwal); Tip tip barsa pani (Alka Yagnik & Udit); Har ghari badal rahi he roop (Sono Nigam) and many more, are liked by the people of all ages.

Popular singers include Bhupen Hazarika (Dil ghoon), Yeshudas, Mukesh, Manna Dey, Hemant Kumar, Noor Jahan, Sandya Mukherji, Sabina Yasmin, Kishore Kumar, Geeta Dutt, Usha Mangeshkar, Anuradha Paduwal, S.P. Balasubramaniam, K.S. Chitra, Udit Narayan, Kr Sanu, Sonu Nigam, Himesh Reshmian, Mika Singh, Shreya Ghoshal, K.K. Sunidhi Chauhan, Mohit Chauhan, A.R. Rahmaan, Mamta Sharma, etc. Songs sung by these singers are the combined products of the talents of lyricists, music directors, composers and singers often determine the extent of success of individual movies.

Soundtracks for movies are released before the movies themselves. Old songs are evergreen and melodious and are sung during family gatherings. Old songs are presented in remixes and this is what the youth likes the most. New gen likes fast music lunggi dance (Chennai Express); tammanche pe disco (Bullet Raja); Sari ke fall sa (R. Raj Kumar); Dhat tere ki mein ghar nahi jana (Gori tere pyar mein) etc. Item songs have become a trend in the films. Chikni chameli (Agnipath); Sheela; Munni; Favicole se, etc. are much liked by youth. But it is a fact that rhythm exites them more than the words. All admire songs but it's youth that enjoys it to the fullest. Songs bring a sense of happiness for them. It is an acknowledged fact that songs have been central to young people's lives from generations. Filmy songs are a driving force among youth. There are some really great lyrical songs that motivate them, that make them smile, that make them cry. Why does that happen? Because it does make an impact. In other words, the most interesting question is-what is the influence of filmy songs on young people? Feeling of a true poet is reflected in almost all the Hindi songs. Songs epitomise romance and pleasure as well.

There are various positive effects songs have on teenagers. Songs have a great effect as on how young think, act and possibly even affecting intelligence. As stated on Reverse spins 101

Website, "Simply listening to music in the background while doing an arduous task can make it seem much easier, or in some case ease the strain of an activity". Listening to songs makes them great and can make their mood change. Whether it is merely a distraction from the stress of a situation or genuinely lifts the mood of the listener, music has been shown in several studies to improve and increase productivity in this manner. Listening to pious, devotional, patriotic songs, one really feels blissful.

In both cases, the listener finishes the activity in a shorter period and time and with less residual stress. Listening to songs can help students improve academically. If music education be imparted right from the beginning, it will definitely aid the youth in understanding the vocabulary and the rhythm of musical language may allow him/her to improve both reading and writing skills. According to our college report done recently in October 2013, students who partake in music performance really score better than those who do not. On the same note, concerning failing students, listening to songs have been shown to pull youth from even the greatest depths of academic failures.

With a step outside of the normal, standardized education system, the failing student may be able to express thought and emotion, make bonds with singers, feel the need for self-improvement both consciously and unconsciously in the classroom and in other areas of life. Through the observations and studies, it seems that the implementation of compulsory music education into the education system could solve many of the problems that test preparatory classes and overbearing focus on core areas of education cannot. Thus listening to songs has even been shown to encourage intellectual growth. Songs can be stimulant to intellectual and cognitive development.

Many youngsters try to compose their own music, which can create healthy emotional expression. Composing/creating new songs are also an economic factor for youth. For most youngsters, songs are an outlet for personal identity, development and expression. Some songs help them to relax and manage their moods and provide ways to connect to peers. The physical effects that filmy songs have on youth are almost the same as emotional. Every emotion can be enhanced through songs. In parlors, gyms, songs played in the background help them pumped up and focused.

Songs are a way to express emotions. Practical investigations have demonstrated that basic emotions such as anger, happiness, fear, sadness can be recognized in and created by songs stimuli in youngsters. Being a youth can be a rough time emotionally as the body goes through a lot of changes. Songs are emotionally 'an art form' covering every type of emotion including happiness, anger, sadness, regret and anxiousness. That is why songs can be especially meaningful to youth when they are able to find song that matches their mood; they can feel comfort, as if they are not alone in their emotions.

Songs teach them valuable lessons as well. Taste and interest in songs can often bring youngsters together. Learning another teenager liking the same rhythm, language, style of song can be an easy way for two teenagers to share, connect and bring a relatively better friendship. Filmy songs are often enjoyed in public, at concerts, dance clubs and places teenagers often hang out. Youngsters attending these concerts and clubs already share a common interest and that particular style or music style. As the youth sometimes feel violated or like outcastes, songs can help bring a sense of community. Filmy songs can teach them a lot about their own culture and other cultures they might not normally be exposed to, musical traditions, musical instruments, history lessons, political issues of that culture and more. Thus, it can be a more fun way to learn about a culture rather than reading a book.

With the new technology, they can bump songs from Iphone to Iphone, stream it on line and watch their favourite videos along with the tune anytime and anywhere.

Many youngsters admit that singing, humming is a source to ward-off worries.

Despite the advantages, songs also have negative effects upon impressionable young minds. The Suite 101 Website has this to say: 'certain lyrics or music with violent lyrics, are believed to have a negative impact on youth. 'Old songs is a new hit and is printed as item.

It can be hard to pry their ear buds from their heads. Enjoying songs may hinder their study skills because brains are only built to do one thing at a time. One would not get the same quality of work done if he focuses on the tone at the same hour.

Pretty much, every emotion can be enhanced with songs. Some teenagers listen to such songs for suicidal tendencies and start making life-affecting decisions.

With the experience of songs being so close to the human psyche, the listener naturally experiences both emotional highs and lows. The troubled mind have been pushed over the edge while listening to sad songs. Many documented suicides have taken place while filmy songs played in the background and there is some speculation that extended listening could lead to anti-social behavior. In some cases, songs are not really the cause of the problem but they clearly affect the actions of troubled youth.

The explicit nature of some modern lyrics has desensitized some to immoral thoughts and actions. Violence in songs also affects the mind. Researches over the years have proved this to be true when it comes to the effects of film songs on young brains. Does not the youth start imitating the styles of singers? Obviously yes. To follow them blindly is not good at all. The constant bombardment of almost impossible to achieve body images leads and leave many youngsters disgusted. They start living in a world of fiction which is dangerous for them. Parents have a great role to play and must help their wards to understand that.

New gen likes rock, hip-hop, and fusion, pop and fast music. In a survey, conducted with the help of president of G.C. Kullu, Raj Soni, in Nov. 2013, it is found that the youth likes fast music but they also like melodious old songs.

"Youth is crazy for the songs of Honey Singh and Mika Singh only because of the rhythm and not the language and the words. Some youngsters use these songs to tease one another. The language used in them is not clear and meaningful whereas old songs are melodious, meaningful and the language is clear in them". "Some youth likes trance music and it is resulting into irritability and rowdism sometimes". "Majority of them likes music that sooth them". Their favourites are Sufi, Semi-classical and Light songs and the favourite singers are Kailash Kher, Javed Ali, Nusrat Fateh Ali Khan, Rahat Fateh Ali Khan, Sonu

Nigam, Harshdeep Kaur, Arijit Singh, Sunidhi Chauhan, Shreya Goshal, Mohit Chauhan, Rekha Bhardwaj etc. Maximum youngsters admitted that they get angry feelings after hearing fast musics songs by Honey Singh and Mika Singh excite them for a moment and the language of modern lyrics is forgotten very soon. Modern lyricists must refrain from using bad language.

Thus, songs have the power to make the world and to mar the world. However, wonderful or terrible filmy songs may be, keeping in mind some important tips, songs are still a cornerstone of human culture, a learning tool, an incredible medium through which young people can interpret, celebrate and share their experiences and emotions. Songs are a powerful medium for leisure and education and to deny its power is a waste of a truly wonderful resource. Old Bollywood songs are still unique and evergreen. Happy singing and listening!

Screen Adaptations of Books : Litteratur's Agony, Audience's Joy 16

DIPALI S. BHANDARI

Ever since the beginning of cinema, filmmakers have tried to conceive newer uses to which it could be put. The movies have a great attraction for the average man because of their life-like quality. In the modern era, films have gradually replaced most of the other forms of entertainment. Taking off from theatre, it covers a varied range of topics for its subjects and themes.

According to Aristotle, Plot is of major importance in the success of a play. By extension, this applies to films as well. One of the tricks for production of a successful film is a gripping screenplay. The audience loves a story well written and associate with the characters at emotional levels. In search of new storylines, filmmakers often look towards the archives of literature. This is why literary classics are often adapted for screen. The baffling question is: Why do some of these adaptations work and the others flop? This paper attempts to analyze the reasons why a book which readers love either fails to set the box-office ringing or invites the wrath of litterateurs for unfaithfulness to the original.

The books adapted for screen are mostly chosen for their success as books. The logic that works here is that if readers loved it as a book, they will definitely love it as a movie. To a certain extent it is true. The unprecedented success of the Harry Potter movie series closely followed the record-breaking success of the books of the series. In reverse, the Twilight books were popularized by the success of the first movie of the series. In Hindi literature too, *Devdas* has been immortalized by three different screen versions in three different eras. Timeless classics have been adapted for the silver screen. With the increasing popularity of television, Epics like the *Ramayana* and *Mahabharata* have been adapted for screen in episodic forms. The popular shows on television that have their roots in literature include *Saraswatichandra, Har Har Mahadev, Lapataganj, Taarak Mehta ka Ooltah Chashma* and other biopics on Hindu gods *Hanumaan, Ganesh, Krishna* and various mother goddesses. In a way, they have enriched the average person in his knowledge and vocabulary of these epics which form the root stock of our culture. Well researched adaptations of literary gems too, acquaint people with the landmarks in literature.

In the contemporary times, people generally do not have the time or inclination to settle down with a book. The preoccupation with internet and television has weaned a whole generation away from books. In a way, this has led to a strong decline in readership. Educationists are expressing concern over the diminishing numbers of readers. It is also a matter of concern that the coming generations may grow up to be entirely unacquainted with our classical and literary heritage. Various efforts are being made to impart the knowledge of our rich past to children to encourage reading habits among them. Formulating the scriptures into comic-book series, promotion of children's books and authors, organizing book fairs in school and establishment of mobile libraries are some of the steps being taken to inculcate and promote reading habits among children. Although these have had a positive impact, still there are clearly many more miles to go.

The parents of today do not have time to read out stories to their young and the nuclear family deprives the child of a chance to learn from grandparents and members of the extended family. With the majority of people opting for a small family and the busy schedule of students, children do not get time to play games or interact with other children. Most of the children spend much of their time with television, Play Stations, mobile phones, i-pads, and internet. In an attempt to attract the children towards the wealth of literature, the concept of animated programmes for children was floated. The most popular of these programmes are based on tales from *The Ramayana, The Mahabharata,* as well as screen adaptations of the Jungle Book, tales from Panchtantra and Karadi tales. Full length movies have also been adapted from epics and books throughout the world. *The Time Machine, The Mysterious Island, The Count of Monte Christo, Arabian Nights* as also fairy tales like *Cinderella, Beauty* and the *Beast, Rapunzel, The Little Mermaid,* etc. are providing education as well as entertainment to the young children. The effort seems to have paid off to a great extent with the children.

However, the effort to replicate this formula with films for the grown up audience does not always work well. Books have been adapted for screen since long for the pleasure that a moving picture provides. When the Lumiere brothers first captured workers streaming out from a factory, people were intrigued by the 'moving' images. Since then films have been made for entertainment and educational purposes.

When a book is adapted for the screen, the criterion for selection of the theme is usually the iconic status of the work or the director's instinct for a potentially successful storyline. However, many of these films do not get the anticipated success on the box office. If a screen version of the book is successful, the critics often charge it with infidelity to the text. In case of a book that has set records of success, the director has a lot to live up to. The adaptation of such a book for screen requires considerable work on the part of the director and the writer as it is not possible to include every detail from the text into the film. The director has to selectively incorporate the essential elements from the book omitting the details that are superfluous owing to time constraints. Apart from this, there are many other problems that the transcreator has to overcome.

The first problem that the writer faces is the difference in the medium. Since the films have a visual aspect, they leave nothing to the imagination. It expresses things explicitly and the audience does not consciously attempt to decipher the symbols employed by the filmmaker to convey his vision. By contrast, literature uses images in a different way and evokes mental images corresponding to the description. At times the literary works are allegorical in nature and any attempt to recreate them in any other medium may not be successful. A reading of the book evokes a different response than watching a movie. The book keeps playing at the back of our mind while we watch the movie. In addition, there is a loss of the aura that surrounds things while they are still inside our minds. As Keats very aptly puts 'Heard melodies are sweet, but those unheard are sweeter'.

The moment a thing transcends the borders of imagination and enters the visual domain the mystery is dissipated to quite an extent. And sometimes the finished products do not match up to the expectations of the general audience who were looking forward to a certain movie with anticipation.

Another problem faced by the writer and director is to align the author's vision to fit in with their own vision. K. Chellappan, talking about translation, says:

> "Creation is thus a paradox: a deep inner language made outer...and this fundamental paradox is intensified in translation because here the translator has to externalize someone else's vision in some other medium in his own medium." (Chellappan, 153)

With a little modification this fits in with the dilemma faced by the writer- director. Very often we find authors complaining that the director/writer 'mutilated' their book or 'did not do justice' with the plot and many more complaints like this. The plea of the director here is that he has to create a 'sellable' product. The screen version of *The Guide* deviates from R.K. Narayan's book in that it rains after Raju dies. In the book, the drought does not end with Raju's fast and death. The Indian audience, according to the director, would not accept the hero dying in vain, especially since he has repented so sincerely. This is why he 'tweaked' the end to make it acceptable to the audience. Understandably, the director cannot do justice to a writer's work unless he agrees with his philosophy and his vision: which are both products of the writer's psychological and cultural make up. Cultural contexts too influence the screenplay of a movie. What is acceptable to the people of one country may not be appropriate for another culture. This is why timeless classics like *Othello, Macbeth* and *Romeo and Juliet* had to be 'retouched' when they were being adapted for their respective screen version in India; namely, *Omkara, Maqbool* and the recently released *Ram Leela*. The films were appreciated by the connoisseurs of literature and movies alike, but the fresh appeal of the works was mainly due to the directors' vision which was in line with the original writer.

The success of these movies proves that movies based on literature, if treated in a just manner will be appreciated and also rake in a good collection at the box office. What is needed is an impartial assessment of the literary work and the target audience, editing for the final screenplay and fidelity to the author's vision.

References

Aristotle, *Poetics*. Chellappan K., The Paradox of Transcreation. *Quality in Translation: Proceedings of the III Congress of the International Federation of Translators (FIT)*. Godesberg, 1959 (Oxford: Symposium Publications Division, Pergammon Press Ltd., 1963.

Quiller-Couch, Arthur Thomas, Sir, The Oxford Book of English Verse. Oxford: Clarendon, 1919, [c1901]; Bartleby.com, 1999. www.bartleby. com/101/. [03/12/2013].

Cinema and Human Values 17

MANDEEP SHARMA

INTRODUCTION

Cinema is a true reflection of almost all the human actions performed in every walk of life in the present scenario, be it within the four walls of house or in wider public gatherings whether these are social, religious or cultural ones. Being a teacher, I feel that such thought provoking undercurrent is noticed even while teaching in the classroom. Any lecture when delivered in cinematic style in order to imbibe human values among the students proves more effective than simple, stereo typed advice. A powerful weapon of man's infinite learning; cinema consciously or unconsciously directs every mind and widens his horizons, whether related to society, polity or economy. In this age of multiple ethnic identities world over and especially in case of India, the moral values are asserted repeatedly in almost all the movies covering wide ranging issues. These issues, not much appreciable amongst the younger generation focus on: Acceptability of the Traditions, Scientific Validity of that Cultural Heritage, youngsters' aggressive support to the controversial modern style of living though sometimes appearing to be immoral are vital to the success of today's movies. On the other hand, some award winning movies of the world bring forth the exploitative angle that feudal tendencies impose on the continuous struggling, surviving or perishing racial groups, the world over.

Such struggles are sometimes fiercely fought and become bloodiest in nature on the name of modernization. Disturbingly, in the majority of government reports, the interests of the poor, the downtrodden, the tribes and the innocent human beings are sacrificed along with their age old ideals in the garb of or on the pretext of development and modernity. These painful stark realities which have been born out of the womb of ideological contradictions explored by the brilliance of cinema have, to a greater extent, shaken this civilized world of today to its very foundations. No doubt, many wonderful movies with their universal appeal brought forth the importance of human values by posing to the viewers some real questions valid for man's existence.

For example, the studies without any interest of the student is bound to prove disastrous, in the same way, development without taking the views of the inhabitants is bound to spell doom for that area. A number of movies have made their everlasting impression in this context. The celebrated movie, *Three Idiots,* leaves a clear question mark on the utility of compulsive education based on reckless and competitive mad race. *Avatar* and *Bagwan* are the other Hindi movies which stratify great virtues of sharing and caring in the context of joint family system in India. Commercially stating, the best approach to cinema is one where a movie is made financially profitable and thematically based on morality.

The movies like *Dabang, Dhoom* and *Krish* are though full of entertainment but with lesser moral values to reflect. Unfortunately, to earn huge profits is the sole aim of the movie makers. It is at this juncture that writer, director or producer has to be ethically reminded that glamour or commercially flavored movies must be restricted to the extent of self-abiding sense and must base itself to family culture. Every kind of nudity or double meaning movies must be justified in the eyes of human values and of course every such compartment be finally a part of totality, i.e. a strong message based on morality in the given society.

The curiosity of a school child while watching any movie is at its best because innocence plays a significant role in lacking clarity of the cinematic themes and the complexities sometimes become hindrance to understand the story at a tender age and sometimes values depicted in the story are misunderstood. For example, when a hero in the story runs away from his home in search of better facilities in life and finally shapes up his career outside by dint of hard work and upholding the human values at the same time, a school child while watching that movie will jump to the conclusion and consequently misunderstand that running away from home can bring fortunes to him. However, he will miss the vital point of hard working as well as respect to the human values at a time when circumstances can be most depressing and forcing. There is no hesitation in accepting that it's the school education that lays the foundation stone for imbibing human values in the personality. It is school environment that brings a sea change in the outlook of any generation at any given space or time.

That's why the role of the school teacher finally comes into picture and is the most crucial in this particular phase of life. Because it is the teacher who can show the path of righteousness to his pupils. Since it is a universal phenomenon that watching a movie has become an essential part of the majority of the people especially the teenagers, therefore, though looks somewhat funny but practical is to hold value based group discussions in the presence of school or college teachers so that good citizens could be produced.

The role of the parents is crucial in interpreting the true sense of the movie. This is true that in Indian system, a child lacks frankness with the parents as far as seeking clarity on any scene or sequence of a particular story is concerned. The parents should either have friend-like relationship with their children and can watch any movie together or be frank enough to freely discuss at length any doubt cropping up in their minds after seeing any movie. There is huge benefit to it, firstly, the instant or brash reaction to any movie will be avoided. Secondly, the human aspect of the movie will be inculcated. Likewise, seeing a movie and watching nude scenes in it, gives rise to crimes against women. The cases of physical assault against the female-folk have increased many folds in recent years. The cinema is also partly responsible for this social upheaval. Because, a large number of such incidents are directly or indirectly motivated by one movie or the other. So the role of the parents becomes indispensable from cinema's point of view.

Finally, the role of the viewers is crucial who owe social responsibility. It's an irony of the fact that the Indian cinema goers sometimes ignore good movies because they lack glamorous touch. For examplc, the movies by Salman Khan prove to be super hits without much stress on moral values but more emphasis on glamorous songs and stunts. However, movies like *Sangharsh* though with lots of moral values do not attract much audience because of no glamour in it. So, the onus is also on the movie watchers. The mindset also needs to be researched and reviewed to give broader horizon to the human outlook right from the school times.

In society, there are many individuals, who have risen from rags to riches while imitating movie themes. This trick is especially successful in the field of business and politics, where human values were kept aside in order to taste success and fame. When such glory somehow short lives and the manipulative angle stands exposed, the chance for damage control slips away and by that time everything seems to be lost forever and crimes are committed. In due course the Hobson's choice is to face trial and then punished. In politics too, some leaders have vertical rise and attain a powerful position or office overnight. Such leaders, to a greater extent, learn this art from movies based on the thinking of reaching at the top by hook or by crook. Shockingly enough, this short route deprives us of human values.

Any civilized country in the world survives any cultural onslaught whether external or internal when its age old heritage is deep rooted among its countrymen, generation after generation. However, the first and foremost condition for such stratification of thoughts to come in, is preaching of human values by the majority of its people and in today's modern world, It is none other than the powerful cinema that can paint the human values in the best way it can and then with the passage of timen layers of such thoughts and beliefs take the shape of human civilisation. Any movie with a powerful theme leaves such an everlasting impression on the human mind that socially speaking it can turn the thoughtful human world upside down in few hours. For example, the movie *'Ek duje ke liye' shakraed* the Indian society and went on to redefine the depth of relationship among the young lovers. Though the lovers sacrificed their lives to immortalize and liberate their soul from the shackles of cultural and caste inequalities, in the end, the love wins but at the cost of lovers' lives. So to conclude, cinema triumphs if it immortalizes humanity and it awaits doom's day if it mortalises human values.

References

Cinema India: The Vishal Culture of Hindi Film Rachel Dwyer, Divia Patel.

Published on July 29th, 2002 by Rutgers University Press, New Jersey, U.S.A.

1. *Five Point Someone* – by Cheten Bhagat.

Published Rupa & Company, Kolkata, 2004.

Science, Technology & Human Values by Edwaral J. Hackett.

J. Hackett.

Journal of the Society for Social Studies of Science, Arizone State University, U.S.A.

Movies

1. *Taare Zamin Par* – Directed by Amir Khan.
2. *Three Idiots* – Directed by Amir Khan.

Cinema : A Boon to Society 18

Sutinder Dohroo

INTRODUCTION

Just as literature is considered as mirror of society cinema also records the reality which is prevalent in society. Cinema refers a noun with its unique consciousness—a word to penetrate the audience's imagination and inspire critical thinking. Human mind cannot help without interacting with outer world, i.e. what is happening around us. Thus, there is an inextricable relationship between these two worlds which takes us closer to the realities of life and hopefully their probable solutions and its traumas, aspirations also if it is seen through that point of view.

Drama is 'an imitation of life' and dramatization of life though cinema leads us to a state of conceiving the factual picture of life positions in such a way that they often portray what is depicted in society. But instead of merely mirroring society films strive hard to bring about considerable and appropriate changes in thinking. Human society has to undergo a transformation—one that brings about democracy, cosmopolitanism, close clustering of different cultures, within the boundaries and across the boundaries a harmonious blending of different ways of thinking and above all sincere and humane attempt for oneness with nature.

Now a question arises in a thought-oriented mind whether cinema acts as a powerful medium of social changes influencing our day-to-day life and its activities? The change adds beauty to life as it is a spice of life which is direly needed in our so called modern and civilized society in which intermingling of diverse point of views occurring in society has made us chaotic and crazy. The answer is 'Yes' as cinema of good faith can help us to sort out many of our problems with its universality of appeal to the common masses.

These 'moving images' administrate our inner world psyche in such a way that we attempt to come out of our 'shells' to see and to respond to what is actual happening around us. The portrayal of different characters in different situations stamps themselves on our psyche that ultimately results in a social change. This is definitely not an easy task for anyone who wishes to make 'real cinema for real people'. Besides being a very important means of entertainment and rejuvenation, cinema has played a significant role to bring out social changes.

METHODOLOGY

My paper focuses on the role of cinema as a boon to society as an educator, encourager, teacher, transformer inspiring analytical and innovative thinking among masses to gear positivism in society by making social changes discarding unwanted negativism that surround us in present times.

To present a clearer view of my opinion and to stress my point of view the characters and situations represented in different films and diverse issues related to us ranging from social and personal life to national, public to political, economical to commercial, raging against set norms leading to conflict between older and younger generation have been studied and assessed to prove what is 'just and fair' in the cinematic culture of 'moving images' as messengers of social change.

BACKGROUND OF CINEMA

Indian cinema has transformed a lot since 1930's. 'Alam Ara' directed by **Ardeshir Irani** was released in 1931. Three big banners in Indian cinema **Prabhat Bombay Talkies and New Theatres** took first initiative in attracting the common masses by depicting social themes. A number of films made during this period projected as a strong plea against social injustices meted out by commoners at the hands of tyrant masters. During 1941's cinema in South India emerged and felt the pulse of the masses and since then cinema came to be viewed as an 'instrument of cultural exchange'.

The period from 1941 to 1960 was the 'Golden Age of Indian Cinema'. After that there was no turning back. By this time we happily witness countless myriad shaped ideas presented by different films coming from different Indian territories. *Tollywood for Tollygunge, Mollywood for Madras, Bollywood – National Hindi films and Hollywood as a world cinema.* Earlier it was approx 1000 films were coming in a year from diverse languages, and dialects. But by 1990, this trend of producing a bulk of films has shown a steady decline. Now-a-days if a film is successful on box-office success it is considered the most popular film.

CINEMA AS AN INSTRUMENT OF CHANGE

People are strongly affected by assessments of what is just and fair in dealing with other. Films as historical documents, beautifully record history with the retrospective and progressive changes occurred in society. With its universal appeal to discard narrow-mindedness of thinking resulting dead traditions, which are no more needed in every-progressing society, cinema becomes an effective mediator to resolve many of problems of struggling human beings heading to achieve better future prospects. In this way, it helps humanity to achieve social justice. History intermingled with social concern and romance is strongly affirmed in **Mugal-e-Azam**.

The daring attempt of revolt by **Shahjade Sabnam** against the authoritative and dictatorial father King Akbar captivated the audience. The thrilling war scenes, soultfull classical musical notes and superb actress and striking actor left an ever lasting impression on the people that touches the core of our heart. The state of parents **helplessness in front before raveling young son** is yet another thoughtful concern depicted in this historical *cum* romantic movie.

After facing Indo-Pakistan wars in 1962, 1965, 1971, the thought shifted over to national concern of peace, progress and prosperity. **Hakikat, Vande Matram Shaheeday Azam Bhagat Singh, LOC**, etc. depicted attention seeking representation of the situations during the war and postwar disastrous effects on society. The beautiful patriotic songs—Batan Pe Jo Phida Hoga, Amar Bo Naujawan Hoga, (Kar Chaale Hum Phida Tan Sathio, Aab Tumeharay Hawaley Watan Sathio (वतन पे जो फिदा होगा, अमर वे नौजवान होगा, कर चले हम फिदा जाना तन साथियो), (अब तुम्हारे हवाले वतन साथियो) Such patriotic songs have delved deep in Indian collective memory and conscience to feel fresh flow of patriotic stream nationality. It evokes deep sense of gratitude and gratefulness towards our motherland. Within the passage of time the plot of many films were nicely woven with the same themes of nationalism attracting younger generations as inspirational and educator films.

At the same time devotional films based on epics **Mahabharat, Ramayana,** etc. were made their way to human psyche making us feel cult of spiritualism in its varied forms. **Jai Santoshi Ma** was released in 1975 and audience's interest shifted briskly from romantic era to religious era. This shift was purposely made to make us realize that almightily administrates the whole universe. He witnesses all of our actions resulting, pain and pleasure in human life. They also encouraged us to lead our life strictly according to the directions laid by our religious gurus and we must become the followers of the path of 'Dharma'. If one accepts cinema as an art form and subscribes to Tolstoy's notion of art being an act of communication and social inter connection, then one can easily believe that cinema has the potential to change thinking of societies. Human kind remains in endless search of fields of mutuality and collaboration among human relations depicted in family, the elimination of stress and injustice created by modernized and urbanized way of living and thinking for facilitation of better future for the next generation and generations after that.

Mahesh Bhatt's Film 'Arth' familiarized us with extra marital affair. The bold theme of the ground realities of family life depicted in a realistic way forced us to re think the threatening situations breaking up of our families. Such a shift involves our understanding of ourselves, our relationships with other humans, natural world created within the family and unnatural world outside the family making us 'miserable being' caught in a web of 'to do or not to do, that is a question'.

This is a universal dilemma of modern man our identification with the processed images presented on the screen unfold reasons of tension in family life. When one compares himself or herself up against the "image" the self vanishes and a transformative role of cinema proves its worth in maintaining peaceful congenial atmosphere with in the family as our major concern in these days because we bear pulls and pressures of modern thinking. Cinema as a transformer shapes our private thoughts and public minds. It has transformed the way we see and understand the world. The visual presentation has indeed taken central place in our consciousness. Films like **Bagwan and Avtar** switched over to other most shattering experiences of the old parents harassed by their own children. When children fail to support them physically and emotionally. The parents are no more needed when the children grow up—is one of the most urgent social issues encountered by older generations. Discarding their parents, the younger generation underestimate their capabilities and potentialities to establish themselves even in their old age without getting least support from their children. The indifference and insensitiveness shown by the children strengthens their will power to make them exemplary character in society. In this way they not only come out of the troublesome situation but become the contributor of spreading optimism in society.

With the passage of time, parents show their excellence by using their creativity and capabilities making their children to feel 'pigmy' as they stood gap-mouthed before them feeling shameful at their insensitive altitude towards them. Cinema is a powerful medium that emotionally affects us and we respond to these situations presented in a film in a unique manner of our own. Thus the role of *cinema teacher* can never be ignored in our day to day life.

It is a matter of great pride that Indian cinema has touched the highest peak of popularity by increasing its boundaries across the world. Movies have really become a powerful medium of 'presentation of realities of life in its diverse colourful forms'. The famous movie **3 Idiots** changed the way of thinking students looked at marks. Its world acclaimed popularity is due to its message "run after knowledge marks and success will follow". It has been shown at the UN for its superb message and performance of its actors. **'I am Singh', 'My Name is Khan'** bring into light the (intelligible) atrocities faced by these communities after 9/11 tragic terrorist attack.

Firaaqa film by Nandita Das lime lights the sorrowful stark realities faced by commoners after Hindu-Muslim riots in Gujarat Post-Godhara in 2002. The British Film Institute (BFI) has claimed the film as "the elegiac document of human traumas." Tsunami of anger, rebellion and bloodshed is blowing and raging within every heart but indifferent state administration takes it as a routine affair. The people of minority are forced to bear the terrified experience yet officials take it as a normal situation. It has already impressed international audiences at the **London, Toronto, Pusan and New York film festivals**. It is ironic besides being extremely tragic that in a democratic setup like India no community can live without fear of being wiped out at the slightest provocation. **Ajay Saklani** film maker selects developmental themes in his documentary films for upliftment of the society. As he says "Documentary and Art cinema helps in the development of people and Nation and I want to play a crucial role in that. Also, the documentary cinema helps me in connecting with the people of different cultures and gives me a chance to learn more about them. I want to do something for all those who are either ignored or deprived from basic amenities. I wish my films will help all these people to live a good and respectful life".

His documentary film Upaasmar 'The Taste of Hunger' presents gruesome act of infant mortality a terrible problem of child deaths for last 3-4 decades due to malnutrition and more than 10,000 children have died. In spite of government declaration to improve the situation the problem remains the same. We ignorant Indians did not know anything about Melghat before the release of the film. We all need to know places like Melghat to actually see how developed our India really is after 66 years of independence.

Comedy film like Rang Rangili takes much of our tensions by its unique laugh therapy. The complex situations of life melt in a lighter spirits making us to realize that every problem has a solution if we deal it with lighter spirits without making ourselves tense and miserable. In 'Jolly LLB' a streak of humour runs though the movie when prosecutions are confused with prostitution. It can be categorized as 'a directive movie' as it dearly highlights the misbehaviour of the Hon'ble Supreme

Court judges and lawyers with Distt./Civil Court with layers working with the highest courts. **'Bhag Milkha Bhag'** is an inspirational movie for the youngsters to face hardships of life as indomitable will power can never defeated and success is the suitable reward after a long struggle.

Even the animal liberation movements in India and else where in the world find its way from meaningful consideration of 'Right to Live' Disney's 1942 Bambi faced severe reaction of those American hunting lobby who profit from animal exploitation. The pro-animal sentiments expressed in The Year of Dog (2007) advocates strongly animal-centric ethics into society. It seems that film has an effective way to create resistance against animal exploitation. The animal issues become visible by placing these issues in people's consciousness. In this way an environmental message circulates among common masses for the protection of animals—which are marginalized both physically and culturally under the impact of industrialization and modernization.

This meaningful consideration in cinematic narrative teaches audience that they are also a part of this world and their existence cannot be suspended as a meaningless entity. It is most tragic that they are reduced to mere raw material, commodities and property in spite of their great usefulness to human beings.

To quote 'Peggy' central character of the 'Year of the Dog' "I believe life is magical. It is so precious. And there are so many kinds of love in this life. So many things to love", delivers a significant message that "Rights to Live" must be given to all. Cinema presents an inevitable prevalence of popular cultures around the globe and thus building a colourful web of 'globe' 'culture' around the commoners. If we are to have a more just world appreciation and tolerance of other cultures, we must focus on cinema as teacher. Inter action and growth is the final ends of social sciences understood from a multicultural perspectives.

LIMITATIONS IN PRESENTATION

In modern life, culture is affected by commercialism and market value of the subjects presented before the audience. As regarding the concept of capitalism, films as a money making machines also play a significant role in shaping our private thoughts and public behaviour. Earlier trend of representation of 'Great Hero' 'his great adventurer' 'his great voyages' and 'his great achievements' leading 'to great success'—these ideas are surely seemed to be dispersed and vanished in the moving wave of modernity, vulgar and vampish presentation of characters in cinema seems to shake the very foundations of our rich cultural traditions in such a way that majestic palace of our rich cultural heritage seem to be in a crumbling stage in this context (Munni Badnam Hue) (मुन्नी वदनाम हुई), Sheela Ki Jawani (शीला की जवानी) (Aab to Loota Hai Bazar) (अब तो लुटा है बाजार) represented women as items commodity rather than a human being. It resulted in suicidal attempts as the poor girls named after Sheela, Muni, etc. fail to bear stress and eve teasing caused by youngsters by these songs in public life.

Bollywood film makers spend most of their time in foreign countries so same of them may lack common Indian touch. Firstly, they should make themselves aware of true indianism by making movie presenting Indian spirit. Some of our movies are nowhere close to our culture. How can people living in the distant villages equate their life with residents of Delhi and Bombay? Instead of copying foreign culture they should endorse our own cultural traditions in a way that compel foreigners to get inspired by our Indianism, they must realize that ours is a poor country even after 66th year independence but our rich culture makes us 'special'. Unfortunately we are losing this richness due to some over ruling rich people of our poor country. The creative expression of cinema serves a commercial goal. The sublime ideas of freedom, getting justice, social issue like democracy, physical mental exploitation fight against social evils created from orthodoxy and narrow-mindedness of opinions. Political issues like terrorism, etc. are used as selling commodities less for solutions more for commercialism.

These crude manifestations of life and extra ordinary exposer to sexualized violence lead to a state of aggressiveness and chaos among the masses. These sexualized violent images devoid of loving feelings are deeply affecting the thought process of younger generations. This aggressiveness finds its way through increase in crime rates suicidal tendencies to get out of this troubled state of mind. In simple terms, the logic of market place destroys the meaningfulness of content turning 'a moving image' into message. For younger generation their helplessness to cope with life presented in films generates chaos as real life problems remain unresolved.

CONCLUSION

To quote Henry Giroux (2002) "A Visual Technology that function as a powerful teaching machine that intentionally tries to influence the production of meaning, subject positions identities and experience suggests how important it has become as a site cultural politics."

People exposed to popular culture with its innovative thinking naturally develop habits of thinking with introspective way of thinking. In modern age of multicultural dimensions of thinking and behaving an average citizen is too uncomfortable with its critical analytical dialogues and complex propositions cinema, as a powerful medium of communication steer up thinking to develop deliberate critical thinking to sort out many of our day-to-day problems. Hence, it place its role as encourager of thoughts for generations.

These thought provoking elements expressed through 'moving images' become a helpful instrument tool to facilitate younger generations for speedy transformation to resolve social issues for getting social justice. This steady change makes way to liberal thinking. So the role of cinema as preacher of aesthetics related to ground reality can never be surpassed or ignored. It plays its part in injecting particular values into collective public consciousness and becomes a medium of social change.

If we want to maintain our existence to sustain a humanitarian society, it is sure that future is supposed to be different from our present. Human society surely transforms gradually to reward us with real democratic set up of with socialistic approach to life, harmonious blend of ideas taken from different cultures corporated with oneness of thinking.

To me, it appears that to a certain extent, cinema has potential to transform those societies that have been exposed to the media of motion pictures with its audio-visual language, into an audio visual human culture. It reveals goodness of cultures economy and politics etc. besides providing us amusement. It is an effective appropriate and appreciative tool for ideological changes in thinking pavin.

Films and Social Causes

19

SHEETAL THAKUR

INTRODUCTION

Films as part of Social media are turning up as an essential mode of interactive and informing media in the recent past. Especially, it is being considered as a platform for both promotion and publicizing social issues. Popular films reveal our ideals and expectations about social life in a myriad of ways. Some of the most common themes in contemporary films revolve around social life and the accompanying problems that living in today's society entails. Using film as a medium to study social life allows us to exercise our sociological imaginations in a way that is easily accessible and relevant. By making connections to our personal lives it can help us make sense of the world in which we live. As Deflem (2005) notes, sociologists "continually endeavor to find new and useful ways to communicate the best of our work to a new generation of learners." Unfortunately, most of the time films show us life not as it is, but as the filmmaker thinks it should be.

The paper starts with the growth observed in the relation between Films and the Social Causes shown to the mass, uncategorized audience as well the informed citizens. The various studies and theories of effect of media and finally on the question for a regulation of social media and a code of conduct for content management in Indian scenario.

CINEMA AND SOCIAL CAUSES

The socially conscious cinemas of early thirties and forties (though regarded as alienated cinema by some) have given way to self styled art cinema with its burden of social consciousness and offering facile solutions for deep social problems, occasionally forgetting that its primary duty is to render truth and beauty without sacrificing one to the other. Indian cinema has had an attenuate streak in them and managed to delineate their feelings through films without hurting the inclinations of others. But all this gradually changed as we reached the 1990s. The film production and distribution system has adapted to contemporary India. Then there was the leitmotif of tackling with exploring propositions for the perspicuous portrayal of the various social issues. As we all know, Indian cinema, over the years, has not only excogitated as a mode of entertainment, but as an alternative form of chronicle as well. So, in all these years, it has not just indulged and captivated the audience with its sheer ingenuity and creativity, for social and political matter as well.

Perception of Social reality is hindered rather than promoted by pat and simple solutions. The Social Problems and issues brought out in films cannot be solved by offering fairy tale and fanciful solutions. Art films with their largely neo realistic format have often offered for their elite consumers *an escape into poverty* just as commercial films have offered *an escape into affluence* for the masses. Basically both are products of the same exploitative system. Cenema is not capable of changing our perception of Social Reality. It is only when our perception of Social reality is undistorted by ideology that social change is possible.

THEORIES ON EFFECTS OF FILMS/ MEDIA ON THE SOCIAL FABRIC

Depiction of Violence and Crime, Promotion of harmful products, superficial value systems, false priorities, values and goals is undeniably noted that it would lead to the following outcomes:

(a) Insensitivity to real violence.

(b) Aggressive behaviour.
(c) Acceptance of violent solutions and equating of weapons with power.
(d) Acceptance of revenge as justifiable.
(e) Acceptance of crime against women as justifiable and abuse of women and children.
(f) Role modeling: Imitative behaviour, Negative (Anti-social) and Positive (Prosocial) results.

However, there are a few theories which help us view the effect of films/media on social fabric.

CATHARSIS THEORY

The first of these theories suggests that rather than harmful, violence in the media actually has a positive effect on society. The central assumption of the Catharsis Theory is that people, in course of daily life, build up frustrations. Vicarious participation on others' aggression helps people release those tensions. In other words, every day we build up frustrations in us. Without a release valve we risk the chance of becoming violent, or at least aggressive. The Catharsis theorist would say that by watching violence in the media you release some of that tension and are less likely to be aggressive or violent.

AGGRESSIVE CUES THEORY

This is the opposite view, that violence DOES have an impact. It has as its central assumption that: Exposure to aggressive stimuli will increase physiological and emotional arousal, which will increase the probability of violence. In other words, all that violence gets the adrenaline juices in us flowing and makes us more edgy, increasing the chance that we'll be more aggressive or more violent. Aggressive cues theorists are quick to point out that watching violence does not mean we'll always be more aggressive or violent, but it increases the chances. And the way in which the violence is presented will have an impact on us, too. If we can relate to the protagonist committing the violence, or if the violence is presented in a justifiable way, we can be led to aggressive behaviour.

OBSERVATIONAL LEARNING THEORY

The Observational Learning theorist would take the Aggressive Cues theory a step further. This theory says that people can learn by observing aggression in media portrayals and, under some conditions, model its behaviour. So the Observational Learning theorist says that not only would the media violence increase the probability of the viewer committing an aggression or violence, it teaches the viewer how to do it.

REINFORCEMENT THEORY

Reinforcement Theory debunks both the above theories. The central assumption of this theory is that media portrayals reinforce established behaviour that viewers bring with them to the media situation. Violent portrayals will increase the likelihood of violent or aggressive behaviour for those who accept violence and aggression as normal. It will decrease the likelihood of aggression and violence for those brought up to believe that violence is bad.

CULTIVATION THEORY

Recent studies, predict that we will turn to or from violence, it looks at how we'll react to the violence. The central assumption of the theory is that in the symbolic world of media, particularly TV, shapes and maintains audience's conception of the real world. In other words, the media, especially TV, creates fantasy world that is mean, spirited and dangerous. It also creates stereotypes of dominant/weak folk in society.

CONCLUSION

We learn many lessons about social life from watching films. Many of the movies produced are unrealistic, escapist, far capitalizing on dramatic situations in order to sell more tickets. However, we still look to films for messages about how we should live our lives. What we learn from the movies provides us with a template for our life which we often use to measure our own experiences. Unfortunately, most of the time films show us life not as it is, but as the filmmaker thinks it should be. Sometimes the images and ideals we glean from film can lead to stereotypical and unrealistic expectations about social life. These expectations also can divert us from the real issues that people face in today's society.

However, there are motion pictures that challenge conventional stereotypes and tell gripping stories about realistic, albeit fictional situations. Films can be a powerful and persuasive vehicle for making us look at the world in a new and different way. Movies can inspire us to critically examine the lives we lead and understand ourselves and our relationships within society more clearly.

Even with the dramatization that makes the stories so compelling to watch, we can see the kernel of truth that lies beneath the surface. Applying our sociological imagination and Social realism to these films, enables us to develop a keener sense of awareness and understanding about the lives of others in our society today.

References

Burton, C. Emory, 1988. "Sociology and the Feature Film." *Teaching Sociology,* 16: 263-71.

Deflem, Mathieu, 2005. "Comment." *Contemporary Sociology*" 34: 92-93.

Huaco, George A., 1965. The Sociology of Film Art New York: Basic Books.

Prendergast, Christopher, 1986. "Cinema Sociology: Cultivating the Sociological Imagination through Popular Film." *Teaching Sociology,* 14: 243-48.

Smith, Don D., 1973. "Teaching Introductory Sociology by Film." *Teaching Sociology* 1: 48-61.

20

The Real, the Unreal and the Reel : Decoding the Scripts for the Texts and Contexts in the Classroom

Manoj Kumar

Education, in every civilization/society, is a tool to socialize people, to orient them about its own culture and to perceive the world in certain ways. Generally, this task is assigned to the schools and colleges which strive to improve knowledge and develop skills through teaching, training and learning. Though it is true that much of human learning occurs outside the classroom, and people continue to learn throughout their lives, yet, so far, books and libraries have been considered the most trusted mediums of imparting education. But today cinema, with its recent heights, is also emergency as a strong, and of course innovative, medium of learning. For, like books, it also records/presents life. True, cinema is not a school yet its sincerity and variety certainly make it a handy tool for a smart teacher. Cinema has enough potential to prove its worth; the only thing required is the creation of some place for cinema in the classrooms. And in the era of intertextuality and interdisciplinarity it is not a big task.

Among various disciplines, the most obvious and close connection of cinema is seen with literature. Literature mirrors life and so does cinema. The only difference is their mediums.

One captures life with the pen and paper, the other through the lens and the reel. As such, they are the two sides of a coin. However, their mutual dependence/relationship is perceived in various ways, the most common being adaptation and appropriation. Adrian Poole has offered an extensive list of terms (though, to represent the Victorian era's interest in reworking the artistic past): 'borrowing, stealing, appropriating, inheriting, assimilating ...being influenced, inspired, dependent, indebted, haunted, possessed ... homage, mimicry, travesty, echo, allusion, and intertextuality' (2004: 2). Julie Sanders continues the linguistic riff, adding into the mix: variation, version, interpretation, imitation, proximation, supplement, increment, improvisation, prequel, sequel, continuation, addition, paratext, hypertext, palimpsest, graft, rewriting, reworking, refashioning, re-vision, re-evaluation. To this list, says Sanders, can be added a wide vocabulary of active terms, mobalised by Adaptation studies: version, variation, interpretation, continuation, transformation, imitation, pastiche, parody, forgery, travesty, transposition, revaluation, revision, rewriting, and echo. (2006:18)

Establishing some useful templates for studying cinematic interpretations of well-known novels, Deborah Cartmell (quoted in Julie Sanders: 20) argues for three broad categories of adaptation:

1. Transposition
2. Commentary
3. Analogue

Wagner (1975) believes that in transposition 'a novel is directly given on the screen, with the minimum of apparent interference' (1975: 222); commentary is 'where an original is taken and ...altered in some respect' (1975: 223), revealing 'a different intention on the part of the film-maker, rather than an infidelity or outright violation' (1975: 224); while an analogy takes 'a fiction as a point of departure' (1975: 223) and therefore 'cannot be indicted as a violation of a literary original since the director has not attempted (or has only minimally attempted) to reproduce the original' (1975: 227).

Julie Sanders have cited many examples of these categories. A fitting example of transposition is Michael Almereyda's millennial *Hamlet* re-envisioned Elsinore as a Manhattan financial corporation with Claudius as a corrupt CEO (2000). In an interesting twist, the disaffected young prince in this version was an anti-establishment art student, who created his 'play within a play' as a video montage to be submitted as a course assignment. The motive behind updating is fairly obvious: the 'movement of proximation' brings it closer to the audience's frame of reference in temporal, geographic, or social terms. On the surface, all screen versions of novels/literature are transpositions in the sense that they take a text from one genre and deliver it to new audiences by means of the aesthetic conventions of an entirely different generic process (here novel into film). Cartmell's second, commentary, has been illustrated through movies like a film version of Jane Austen's *Mansfield Park* (Dir. Patricia Rozema, 2000) that made explicit that novel's context in the history of British colonialism and the practice of slavery on Antiguan plantations. Rozema made visible facts that the novel represses. The absence or gap in the original narrative being remarked upon in the transpositional film was one that had been identified by postcolonial criticism. As such commentary comments on the politics of the source text, or those of the new *mise-en-scène*, or both, usually by means of alteration or addition. Here the process of adaptation starts to move away from simple proximation towards something more culturally loaded. The third category, analogue, is revealed through Francis Ford Coppola's Vietnam film *Apocalypse Now* (1979) and its recontextualization of Joseph Conrad's dark nineteenth-century exploration of the colonial enterprise in the Congo, *Heart of Darkness*. Cartmell's third and final category of adaptation, analogue, may enrich and deepen our understanding of the new cultural product to be aware of its shaping intertext, it may not be entirely necessary to enjoy the work independently.

However, the full impact of the film adaptation depends upon the audience's awareness of an explicit relationship to a source text. In expectation of this most formal adaptations carry the same title as their source text. The desire to make the relationship with the source explicit links to the manner in which the responses to adaptations depend upon a complex invocation of ideas of similarity and difference. These ideas can only be mobilized by a reader or spectator alert to the intertextual relationship and this in turn requires the deployment of well-known texts or sources.

Now if we look into the history of adaptation studies it will be found that the authors and auteur were at odds for a long time. As Mireia Aragay (2005: 13) tells us that around the year 1957 writers like Bluestone considerd cinema far inferior. The novel, Bluestone claims, is 'more complex' than film (1957: 7); the fact that it is a linguistic—hence symbolic—medium means that it is more self-conscious and self-reflexive, far more deeply steeped in metaphor, far better equipped to render thought and other mental states. Film, as a primarily visual medium, can only aspire to metaphor 'in a highly restricted sense' (1957: 20)—mainly through the uniquely cinematic technique of editing, Bluestone claims (1957: 27)—and is singularly inadequate when it comes to rendering thoughts and feelings (1957: 48).

Then, there was the question of the originality, for the writers considered their works as the original creations and that of the film makers as an inferior copy. But with writers like T.S. Eliot the shift began. Eliot sought to rethink notions of originality and value, querying the 'tendency to insist, when we praise a poet, upon those aspects of his work in which he least resembles anyone else' (Eliot 1984 : 37). Eliot questioned why originality was valued over 'repetition': 'No poet, no artist, of any art, has his complete meaning alone' (38). He was not advocating blind adherence to precursor texts or ages, an action that would after all be little more than literary plagiarism; his notion of the 'individual talent' was that it created new material upon the surface and foundation of the literary past. And then came Barthes's seminal 1968 essay, *'The Death of the Author'*, which 'killed' the Author-God and his finished, self-sufficient work, replacing it with the text as a 'multi-dimensional space in which a variety of writings, none of them original, blend and clash' (Barthes, 1988: 170). And finally, Jacques Derrida's deconstruction of the hierarchical opposition of original and copy, as meaning is always-already 'disseminated', both dispersed and dissipated, so that in every text and every word other texts and words inevitably resonate, landed us into intertextuality and thus lead adaptation studies in the direction of problematising so-called 'originals'—as Cattrysse succinctly puts it, 'how original are originals?' (1992b: 67).

But then cinema is not just literature alone. A cursory glance at the catalogue of any film site reveals the scope and potential of cinema. Apart from pure entertaining genres like comedy, tragedy, romance and horror, etc. we have films showcased as history, biography, religion, adventure, war, sci-fi, family/ society, adventure, animation and sports, etc. i.e. almost every aspect of life, and every discipline of an education system. Though doubts can be raised about the authenticity of information in cinema even then the mass appeal can be safely utilised in teaching a number of disciplines in various ways. For example, one can trace some kind of correspondence between Indian cinema and the socio-political history of india after its independence. The first and foremost needs were food and security. Hence, the slogan 'jai jawan, jai kisan' was projected through movies also. Movies like *Naya Daur, Do Bigha Zameen, Mother India,* etc. catered for the kisans while *Shaheed, Haqeeqt, Gandhi,* etc. served the nationalistic/patriotic values. But with the era of angry young man came Amitabh Bachchan (*Zanjeer, Diwar, Coolie*). [here, it would seem an oversimplification to say that actors like Dev Anand, Rajesh Khanna, Rajender Kumar, and Dharmendra all remained clinched with the romantic hero image and did not correspond to the contemporary phase of anger and unrest and thus Amitabh's fame got a huge hipe].

Later, with the advent of industrial phase a new kind of hybrid cultural assimilation occurred hence *Disco Dancer.* Dark days of Punjab were captured in *Machis;* of Kashmir and Assam and other naxalite states in *Roja* & *Dil Se,* etc. With Kargil and the tensions mounting on the borders came J.P. Dutta's *Border, & LOC.* Presently the silver screen is dominated by the corporate culture.

Here, it would be necessary to present a glimpse of the labour/details involved in the making of a film. Colm Hogan's analysis of the operation of color and lighting in Deepa Mehta's controversial, award-winning film *Fire* will serve as a fitting example, to take just one, of the relentless efforts, of the whole dedicated industry, and will surely help us to understand the sincerity of the film-makers. Hogan believes that *Fire* is a film that is almost impossible to understand if one does not pay attention to visual style for Deepa Mehta makes systematic use of colors to communicate her main themes and manipulates lighting for both thematic suggestions and emotional effects:

> Mehta repeatedly associates the women in the film with the colors of the Indian flag (orange, white, and green), suggesting that the hope for India's future lies in new forms of connection undertaken by women. The first sexual union of the two main characters—Radha and Sita—presents the viewer with a particularly striking image. One of the women is in orange. The other is in green. They are separated by the white bedsheets. But this is not only a union of women. It is also a union of communities (orange representing Hinduism; green representing Islam). When they are finally and fully joined at the end of the film, Radha and Sita meet in a *Sūfī* shrine, *Sūfism* itself being a union of Hinduism and Islam. Mehta stresses and emotionally enhances her thematic points by the systematic use of two lighting techniques. First, she associates diffuse, unbounded, bright light with repressive religious orthodoxy. In contrast with this, she gives us sharply outlined silhouettes to communicate an almost tactile sense of union between the women. (Holgan, 2008, p. 12)

Similarly, the directors of the blockbuster *Dhoom* tell us that the colours of the bikes and the t-shirts of the characters in the movie were finalised after matching more than two million design combinations and the bikes were painted in Japan. As far as the costs of cinema are concerned, Kamal Hassan, (Actor, Director, Producer and Chairman, FICCI—Media and Entertainment Committee-South,) in his article in *The Hindu*, Dated November 15, 2013 tells us that as *per the FICCI Deloitte Report for 2013, the overall South Indian M&E industry is estimated to at 23,900 crore and expected to grow at a CAGR of 16 per cent to reach Rs. 43,600 crore by 2017.*

So, are these few facts not sufficient to give cinema a respectable place? Now, the question is—why do movies appeal us? Is it just because of the glamour or the money involved? Why is cinema so much charismatic or alluring? Certainly they are there to make money and hence every possible mean to attract the audience are used. And all this is based on a highly professional, well researched and scientifically proved system. An example of such professionalism is seen in *advertising*, which uses proven theories and concepts, good enough to make us change our mobiles every now and then. May be a lot of planning or tactics is involved in cinema but the best reason, perhaps, is what Aristotle called the pleasure of 'learning'. Learning is our basic instinct. No movie, however thrilling or luring, will hold us for long unless we get some learning there.

PART TWO

In Teaching we process real life information to learners in classrooms or lecture theatres. Similarly, the directors of Cinema also process real life information, of course not to learners but to an audience. Though the two systems operate with entirely different mediums yet the end result is more or less the same—some kind of learning takes place, some kind of awareness, however little, is created and the mind of the recipient is stirred, which precisely, is the aim of education. And at times, cinema has far better impact in reaching/sensitising the masses, e.g. *Bandit Queen, 1084 ki maa, Maachis,* and quite recently *Table No. 21*. May be a large part of cinema is pure entertainment only, but we do have films under serious film genres namely history, biography, documentry, sci-fi, adventure, war, epic, family, sports and so on i.e. every aspect of life (much more than the curriculam of any university) is there. So, should a smart learner opt for a movie theatre rather than a classroom? May be not. For, the movies can't be trusted for authenticity of the information and certainly, the teacher can't ever be substituted. Moreover *cinema is not a school*. But then, school is not the only custodian of learning and imparting knowledge today. Certainly, cinema can't replace the teacher but can't a teacher give it a place in his classroom? As a matter of fact many smart teachers have been making successful use of examples direct from cinema for illustrating various concepts, thereby not just making the understanding easier but rather livelier. But today, we are living in the era of intertextuality and interdisciplinarity. Further, focus of teaching has shifted from the teacher-centric to the learner-centric approaches and hence seeking assistance from cinema as a teaching tool seems justified because here a few preliminary conditions of learning are satisfied, namely—receptibility, attention, time management, and 'passive learning', etc. There is no denying that Audio-visual methods are more effective and hence the demand for smart classrooms is increasing even in

Govt. schools. The CBCS/RUSA guidelines also emphasise interactive learning methodology.

All this is further supported by the contemporary pedagogical research. For example, Krashne's *Affective Filter Model* tells us about the various psychological filters used by the learners in different situations. But the most suited for the present purpose is the Zeigarnick Effect (Amblyn, 2003) developed in the 1920s a German researcher named Bluma Zeigarnick using the phenomenon of 'the Primacy and Recency Effect' i.e. the tendency of the people to remember what they heard at the beginning and end of any cluster of information, be it a learning module, a speech, a list, a story, or a performance. Zeigarnick observed that if people tend to remember beginnings and endings best, a good strategy might be to create more beginnings and endings. He found that interrupting a task periodically—even one that was going well—could lead to substantially better recall. The phenomenon came to be known as the "Zeigarnick Effect."

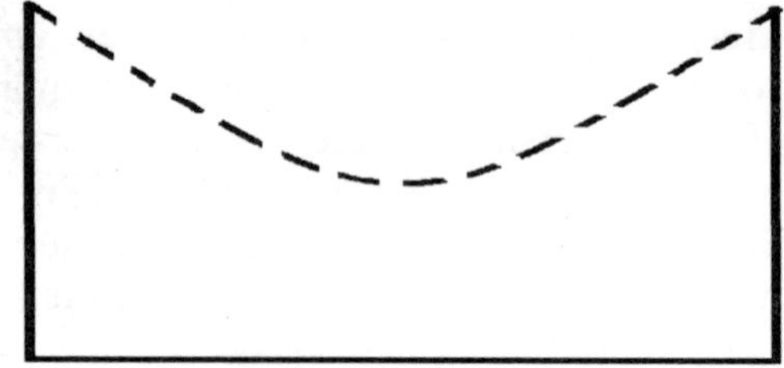

Figure 1 : Curve of recall

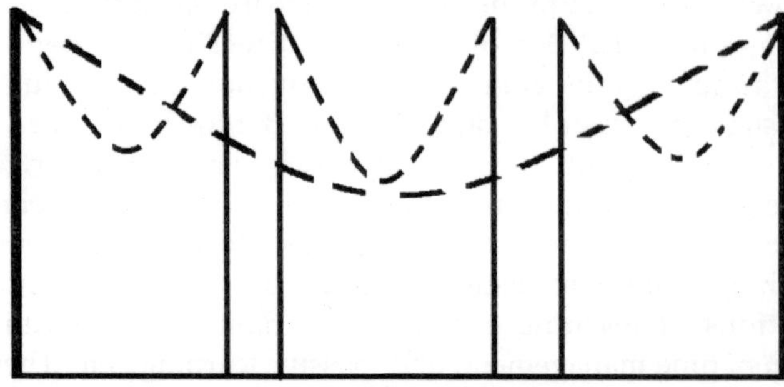

Figure 2 : Zeigarnick Effect

While teaching, the gaps/breaks shown in Fig. 2 can smartly be filled with appropriate parallels in cinema.

But the most important role of cinema in classroom pertains not just to effective teaching but to the real challenge of teaching in the post-modern world. And the challenge is what Baurdrillard calls the death of the real. In his Code of simulacra he maintains that in the postmodern world copy is more true than the real. In such a hyperreal world the need of the hour, besides better teaching, is to develop a kind of critical faculty in our students that will enable them to clearly differentiate the real and the unreal. And cinema is perhaps the best platform for every teacher to begin with. Decoding the scripts from the viewpoint of the texts and contexts of different disciplines would not only initiate the students to differentiate the real and the unreal in the reel but will also serve as the first lessons for realising the realities of real world.

References

Cartmell, Deborah, and Whelehan, Imelda (eds.) (1999), *Adaptations: From Text to Screen, Screen to Text*, London: Routledge.

Doni Amblyn (2003), *Laugh and Learn: 95 Ways to Use Humor for More Effective Teaching and Training*. New York: AMACOM Books.

Eliot, T.S. (1984), *'Tradition and the Individual Talent'* in Frank Kermode (ed.) *Selected Prose of T.S. Eliot*, London: Faber.

Jim Powell (1998), *Post-modernism for Beginners*. Chennai, India: Orient Longman.

Kamal Hassan's article in *The Hindu*. Dated: 15th November, 2013.

Patrick Colm Hogan: *Indian Movies. Culture, Cognition, and Cinematic Imagination*. University of Texas Press, Austin (2008).

Poole, Adrian (2004), *Shakespeare and the Victorians*, London: Thomson Learning/Arden Shakespeare.

Sanders, Julie (2006), *Adaptation and Appropriation*, the critical idiom series, New York: Routledge.

Wagner, G. (1975), *The Novel and the Cinema*. Rutheford, Madison and Teaneck: Farleigh Dickinson University Press.

Impact of Cinema on the Indian Society : A Study of Hamirpur District

21

RAJNEESH KUMAR SHARMA

ABSTRACT

Cinema is a powerful medium. It speaks with the language of universality. Hindi cinema produced in Bombay, now superficially well known as Bollywood, is essentially a generic cinema that pervades India. But of late the products of Mollywood (Madras) have quite markedly influenced its aesthetic strategies while Tollywood (Tollygunge, Calcutta) has been constructing its popular idiom following Bollywood. Hindi cinema is also considered as an "all-India formula film" [critic Chidananda Das Gupta]. However, one has to be cautious not to generalize Hindi cinema as such. The social impact of the cinema in India is also seen in the nationwide popularity of film-based programs on various television channels. It's mostly the young generation that has been caught up by the film-song programs. Popular film songs have gone very deep into the Indian collective memory and conscience.

INTRODUCTION

The birth of Cinema in India can be attributed to the Lumiere brothers. Only a few months after the Lumiere brothers introduced the art of cinematography in Paris in 1895, cinema made its presence felt in India. The Lumiere brothers held their first public showing at Watson Hotel in Mumbai on July 7, 1896 and the *Times of India* glowingly referred to it as the miracle of the century. Westerners, who were quick to realize the value of India as a site of filmmaking both because of its natural beauty and its exotic culture, were inspired to make films that used Indian scenery and culture. However, this phenomenon did not create much of a ripple. The Indian viewer took the new experience as something already familiar to him, thanks to the art of shadow play and the tradition of story-telling with hand-drawn images accompanied by live sound.

The unique properties of attending the cinema can have decisively positive effects on mental health. Cinema attendance can have independent and robust effects on mental well-being because visual stimulation can queue a range of emotions and the collective experience of these emotions through the cinema provides a safe environment in which to experience roles and emotions we might not otherwise be free to experience. The collective nature of the narrative and visual stimulation makes the experience enjoyable and controlled, thereby offering benefits beyond mere visual stimulation. Moreover, the cinema is unique in that it is a highly accessible social art form, the participation in which generally cuts across economic lines. At the same time, attending cinema allows for the exercise of personal preferences and the human need for distinction. In a nutshell, cinema attendance can be both a personally expressive experience, good fun and therapeutic at the same time.

A significant amount of research into the physiological effects of emotion involves showing the research subjects whole films or film clips in order to induce the relevant emotive state being studied. For example, Baldaro *et al.*, show subjects a film of a live surgery to induce a fearful or stressful emotive state (2001). The visual queues present in the gory film seemed to induce heart rate deceleration and increased respiratory sinus arrhythmia—both parallel responses in non-humans to fear. Von Leupoldt and Dahme found that they could induce restricted then normal breathing among healthy adults by showing them negative followed by positive movie clips (2004). In a rather ground breaking study, Konlaan, Bygren and Johansson found that frequent cinema attendees have particularly low mortality risks—those who never attended the cinema had mortality rates nearly 4 times higher than those who visit the cinema at least occasionally (Konlaan, Bygren, and Johansson, 2000). Their finding holds even when other forms of social engagement are controlled, suggesting that social engagement specifically in an artistic milieu is important for human survival. As epidemiologists, the authors explain that strong visual and auditory stimulation of the type associated with experiencing artistic expression has positive physical effects in non-humans. The authors believe that such stimulation reduces the chances of disease and outline how such stimulation can promote autoimmune responses in humans.

Given these emotive responses, and attendant physiological effects, to viewing film, it is not surprising to note significant research into the deleterious effects of film content on social and psychological development. Films can reinforce gender stereotypes (Oliver and Green, 2001), pro-violence attitudes among children (Funk, Baldacci, Pasold, and Baumgardner, 2004), or even encourage suicide and provide the appropriate means (Ohberg, Lonnqvist, Sarna, and Vuori 1996). Ohberg *et al.* found that age specific suicide rates through the use of auto-exhaust fumes significantly increased shortly after a 1982 popularly released film in Finland featured this method. On the other hand, the content of films need not have deleterious effects. In a controlled experiment, Mazur and Emmers-Sommer found that subjects shown a film featuring a positive portrayal of non-traditional families experienced more favourable attitudes towards homosexuals (2002).

Hindi cinema produced in Bombay, now superficially well-known as Bollywood is essentially a generic cinema that pervades India. But of late the products of Mollywood (Madras) have quite markedly influenced its aesthetic strategies while Tollywood (Tollygunge, Calcutta) has been constructing its popular idiom following Bollywood. Hindi cinema is also considered as an "all-India formula film" [critic Chidananda Das Gupta]. However, one has to be cautious not to generalize Hindi cinema as such. As it is well known India produces a massive number of feature films in many different languages, including several dialects. In 1999, the total number of films produced, in as many as 35 official languages and dialects, was 601-up to

October but one could add about 30-40 feature films to this number up to end December, 1999. The production figure has been steadily declining since 1990 when India produced little less than a thousand films a year. The debate, however, keeps going whether it's cinema that influences society or *vice versa*. Most of the dominant formula films get their narrative base, in one way or another, from the two Indian epics *Mahabharata and Ramayana*. The dream merchants seem to know this fact well to extract an impact as wide as possible for a box-office success. This holds true of the generic Bellwood, including television.

The reality that obtains in southern India (especially in Tamil Nadu and Andhra Pradesh) is substantially different from that in northern India. The cinema politics nexus in Tamil Nadu, for instance, is quite interesting. All five chief ministers who have governed Tamil Nadu since 1967 have been associated with cinema. "The immense popularity of film as an entertainment form and its emergence in Tamilnadu as a major cultural preoccupation underscores the significance of the role of audio-visual communication in Tamil society" [S. Theodore Baskaran]. Superstars MGR and NTR - doyens of Tamil and Telugu cinema respectively - were quite active in regional and national politics. The social impact of the cinema in India is also seen in the nationwide popularity of film-based programs on various television channels. It's mostly the young generation that has been caught up by the film-song programs. Popular film song has gone very deep into the Indian collective memory and conscience. In a nutshell, my presentation will take up some concrete examples of what impact the cinema has on Indian society by and large – including how the classical villain eventually turned into a hero or how social values underwent a certain change. Popular films have even been changing people's dress and hair styles; in Bombay, I remember even shoes would be branded after a box-office hit film. The cinema's social impact is reflected in the way censorship operates in India. In colonial India, the local police controlled film censorship, was mainly political in nature, but in post-colonial India it has acquired moralistic overtones; I'll touch upon some recent examples in this realm. I think it's the state that constantly finds itself insecure *vis-a-vis* society at large and artists in particular. All said and done, the cinema hasn't yet shed its mystical hallow in India.

OBJECTIVES

1. To examine the impact of the cinema on social status, employment, economic development and enhancement of the knowledge.
2. To analyse the impact of the cinema on moral value of society, younger generation and crime and violence.

METHODOLOGY ADOPTED

The study is based on primary data which is collected from Hamirpur district of Himachal Pradesh. 200 respondents have been selected with the help of simple random sampling. A questionnaire was developed exclusively for the purpose of collecting the primary data, particularly to examine the impact of cinema on the society. The SPSS package has been used to analyze the data. Consistent with the objectives of the study, different techniques like the simple percentage, mean, standard deviation, skewness, kurtosis and chi-square have been used for the analysis of the collected data.

RESULTS AND DISCUSSION

Positive Impact of Cinema on Society

It is evident from the Table 1 that the mean score of the respondents' views regarding the impact of the cinema on increase in the employment opportunities, social status, economic development and enhancement of the knowledge is much higher than the standard average score at 3 point scale. The variation in their opinion is noted at 0.648, 0.663, 0.661 and 0.616 respectively. Further, it is observed that the values of skewness are negative in all cases. It shows that the opinion of the respondents is skewed more towards the upper and to the standard average score.

The calculated values of kurtosis reveal that distribution is platy kurtic which also support the same. While applying c^2 test, it is found that the calculated values are much higher than the table value at 1 percent level of significance. It rejects the null

Table I

Positive Impact of Cinema on the Society

Attributes	*Strongly Agree*	*Agree*	*Not Agree*	*Total*	*Mean*	*S.D.*	*Sk.*	*Kt.*	χ^2	*P-Value*
(1)	*(2)*	*(3)*	*(4)*	*(5)*	*(6)*	*(7)*	*(8)*	*(9)*	*(10)*	*(11)*
Enhance the Knowledge	61 (30.5)	111 (55.5)	28 (14.0)	200 (100.0)	2.165	0.648	-0.173	-0.657	52.3 90	<0.01
Increase the Social States	98 (49.0)	82 (41.0)	22 (10.0)	200 (100.0)	2.39	0.663	-0.632	-0.636	50.92	<0.01
Increase the Employment	66 (33.0)	114 (57.0)	20 (10.0)	200 (100.0)	2.23	0.616	-0.184	-0.547	66.28	<0.01
Economic Development	96 (48.0)	84 (42.0)	20 (10.0)	200 (100.0)	2.38	0.661	-0.601	-0.655	50.08	<0.01

Note : Figures in parenthesis indicate the percentages of the row total.
Source : Various Questionnaires from Respondents.

TABLE 2

Negative Impact of Cinema on Society

Attributes	*Strongly Agree*	*Agree*	*Not Agree*	*Total*	*Mean*	*S.D.*	*Sk.*	*Kt.*	χ^2	*P-Value*
(1)	*(2)*	*(3)*	*(4)*	*(5)*	*(6)*	*(7)*	*(8)*	*(9)*	*(10)*	*(11)*
Crime and Violence	59 (29.5)	121 (60.5)	20 (10.0)	200 (100.0)	2.195	0.599	-0.1	-0.401	77.83	<0.01
Negative Impact on Younger Generation	92 (46.0)	98 (49.0)	10 (5.0)	200 (100.0)	2.41	0.586	-0.4	-0.702	72.52	<0.01
Decline Moral Value of Society	91 (45.5)	93 (46.5)	16 (8.0)	200 (100.0)	2.375	0.63	-0.494	-0.642	57.79	<0.01
Impact on Indian Culture	86 (43.0)	87 (43.5)	27 (13.5)	200 (100.0)	2.295	0.693	-0.469	-0.85	35.41	<0.01

Note : Figures in parenthesis indicate the percentages of the row total.
Source : Various Questionnaires from Respondents.

hypothesis and reveals that the opinion of the respondents is not equally distributed.

NEGATIVE IMPACT OF CINEMA ON SOCIETY

It is observed from the Table 2 that the cinema has decreased the moral value of the society, increased the crime and violence and the negative impact on the younger generation. The mean score of the respondents' views regarding theses parameters are much higher than the mean standard score i.e. 2 at 3 point scale. It reveals that the major chunk of the respondents either agree or strongly agree theses negative attributes.

The variation in their opinion is noted below 0.70 which may be considered satisfactory. The negative values of skewness depicts that the opinion of the respondents is scattered more towards the higher side of standard average score. The significant value of the c^2 test at 1 percent level of significance manifests that the opinions of the respondents is distributed unequally regarding development of the above-mentioned attributes. It also supports the above analysis.

CONCLUSION

From the analysis it can be concluded that the cinema has great responsibility to give proper direction to the society. The cinema is helpful for increasing the social states, economic development, and enhancement of knowledge increasing the employment etc. Unfortunately, in recent years it has deviated from its social obligation where films are produced just to earn more and more money. The producer and financers are merely concerned about the commercial value of the films. It leads to decline of moral values of the society. It is causing great harm to social responsibility. This needs to be checked without any delay. The cinema has a major role to play in a country like India. The need of the hour is that cinema should be exploited as a power tool to educate, inform and aware the masses apart from entertaining them producing films with themes that generate awareness against greed, power and the downward spiral that they can cause.

REFERENCES

Alesina, A., R. Di Tella, and R. MacCulloch, 2004. "Inequality and happiness: are Europeans and Americans different?" *Journal of Public Economics* 88:2009-2042.

Argle, Michael, 1987. "The Psychology of Happiness." Chapter 6 in *Personality and Subjective Well-Being,* edited by E. Diener and R. Lucas.

Baldaro, B., M. Mazzetti, M. Codispoti, G. Tuozzi, R. Bolzani, and G. Trombini, 2001.

"Autonomic reactivity during viewing of an unpleasant films." *Perceptual and Motor Skills* 93:797-805.

Blanchflower, David G. and Andrew J. Oswald, 2000. "Well-Being Over Time in Britain and the U.S." *National Bureau of Economic Research Paper No. 7487.* London.

Bourdieu, Pierre, 1984. *Distinction: A Social Critique on the Judgement of Taste.*

Cambridge, MA: Harvard University Press.

Clark, Andrew and Andrew J. Oswald, 1994. "Unhappiness and Unemployment," *Economic Journal,* 104:648-59.

Di Tella, Rafael, Robert MacCulloch, and Andrew J. Oswald, 2003, "The Macroeconomics of Happiness," *Review of Economics and Statistics* 85:809-27.

Gumbel, Andrew, 2005. "This Season's Disaster Movies." pp. 24-25 in *The Independent* (28 June 2005). London.

Cinema as a Cultural Heritage of a Nation

22

ANIL GAUTAM

Cinema is that particular language whereby the film maker shares his dreams with the audience. Cinema has the unique power to lead audience on in a sort of dream, leaving a very little freedom in regard to the particulars of that dream. One studies poetry or drama through the works of great poets and dramatist. One comes to know whole passage by heart. The same method can be employed in the study of cinema as a cultural heritage of a nation.

Much of what a man is pertains to his imagination. Indeed, imaginary are his hopes, his intentions, his ideas of himself. People dream of their lives and live on their dreams. The dividing line between living and dreaming is not always clear. Films are collective dream of society. They provide society with methodology or patterns of behaviour. However, the mass appeal of the movies is a clear indication that most people today respond in one way or another to the dream like fantasies projected on the screen. Cinema is an appearance of continues motion created by motionless images which we have been arranged in an appropriate succession so as to produce fiction out of reality. In fact, cinema cover the range of all films taken collectively. If we, point out the role played by cinema in the life of human being we find that the mental universe created in its mass audience by the film itself. This knowledge is necessary in order to grasp the significance of the movies in the life of the people.

During the 20th century, film has been a powerful media in which to influence people's lifestyles and human behaviour. Film is for people who do not enjoy reading or other more stimulating leisure and want to be entertained or escape from everyday life. Movies gave society a great way to see vintage fashion, including how to wear period accessories that accompany the clothing. Movies also gave society a view of actors portraying wartime heroes, rebels or gangsters, which may influence peoples human behavior.

The American film industry was extremely prolific, affluent, powerful and productive during the war years. The world was headed toward rearmament and warfare in the early to mid-1940s, and the movie industry, like every other aspect of life responded by making movies, producing many war-time favorites. These movies offered escapist entertainment, reassurance, and patriotic themes and morale boosters for the audience.

In the period following the war, post-war affluence increased choice of leisure time activities, conformity, middle class values, a baby boom, the invention of television, drive-in theaters, and a youth reaction to middle aged cinema. When most of the films were idealized with conventional portrayals of men and women, young people wanted new and exciting symbols or rebellion. The film industry responded by producing a number of movies with portrayals of young men and women rebelling against the establishment. "Rebel Without A Cause" was a movie about a rebellious, misunderstood, middle class youth who had difficulty relating to his parents. This movie influenced the audience that it was okay to act in a rebellious way to get attention.

When looking back on the film history of the 20th century you begin to realize the great impact these films had on people's lifestyles and human behaviour. Movies influenced the way people dressed and the way people are acted. We as, movie goers, must choose what is morally right or wrong and not be influenced by the film industry. We must also choose what a fashion statement is and what is not. The film industry may be protected under the freedom of speech amendment, but we do not have to be influenced by what they project in their movies.

The film industry introduced flapper movies in the early days. The flapper wore short hair and a short skirt, with turned-down hose and powdered knees. The flapper must have seemed to her mother like a rebel. Flappers offended the older generation because they defied conventions of acceptable feminine behavior. They used make-up and wore baggy dresses, which often exposed their arms as well as their leges from the knees down. The flapper movies were modren and influenced a revaluation in fashion.

During the time of the Great Depression, film was a source of cheerful escapism for most. People were out of work, but they did manage to find money to go the movies. Even during the darkest days of the Depression, movie attendance was between 60-75 million per week. The balancing act for film making was to both reflect the realism and cynicism of the Depression period. They also provided escape entertainment to boost the morale of the public by optimistically reaffirming values such as thrift and perseverance.

During the golden age of Hollywood, movies were under strict enforcement and censorship. Film studios submitted their films for review and if they met the strict standards of decency they could be released. Regulations of the code included censorship of language, references, to sex, violence and morality. Without a seal, films were threatened with negative publicity and potential box-office failure. Movies were not allowed to portray gangsters as heroes. Movies of this time, basically influenced people to have better moral standards.

Contact between Indian and western cinemas was established in the early days of film in india itself. Dadasaheb Phalke was moved to make Raja Harishchander after watching the film life of Chirst at P.B. Mehta's American Indian Cinema. Similarly, some other early film directors were inspired by Western movies.

In Indian at least 80 percent of films shown in the late 1920s were American even though twenty-one studios manufactured local films, eight or nine of them in regular production. American serials such as Perils of Pauline and Exploits and the spectacular sets of films like Quo Vadio and Cabira were popular and inspiring during the World War I era. Universal pictures set up an Indian agency in 1916, which want on to dominate the Indian distribution system. J.F. Madan's Elphinstone Bioscope Company at first focused on distribution of foreign films and organization of their regular screenings. Additionally, J.P. Madan's the prolific produces, employed Western directors for many of his films.

CINEMA AND SOCIETY

Every person has the right freely to participate in the cultural life of the community to enjoy the arts this is required in order to develop fully as a human being. Cinema as a medium of art can be a unique communication between the artiest and his/her fellow-men. The artist raises about the barriers of language and nation when he/she expresses himself/herself in all sincerity and earnestness. What the artist says about life, death, love. Joy and suffering acquires universal significance for the speaks of experiences that are familiar to all. Thus the artist helps his/her fellowmen to acknowledge one another as brothers sharing the same human existence. For instance, Satyajit Ray's Aparajito has gone a long way to make Europeans and Americans understand and love India. At the same time, foreign audiences recognize something of Sarbajaya tried to be an All India artist, or an international astist?

IMPACTS OF CINEMA AND SOCIETY

We can discuss the above topic in two distinct ways:

(i) **Material aspect of life**—Impact of cinema on the material aspect of life implies the elements of impact, which can be perceived through sensory organs and/or move evident, which are explicit and visible. These are as follows:

(a) **Fashion, dress and personal decoration**—Fashions and dresses are said to have been greatly influenced by general and film- stars in particular. In recent years, the film heros and heroines have acquired the great currently under the guise of being mod. People very often fell in lively discussion regarding the spread and day to day ongoing changes in fashions and dresses in society. In the late forties and early fifties, a number of popular film stars like Dalip Kumar, Dev Anand, and Raj Kapoor became the trendsetters in personal decoration and styles.

(b) **Etiquette and manners**—Cinema in general, which also served as a vehicle of westernization and secularization expecially in 1950s, led to gradual decline of tradition, etiquette and manners pertaining to either intra-family relations between parents and children, brother and brother or those elders, whch in traditional societies were characterized by some amount of social distance, restrain and damily decorum. Etiquettes and manners pertaining to the relationship between boys and girls is another area of life, which seems to have been deeply affected through cine relationaship between boys and girls is another are of life, which seems to have been deeply affected through cinema.

(c) **Crime**—It is often said that one of the reason of increasing crime in society is due to the influence of films, which irrespective of their thematic requirements, in unending ways have shown tendencies to incorporate and as well as glamourize one or the other elements of crime. The incidents of crime happening in society by large, show some what similar use of different elements of crime like that of films.

(ii) **No-Material aspect of life**—The impact of films on the non-material aspects of life relate to the realm of ideas viz. belief system, values and ideals, aspirations, knowledge and awareness to certain problems and evils in our society. These are as follows:

(a) **Belief Systems**—The religious, mythodological and devotional films are well known to have been creating their significant impact on belief system of the people.

(b) **Values and Ideals**—Compare to the Western cinema, we find that most of the Indian cinema, barring those which are religious ones or especially those made after independence or even before that have been inculcating the values pertaining to identity which implies within it secularization and equalitarian values.

(c) **Aspiration**—A number of entertaining and so called commercial cinema depict that people born in poor circumstances, by dint of their perseverance or that of their gather mean they adopt and their success in guardians, rise to that of great social and economic heights though usefully shorter span of time may not be rational and viable.

(d) **Knowledge, Education, Problems and Probable solutions**—Cinema also add to the knowledge of the people and educate the masses in different ways. In this regard we may see that the documentary and the ethnographic films remain supreme because of their direct and meaningful relevance to broaden our horizon of knowledge or to tell something about the people.

CONTRIBUTION OF CINEMA TO THE NATIONAL INTEGRATION OF A NATION

India is an example of multiple societies characterized by diversities of all types. The pre and post-independent India witnessed eruption of disintegrating forces in the name of region, religion, caste and the like/there have been various religious riots at different points of time, instances of caste discrimination or caste riots in recent decades and assassination of Mrs. Gandhi and the like factors, operating in the country, very often created an atmosphere to emphasize on national integration. Debates are held and efforts are also being undertaken to reach the goal of national integration. The national integration has been a much talked about subject in the cinema world. Indian cinema has also served "as an integrating force" and as well contributed to the "national Unity". While looking at Indian cinema from this point of view, find that it has "contributed to national unity" and this impark in two different ways. Firstly on the organizational level of cinema it presents an ideal model of unity and integration whereas Secondly, it is the impact which the Indian cinema wields through its various films.

By its very nature, cinema is an integration force. It reaches out to the people scattered all over the country and brings them closer by enabling them to share common experiences. We may describe the atmosphere of a cinema hall like a person have no idea who is his next seat neighbour- He may be Brahmin Hindu of orthodox of liberal views, orthodox of liberal Muslims, or a Harijan. You are all packed in this black-box which is the neighborhood cinema theatre, air-conditioned or otherwise amidst a diversity of people. That means the atmosphere id conducive to National integration—as all sorts of people are intermingled together.

References

Representing moving images: Implications for developers of digital video collections. Proceedings of the 1998 Meeting of the American Society for Information Science by Goodrum, Abby (1998).

How has film influenced life styles and human behaviour in the 20th century research, "Fashion term papers, 14 November 2013".

Globalization of Indian Cinemas-Bidvertiser cinema of India, August 04, 2008.

Preservation of Cinema as Cultural Heritage of a Nation with Special Reference to Indian by Sajukta Ray Pahari in 7th International CALIBER, 2009.

Cinema—A Reflection of Society 23

BANDANA VAIDYA

Cinema is meant and believed to entertain, to take the viewer to a world of fantasy that is different from the real world, a world which provides an escape from the daily grind of life. Vidya Balan's character in *The Dirty Picture* says that a film works because of, three reasons "entertainment, entertainment, entertainment." This statement is true to a great extent but producing quality cinema is an art and it must reflect human emotions, connect with the hearts and finally awaken our humanness. In this paper an attempt will be made to show that cinema from the time of Dadasahib Phalke to the present time of Farhan Akhtar has not only entertained but has also shown the dreams, aspirations and desires of the common man. The various hues and aspects of real life have been reflected on the reels of cinema.

Cinema over the decades has reflected the changing social, political and economic scenario of India. The gradual breakdown of the feudal order, class conflicts, India's struggle for independence, the rise of the middle class, the emergence of small town India, the despair, anger and alienation of the common man, the loss of faith in those in power, the new found confidence of the ordinary man, patriotism and new threats to the country like terrorism have all found expression in the Indian cinema.

The journey of India cinema began over the hundred years ago when Dada Sahib Phalke, the father of Indian cinema released his first silent movie *Raja Harishchandra* in 1913. A visionary, Dada Sahib Phalke could foresee the tremendous potential films had. He integrated centuries old mythological narratives with the emerging medium of cinema and made films like *Raja Harishchandra, Lanka Dahan, Mohini Bhasmasur* and *Kaliya Mardan*. These movies were successful as they catered to the spiritual bent of mind of the society of those times. *Satyavadi Raja Harishchandra* had all male castes as there were no females available to play the roles. Cinema during those times was a taboo for the Indian woman who spent most of her time within the four walls of her house.

Times changed and so did the movies. *Achutt Kanya* released in 1936 deals with the social position of Dalit girls in Indian society. Ashok Kumar starrer *Kismet* released during the Quit India Movement was a cinematic rendition of resistance against imperialist British by Indians.

Post-independence, Nehruvain era was a period when director like Bimal Roy, Mehboob Khan, Satyajit Ray, Guru Dutt and Raj Kapoor left an indelible impression on the minds of Indian movie viewers. Mehaboob Khan's Mother India, Satyajit Ray's *Pather Panchali*, Bimal Roy's *Do Bigha Zameen* show the grim struggle for survival of the poor living in rural India. These movies are also a celebration of the human spirit and the never say die attitude of the Indian farmer. Mother India film publicity said "The grain of rice on your table does not tell the grim of take the toil that grew it". Movies of Raj Kapoor had a patriotic theme. His films *Shree 420, Jis Desh Me Ganga Behti Hai* celebrate the newly independent India and encouraged film goers to be patriots. His song Mera Joota Hai Japani fills the heart of every Indian even now with patriotism.

The movies of the sixties were romantic and fun filled. Heroes like Shammi Kapoor and Rajesh Khanna danced into the hearts of the people. Even in this decade, movies were made to find solutions to the numerous problems being faced by the country. Manoj Kumar's Upkar was based on the slogan *Jai Jawan Jai Kisan* given by the then Prime Minister of India Lal Bahadur Shastri. *Haqeeqat* released in the 1964 was a war film based on 1962 Sino-Indian War.

The seventies was a periods of disenchantment of the common man with those in power. The young Indian were unhappy with governance, rising prices food scarcity and corruption. It was a period when emergency was imposed upon the nation and liberties were suspended. Manoj Kumar's *Roti Kapad aur Makan* showed the struggle of "aam admi" for the bare necessities of life, i.e *Roti Kapda aur Makan.* Amitabh Bachchan beautifully portrayed the role of an angry young man in movies like *Zanjeer, Deewar* and *Sholay* who is hell bent on changing the rotten system. The 70s and 80s also saw the emergenc of parallel Indian cinema. Directors like Mrirnal Sen Gulzar, Rajinder Singh Bedi, Govind Nihlani, Saeed Mirza to name a few departed from the traditional song-dance formula films and authentically portrayed the growing existential problems of the people, their simmering discontent and the exploitative power structure.

The decade of the nineties in Hindi Cinema was one which popularized the genre of family darma. *Hum AApke Hai Kaun/ Kuch Kuch Hota Hai, Kabhi Khushi Kabhi Gam* are some of the movies of this genre. These movies reinforced the patriarchal values of Indian society and talked about family bonding. The nineties was also a period when terrorism had begun to raise its ugly head. Mani Ratnam's *Roja, Bombay* and *Dil Se* depict human relationships against a background of Indian poltics and military *Machis 1996* by Gulzar portrays the circumstances surrounding the rise of Sikh insurgency in Punjab in 1980s and traces the transformation of a youth from a boy next door into a dreaded terrorist. Border is based on Indo-Pak war of 1971. In the beginning of the next century, movies like *Loc Kargil, Refugee, Mission Kashmir* based on Kargil war fought between India and Pakistan were made.

In the new millennium India society woke up to liberalization and globalsation. New age cinema makers too broke traditional Bollywood's definitive cinematic boundaries. The modern era is an era of marketing and consumerism and in this new age, films are being promoted, marketed and sold as products. However, even in this age there are directors who delve deep into the stark realities of life. Bhandarkar's film the utmost details of page three category people belonging to the upper class society. Fashion is about the dark and pitiable state of affairs in to the world of fashion. Company show the stronghold of underworld while *Gangajal* and *Omkara* are about the rule of *bahubalis. Arakshan* touches the controversial topic of caste-based reservation given in India government jobs and educational institutions. Even blockbuster like *Munna Bhai MBBS* and *Lage Raho Munna Bhai* showed that the greatest gift of God to man is love and all human beings yearn for that '*Pyar Ki Jhappi*'. '*Dil Chahta Hai*' and 'Three Idiots' conveyed an important massage that true happiness in life comes by doing what the heart desires. Aamir Khan's *Lagaan* and *Rang De Basanti* showed the patriotic fervor of Indians. Thus, movie in the present time have not merely provided a visual treat to the audience, they have also shown the economic, social and political set-up in which we live.

Since its inception over a hundred years many film makers have dared to make women centric movies. They have shown women at the centre stage and have highlighted their trials and tribulations, their fight to break the shackles of their social milieu and their desire to find their place under the sun. *Mother India* was the avant grade in introducing a woman to her own strength. Movies like *Arth, Bhumika, Mirch Masala, Damini* have shown the struggle of a woman to fight all odds in order to establish her identity. Contempoaray movies like *Cheeni Kum, Astitva, No One Killed Jessica, Paa, English Vinglish* show tcomplex nuances of the feminine psyche. They also show the changing face of the Indian Woman her no nonsense desire to lead her life on her own terms.

To conclude one can say that Indian cinema has evolved and changed during its journey of over a hundred years. To quote Alfred Tennyson "The old order changeth yielding place to new" Co Actors of the yore have been replaced by new ones, the art of film making has changed yet one thing remains- the human connection of films. It was there in the past and will remain as long as movies are made in India.

References

Dawar, Ramesh, Bollywood: Yesterday. Today. Tomorrow. Star Publications (2006)

Rayadhyaksh. Ashish. Paul Willemen: Encychopedia of Indian Cinema. Routledge (1990).

Unheard Voices of Widows of Vrindavan : From Real to Reel Introduction

24

SANGEETA SINGH

Feminism in Indian cinema is most commonly conceived as a very sensitive concept which is most subtly handled under restricted circumstances of opposition in the name of religion and national identity. The traditionalists perçeive feminist discourse as alienating women from culture, religion and family responsibilities. And nationalists are of the opinion that feminism has its roots in the West and it will only result in eroding the culture and national identity of women, they believe that women are the best custodians of a nationalistic identity. The construction of a nationalistic rhetoric on the basis of religion has always attempted to erase internal differences and conflicts within India in the name of national identity. "For nationalists, history has always meant, in fact, selective history. Nationalists, whose objevtive is to foster a sense of identity and solidarity, to establish a chain of heroes, or to prove their case for a certain historical boundary, pick up those raisins from the cake of history which support and rationalize their cause" (Benyamin Neuberger: 43)

FOCUS OF THE STUDY

This paper foregrounds the unheard voices of widows

presented through the medium of a film *Water* by Deepa Mehta. It is a feminist film that has been interpreted as an eye opener about the issues that are unique and originate due to the contextual exigencies of women in India. The film *Water* depicts the harsh reality of widows in India and also upholds the belief that 'the problem before majority of women (in India) today is not equality but survival' (M. Mulhopadhyay: 50) *Water* deals with the struggle of basic human rights which were denied to the widows in India during the pre-independence time. In this paper the ideological thrust of Deepa Mehta is analyzed *vis-a-vis* her work.

I have tried to develop an argument as to how the empowerment of widows is challenged by the religious sanctions associated with them. Women in India find themselves implicated in the system of dharma codes at various levels as depicted in the film. This is also expressed by Rajeshwari Sunder Rajan in her essay "Goddess Inspired Hindu Feminism". As she says, "This tradition has not only marginalized and alienated women in minority communities, but has also opened by possibilities of further exploitation of these very communities by the Hindu Right and demarcation of more restrictive and repressive cultural lines."

The narrative of *Water* grapples with the legacies of old traditions and their interface with newer knowledge. The film attempts to sensitize the reader about the changing times and issues related to widows. The film depicts how widows are reduced to a virtual non-status through a series of rituals masquerading obscurantist religious sanctions—the breaking of a widow's bangles or banishing her from auspicious functions.

The film was surrounded with a lot of controversy. The deplorable condition of widows in the widow ashrams and their subsequent involvement in prostitution for survival as depicted in the film incurred the wrath of the Hindu activities. They stalled its shooting in Varanasi and blamed Deepa Mehta for tarnishing the image of Hindu religion to gain favours from the West. However, I would defend Deepa Mehta who has tried to unravel how discourses of truth operate in relation to the dominant power structures in Indian society. She has unveiled the hypocrisy within our dharma codes. The movie *Water* is a cinematic counter narrative of the dharma codes as prescribed for widows in the dharmashastras particularly the *Manu Samiriti*. Deepa Mehta has tried to re-do history from a woman's point of view. She has tried to revise the world view that women have inherited from the society. The film *Water* is a non verbal revolt against patriarchal sexual ethics unique to the Indian continent. It is a critique of the silencing of women's voices, the denial of their right to their own bodies and the thwarting of choices; a kind of forced exile from the societies' main stream. The women who were pressurized by all kinds of visible and invisible contexts have been depicted in the film. *Water* highlights the plight of widows it urges women to liberate themselves from paying obeisance to those religious codes and social conventions of patriarchal agenda that function in complicit with culture and religion to exploit them.

"In Brahmin culture, once widowed, a woman was deprived of her useful function in society—that of reproducing and fulfilling her duties to her husband. She ceased to exist as a person; she was no longer either daughter or daughter-in-law. There was no place for her in the community; she was viewed as a threat to society. A woman's sexuality and fertility, which was valuable to her husband in his lifetime, was converted upon his death into a potential danger to the morality of the community" (Sidhwa, 24).

One of the sacred Hindu texts, *The Laws of Manu*, states, "A widow should be long suffering until death, self-restrained, and chaste. A virtuous wife remains chaste, when her husband dies, goes to heaven. A woman who is unfaithful to her husband is reborn in the womb of a jackal" The ritual of making the widow toensure her hair is associated with religious conjectures to avoid any kind of objection and rationalization. However, the real reason for it was to make the widow look ugly and physically unattractive. The narrative articulates the brutal treatment meted out to the widows in the name of religion and righteous codes of conduct. The complexity of the social codes are seen and comprehended in the film through the eyes of a girl child Chuhiya, who becomes a widow at the outset of the movie.

Pandita Ramabai's book *The High Caste Hindu Woman* discussed at length the social practices that degraded and dehumanize widows and reason as to why it was so. Reflecting her views, Uma Chakarvarti writes that 'the young widow was the object of suspicion and, therefore, closely guarded for the fear she might ruin the family's honour through her lapses'. In order to make her less attractive to "man's eyes" she is disfigured and made to fast so that her youthfulness and desires are suppressed. The anxiety about family honour makes even the parents impose on her an entire set of oppressive social and cultural practices. Faced with an unending cycle of degradation with no possibility of employment, the high caste widow had no option. The only available choices were suicide and prostitution. However, these were not real choices but ones forced upon them because of cruel customs and traditions. (Chakarverti 283) Circumstances force them in to a life of compromise.

Water is a powerful film against social ostracism and culture prejudices against widows. The film is a harbinger of social and moral debates and also raises the ethical issue of human invasion through her presentation of the widows.The condition of widows in traditional Indian societies enforces cruel sexual and social abstinence that, in fact, mask economic reasons sanctioned by religion. A widows gnawing, anguish her solitude and her alienation have been depicted through Shakuntla's quest of righteous living . Sad experiences and bitter disillusionment with realities of life force her to question her belief system .The movie traces the self-actualization of Shakuntla who feels solidarity towards widows as ill-fated as herself and commits herself to bring about a change. She takes a step against the grain of custom and expectations. She assists Kalyani in freeing her from the bondage of the ashram and forced prostitution. Shakuntla also becomes instrumental in brining out an affirmative future for Chuhiya, a child widow who becomes a constract to question the ways of Dharmashastras for widows.The film also establishes a link between private sorrow and collective social trauma of the marginalized widow. The narrative becomes an oblique voice of all the widows who have suffered endlessly under the process of such grand narratives of patriarchal ideology. And they do not offer any scope for alternative way of living.

The attempt of Deepa Mehta to establish a dialogue with tradition with the objective of searching for theoretical possibilities available within the tradition that may serve as new vantage points in the struggle for empowerment is quite commendable. The film also exposes the fact that the same glorious Indian tradition is also struck by paradoxes and forgery of its own kind. On one hand in India women are treated with utmost respect at certain occasions and shunned when they become widows. The novel exposes the hypocrisy and double standards of Indian society. The film constitutes a critique of conventional patriarchal values and satirizes the honour with which women are placed in society. It makes a shocking statement in a land where women are worshipped, they continue to be tortured, abused and humiliated in the name of religious sanctions.

The film is a post-conventional analysis in the opposition of hierarchies that underpin our understanding of ourselves; it is an attempt by Deepa Mehta to uncover the constructed nature of our epistemology and ontological categories.

If we look into the conditions of widows in other parts of the world, we find similar ostracism meted out to them in other cultures. Though the degree of discrimination and level of inhuman treatment may differ, yet self-similar constructed structures were also found in African society as well. Across a wide range of cultures, widows are subject to patriarchal customary and religious laws and confront discrimination in rights. Widowhood is a kind of living death for women in almost all cultures. A recently published book–*Invisible, Forgotten Sufferers: The Plight of Widows around the World* – reveals that there are an estimated 245 million widows worldwide, 115 million of whom live in poverty and suffer from social stigmatization and economic deprivation purely because they have lost their husbands. These are women who still jostle with basic human rights and struggle for existence. They are so caught up with their insecure existence that they cannot think in terms of identity and selfhood. They are unaware of their strengths or the human right laws. They are un-educated, live under economic dependence, and have a servile existence. Deepa Mehta's film, *Water*, depicts the plight of such women and their struggles. The film delineates the harsh injunctions that are imposed on widows. The film is an urge to re-tell and re-encounter the lives of widows that have been left mute in history.

Though the movie has a backdrop of pre-independent India, but the story is still just as relevant; the violent protests that nearly aborted Deepa Mehta's film are a reminder of how unthinking adherence to tradition can lord it over reason and humanity. A lot still needs to be done to improve the condition of widows in India even today the laws are not just enough, there is a need to change the mind-set of people against their treatment of widows. It is an attempt by Deepa Mehta and to uncover the constructed nature of our epistemology and ontological categories. Deepa Mehta's concerns as an artist and a woman engaged in her world have given rise to a film that demands that we recognize the complexity of the historical matrix in which the Dharmashashtras were embedded and question its relevance in later times. Her work actively seeks to engage her audience in a process of self-criticism and education.

Deepa Mehta has been criticized for looking at India in negative terms, exoticizing it and freezing it through stereotypes. The same thing was said about the Oscar winning movie *The Slum Dog Millionaire*. We blameall the diasporic representations as essentialist and homogenizing the Indian reality, but are we also not being essentialist in trashing all creations by diasporic writers as politically motivated. When an artist chooses to create a narrative around a particular issue he/she has to limit his canvas as it is not possible to include everything in a limited space. Deepa Mehta too has been taken to task for "scandalizing the national sentiment" The filming of water at Benaras had to be stalled owing to the propests from fundamentalists backed by political parties. They were of the opinion that Deepa Mehta was trying to show the Hindu Tradition in bad light. Artists often have to confront such opposition from the people in power if they attempt to portray anything contrary to what they uphold as truth. There is also a larger question of artistic freedom in this horrific experience of opposition in the name preserving the national identity. Today, across the cultural spectrum, artistic freedom is under assault. Self-appointment guardians of morality in the name of religion have become militants. Without the guarantee of freedom of expression, of conscience, our story tellers will be silenced and we shall be poorer for it. In this age, a reluctance to speak out against what one perceives as root cause of an injustice may grow into a state of sanctioned violence, exploitation and even genocide. The writers who choose to write about these issues and initiate a conversation are able to build up a "community of conscience". They should be provided with a security against forces that try to silence such artists with activism of transformation. "If art is to nourish the roots of our culture, society must set the artist free to follow his vision wherever it takes him." (John F. Kennedy)

Deepa Mehta has taken a brave step to publicize one of the most hidden and veiled areas of violation of women's human rights. The widows are the most under-represented section of Indian society. Very few movies have depicted the plight of the widows. Rabindernath Tagore's *Chokkher Bali,* a novel that deals with the psychology of a young widow was very successfully adapted into a film of the same title by the famous Satyajit Ray. Thus, artists like Deepa Mehta are catalysts in bringing social justice to those sections of women who have no representation in the mainstream of the feminist movement. They become instrumental in bringing about a transformation in the social condition of women through their counter narratives. The subject matter of such films and fictional work which draws its inspiration from the real life situations bring into focus the aspects of women's life which were hitherto ignored to a wider hearing.

The narratives depicted in films attempt to question those cultural signifiers in the Indian society which are responsible for the marginalization of women from the mainstream. It is a covert strategy to speak back to the power structures by a woman artist. The diasporic identity of Deepa Mehta becomes an advantage as well as a disadvantage in her representation of India in her film. The challenges faced by artists like Deepa Mehta who dares to subvert the patriarchal hegemony by puncturing the self-righteous smugness of religious codes is also noteworthy. Deepa Mehta in an attempt to start a dialogue first exposes the hypocrisy of the embeddedness of religion and national identity in the gender politics of India.

Also, the zooming in process in the film has been effectively used by Deepa Mehta, where the lowest denominator Chuhiya has been identified as the focal point of her narrative. In the film, Deepa Mehta has interwoven gender politics with the politics of religion. The film also shows how the individual stories coolesqueto become collective misery of widows of India. The female gaze on the religious codes is given a due space. Women who are marginalized by society are given a space to re-write it from their perspective in the film. Woman's body as a territory vulnerable to physical assaults is also one key theme in the film. The director has tried to bridge the gap between reality and representation through her film.

This imaginative film acts as symbolic representation of the voices of all the widows silenced by dominant discourses of Dharmashastra. The film provids the definitive account of the female gaze of a director who presents 'her story' as opposed to 'his story'. Deepa Mehta's concerns as an artist and a woman engaged in her world have given rise to a film that demands that we recognize and hear the silent cries of victims of Dharma shastra.

References

Chakravati, Uma, *Revisiting History: The Life and Times of Pandita Ramabai.* New Delhi: Kali for Women, 1998. Print.

Manu, *Laws of Manu.* Trans, Wendy Doniger with Brian K. Smith Harmondsworth: Penguin Classics, 1991, Print.

Mukhopadhyay, Maitrayee, *Silver Shackles: Women and Development in India,* Oxfam in Oxford 1984, Print.

Neuberger, Benyamin, *National Self-determination in Post-colonial Africa.* Lynne Rienner Publishers Inc. Boulder: Colorado, 1986. Print.

Rajan, Rajeshwari Sunder. "Goddess Inspired Hindu Feminism." in Chandhari, Maitaryee, ed. *Feminism in India.* Zed books, 2005. Print

Sidhwa, Bapsi, *Water A Novel: Based on the Film by Deepa Mehta,* Penguin. Viking 2006. Print.

Water. Dir. Deepa Mehta. Prod. David Hamilton, 2007 Film.

Indian English Films Based on Novels in English Literature 25

Abhiyudita Gautam

Cinema has been a greatest unifying factor in India as people from all caste, creed, colour and speaking different languages sit together to watch this visual experience. It has emerged as the strongest source of entertainment in the last century after the development of electronic media.

There is an immense diversity as far as the languages in the Indian cinema are concerned, ranging from the languages from the North India like Panjabi to Bhojpuri and Bengali, Assamese in the east and the languages like Tamil, Telegu, Kannad and Malayalam in the South to Marathi and Gujarati in the West.

English movies were the first entrants into the Indian Cinema. In the 1920s, films directed by Franz Osten and Himanshu Rai including *'The Light of Asia'* and *'A Throw of Dic'e,* could be considered as English-language films because the titles were in English. With the coming of sound, directors such as Osten and Rai chose Hindi as the language, thus effectively bringing to a close this phase of English-language films made in India.

Indian crossover films appeared in Indian Cinema with international productions with Indian themes, starting with Merchant Ivory Productions first venture, *'The Householder'* (1953), which has an India story, setting with an Indian cast, which included, Shashi Kapoor, Leela Naidu and Durga Khote, followed by a number of Indian-themed films largely propelled by Indian-born producer, Ismail Merchant. However, it took a while before an Indian director would commercially take up making films in the English language.

The first such film came at the peak of the Parallel Cinema movement, when Aparna Sen directed *'36 Chworanghi Lane'* (1981) to critical acclaim. Its lead actress, Jennifer Kendal was even nominated for a BAFTA Award. The genre was able to stand on its own with Dev Benegal's *English August'* (1994) which was widely accepted by urban audiences and became its first hit, drawing an audience of 20 million.

This paved the way for other directors to look at using English language as a viable medium, like Nagesh Kukunoor who made *Hydrabad Blues* (1998), Kaizad Gustav's *Bombay Boys* (1998) and more recently 'Being Cyrus' (2006) by Homi Adajaniya, and Rituporna Ghosh whose *'The Last Lear'* (2008), starring Amitabh Bachachan as the lead, won the Best English Feature film Award at national film Award Meanwhile, film directors of Indian descent, such as Mira Nair, Deepa Mehta and Gurinder Chadha, continued to make English-language films on Indian themes to international acclaim; this has opened up the genre further both creatively and commercially.

A PASSAGE TO INDIA: SUMMARY

E.M. Fotster's *A Passage to India* concerns the relations between the English and the native population of India during the colonial period in which Britain ruled India. The action takes place primarily in Chandrapore, a city along the Ganges River, notable for the nearby Marabar caves. The main character of the novel is Dr. Aziz, a Moslem doctor in Chandrapore. After he is summoned to the Civil Surgeon's home only to be promptly ignored, Aziz visits a local Islamic temple where he meets Mrs. Moore, an elderly British woman visiting her son, Mr. Heaslop, who is the City Magistrate. Although Aziz reprimands her for not taking her shoes off in the temple before realizing she has in fact observed this rule. The two soon find that they have much in common and he escorts her back to the club.

A Passage to India (1984) : The film, a classic drama is one of the most memorable English film based on the Indo-British relationship and its impact on the day-to-day life during English

Rule in India. Written and directed by David Lean, based on the 1924 novel by E.M. Forster, won various awards including Academy Awards and Golden Globe Awards. The brilliant acting comes from Judy Davis, Victor Banerjee, Peggy Ashcroft and James Fox in the key role.The novel is set against the backdrop of the British Raj and the Indian independence movement in the 1920s.

A Passage to India is a critique of British rule in India. The British are not shown as tyrants, although they do fail to understand Indian religion and culture. They are also convinced that the British Empire is a civilizing force on the benighted "natives" of India, and they regard all Indians as their inferiors, incapable of leadership. And yet, in their own way, the English try to rule in a just way. Ronny, for example, the City Magistrate, is completely sincere when he says that the British "are out here to do justice and keep the peace" (chapter 5). And there is no trace of satire in the passage that shortly follows this, which describes Ronny's daily routine: "Every day he worked hard in the court trying to decide which of two untrue account was the less untrue, trying to dispense justice fearlessly, to protect the weak against the less weak, the incoherent against the plausible, surrounded by lies and flattery". Ronny is also aware of the hostility between Hindus and Moslems, and believes that a British presence is necessary to prevent bloodshed. Even Fielding, the most sympathetic of the English characters, does not argue that the British should leave India. However, the British lack any ability to question their own basic assumptions about race and Empire, and as such they become the objects of Forster's biting satire.

CITY OF JOY

City of Joy, a Novel by Dominique Lapierre

Stephan Kovalski (a Catholic priest), Max Loeb (an American doctor), and Hansari Pal (an Indian rickshaw driver), dominate the narrative. All three reside in the slum and represent the juxtaposing of Western religion and science with Indian misery. Their lives are interwoven with that of the slum, its filth, poverty, starvation, hopelessness, and outbursts of violence. Kovalski becomes particularly engaged in the problems of the slum's lepers, the absolute bottom rank of Anand Nagar's society.

Lapierre demonstrates how social Darwinism rules the life of Hansari Pal. Pal realizes that his struggle to provide for his family involves both luck and survival of the fittest. When another rickshaw driver dies and Pal seeks to take his place, he is caught in a web of union corruption. Pal, however, manages to fight through its entanglements. With incredible luck and tough fighting, he makes a "relative" fortune by retrieving used hospital dressings from the city dump. After this good fortune, however, Pal succumbs to the ravages of tuberculosis, but not before his son is married and his line assured.

Max Loeb enters Anand Nagar as a young doctor from a heritage of American upper-class opulence. Initially idealistic, Loeb soon grows to a realism and a genuine loving commitment to his pitiable patients.

Lapierre sees hope in Kovalski's reconciliation of his religion and his growing vision of joy as perceived by his slum...

City of Joy (1992), the film is excellent in terms of making us aware of the world's needs. There are too many disturbing elements for younger children, but viewers from the United States or other first world countries will be prompted to count their blessings anew. Three lives become intertwined in the City of Joy, a very poor area of Calcutta, India. Joan Bethel, Max Lowe a disillusioned American surgeon who is, robbed and beaten by some local "godfathers" while on vacation. Hasari Pal (Om Puri), who has brought his family to Calcutta in a desperate search for work after his farm was repossessed during a drought, helps bring Lowe to the clinic. From there, the film's theme is the conflict between those trying to make a difference and those who want everything to stay just as it is. Hasari comes to Max's aid and takes the injured doctor to the "City of Joy," a slum area populated with lepers and poor people that becomes the Pals' new home and the American's home away from home. Max spends a lot of time in the neighborhood, but he doesn't want to become too involved with the residents because he is afraid of becoming emotionally attached to them. He soon, however, is coaxed into helping his new-found friends by a strong-willed Irish woman who runs the local clinic.

Eventually, Max begins to fit in with his fellow slum-dwellers and become more optimistic. There are many around him whose lives are much worse, but they look on each day with a hope that gives new strength to the depressed doctor

BRIDE AND PREJUDICE (2005)

Published in 1813, Jane Austen's *Pride and Prejudice* follows the process of an upper class family's search to marry their daughters off before the death of their father. As mentioned in our class lecture, one main theme of this novel is the relationship between class and gender, where becoming an eligible bachelor weighs heavily on his socioeconomic status. Through the narrator's choice of alternating temperate and solemn voices, this novel also shows Austen's views of marriage and its importance. What also becomes clear is how the time period of the novel plays a role in explaining the situation and need for marriage.

Gurinder Chadha's film, titled *Bride and Prejudice,* inspired by Jane Austen's *Pride and Prejudice* focuses on the differences around an American idea of marriage and weddings and an Indian idea of marriage and weddings. In this film, due to the occasional breakout of song and dance, it can be considered a musical. Some of the main themes in this film are the ways of dealing with the pride of a foreigner and the personal effects of international economic disparities. This film being filmed in three different countries was an excellent way to display and play out the supporting elements of these themes.

The musical (singing and dancing) aspect in Chadha's *Bride and Prejudice* is included as an introduction to India's Bollywood culture and cannot be considered similar to the theme park atmosphere Lalita accuses Darcy of wanting. Lalita's accusation of Darcy wanting to turn India into a theme park refers to the foreign American business that has been built in her country. Darcy tries to make the claim that he wants to show Americans the Indian culture, but the upscale American styled hotel Darcy is deciding on is nothing like India and would only be a theme park in India, due to having very little to do with Indian culture. Chadha's inclusion of song and dance in the streets on Amritsar and during wedding ceremonies is a catalyst for showing Bollywood culture and the celebration of a marriage. To those who live in India, some of these songs and dances are ritual and an act of celebration, and cannot be considered as having a theme park like nature. But for those Americans traveling to a five star hotel located in India with only generated bits of Indian culture, they would be entertained and enjoy their time as one visiting a theme park.

Journalism for Films 26

SUDHIR SONI

FILMS AS AN INDUSTRY

Film-making is not an easy task. It involves combination of many aspects; being a collective art, the film-making is an industry; and it is a full-fledged profession involving production, distribution, earnings to make up the expenditure, methods of profit-making, advertisements, publicity, etc. Truly speaking, it is a triangle of art, industry and profession. All these factors—art, industry and profession—have equal influence on the film-making from beginning to the end of production and exhibition.

The whole concept of the films has undergone a great change at present. Big budget films are being produced films made using hube and costly sets, costly stars, the framework and huge investments, etc. are expected to not only recover the expenditure on their production, but also to make some profits like an industry. The film producers leave no stone unturned to make the films profit-making from every point of view. The increasing tendency to make more and more profits has told the knell of art and values. A tendency of making use of the film masala in the script and its picturisation has developed; the main aim of which is to earn profits even at the cost of art and values.

Today, there is a race for making costly sets, glitter and splendour, shooting at foreign locations, cheap songs and dialogues for making films. Such films are misleading the young generation; the producers who claim making films for pure entertainment also have only one aim, encashing the public mentality and interest.

With the changing times and society, it has been installed in the mind of the audience that no one sees films for getting an education after purchasing costly tickets, but they go to the cinema halls for entertainment and spending some time in the dreamworld. They, therefore, need no advice or logic. Under such circumstance, the only aim to the film-makers is making money out of the pockets of the audience by luring them to see these films. This is the element, which has made the films and cinema a market and the industry makes use of this market like any other markets. It, first of all, develops in the audience the habit of films seeing thereafter the consumers are made victims of the addiction to these products. Films are developing a class in the society which become a source of making profits, like any product of an industry.

For most of the producers and directors, film-making is no more a means to present idealism, like the days gone by. It is no more a mission for the positive development of the society, it is just a money making business, for which values do not matter much. At time, some films come out with some ideal, but most of the films are the products of arithmetic of profit-making alone.

DIFFERENT TYPES OF FILMS

The films can be classified as under:

1) Feature Films

Feature films are the main sources of the world of entertainment. The era of the feature films in India was marked by the film *"Raja Harishchandra"* made in 1913. With the development of the technology came the *"Talkies"* followed by the colour pictures; the feature films, thus, become pervasive in the society.

Based on some story, the films are woven with the fabric of colour and audio-visual effects in such a way that the audience find themselves in a dream-world. India is the largest producer of the feature films after Hollywood. Moving around diverse subjects, these films, in addition to the Indian sub-continent, are seen in the other parts of the world; the gulf countries, Russia, America, Britain, etc. Films like *"Do Bigha Zamin"*, *"Hathi Mere*

Sathi", "Uttar-Dakshin", "Ghayal," etc. shown in Cinema, became very popular. Raj Kapoor's film *"Awaara"* was most popular in the contemporary USSR. The feature films produced in India are permitted to be screened only after getting a certificate from the Central Board of Film Censor, which was constituted on 15 January 1851.

Many films of the social themes and issues have been in India, some classic films have also been produced. Every film leaves its impression on one class of the society or the other. The feature films have, today, become an addiction in the society. The stars have become the role models for the youth, who copy their style of living. They try to emulate the film characters with blind faith. Despite all these evil aspects and bad influence there are many films, which have been able to bring out the best in the society and individuals as well through better music and dialogues, etc.

Child Films

The aim of producing the child films is to develop creativity and social values and child psychology. The world of the children is a wonderful world, in which everything is positive and there is nothing negative. Making films suited for children and adolescents is an art. Children are instinctively influenced by nature and cartoons; the child films have, therefore, to be made selectively and imaginatively.

The Children's Film Society of India was set-up in May 1955. It is also known as the National Children and Youth Film Centre. The main objective of this organization is to undertake, sponsor, promote and coordinate production, distribution and exhibition of films suited for children and adolescents. The headquarters of this organization is located at Bombay.

Advertisement Film

The modern age is the age of advertisements. Advertisements are seen displayed virtually at every place, nowadays inside and outside the houses, offices, shops, walls, etc. one has to encounter these advertisements while walking sitting at some place or travelling.

The basic factor behind the advertisement films is the economic and industrial development. Advertisement is considered to be a strong weapon for the disposal of huge products available in the markets. This importance of the advertisements attracted the film-makers to produce advertisement films.

Today, thousands of advertisement films are made every year. These films are the products of consumerism; and this profession is also full of glamour. The advertisement films are made by the advertisement agencies and the renowned producers. They take care of all the aspects of the advertisement, the ideas of the advertiser and presentation form, etc. In the advertisement films the whole process of pasteurization revolves round the product. The main objective of the advertisement films is to achieve growth the sale of the advertised products. That is the reason, these advertisement films are far away from the reality; their aim is to create a dream world for the fulfillment of the desires of the middle class people.

India today, is badly under the influence of the international consumerism. The concept of free trading exercises many pressures on the mind of consumers. With the use of computers, digital audio-visual effects and graphics, etc. have created a new world markets. The Advertisements dominate all the means of mass communication It is strange, but true, that most of the films newspapers, magazines, serials, etc. are selling on the strength advertisements alone. There are some positive aspects also advertisement have proved positive in highlighting the issues of public interest like family welfare, public health, electricity and other consideration, etc.

Documentaries

The short films made with the objective of public information, education and instruction are called documentaries. These films of short duration have a long history of their own; although, these films are shown by way of a filter, but it is an historical fact that the documentaries gained ground much before the feature films.

The main subjects of the documentaries are government public welfare schemes, revolutionary events of the history and society festivals, fairs, functions, like sketches of the great personalities, literature and culture, etc. The audience gets knowledge on these aspects through these documentaries. These documentaries are also made use of by Doordarshan in the functions and the cinema halls, as per their usefulness, the documentaries depicting the episodes of the India freedom struggle, lectures of Gandhi and Nehru and other issues connected with independence of India, etc., provide impetus and motivation to the coming generations.

Educational Films

Like the documentaries, the films made for public awaking are termed the educational films. These films provide education and instruction for the general awakening of the public.

The education films like *"Aao Parayen, Kuchh Kar Dikhayen"* brought a revolution in the literacy campaign; the people were convinced that literacy plays an important role in the uplift of life.

The useful films like *"Paani Bachaiye", Bijali Ki Bachat"* and *"Bharat Gas"*, etc., etc., make the public aware to stop the misuse of these values sources of general life.

The educational film on *"AIDS"* has played an important rule in making the people aware of the deadly effects of unsafe sexual contacts. The film on *" Sarak Niyam"* (road rules), educates the people on the various aspects of traffic. The educational films on various rural schemes, government policies and plans, family planning, public health, vasectomy/tubetomy, vaccination, pulse polio, etc. have shown their effectiveness. These films educate the public to bring improvement in their routine life.

The educational films are very important for the society. These films are the mirror of the society. These films not only take up the issues in an interesting way, but also bring awareness among the public. Today, even the people of the remote area send their daughters to schools; the awakening for the education of the female children is the result of these educational films. These films play important role about bringing awareness on various rural schemes, environment protection, public health and other issues of the public interest.

FILM ORGANIZATIONS IN INDIA

India is today, much ahead in the field of film-making; India is the first place in the world in terms of number of films produced per year. The history of feature films dates back to 1912. Following are the main and important organizations:

CENTER FILMS CERTIFICATION BOARD

Any film certified by the Certification Board can be exhibited in India. This board set-up under the Cinematography Act, 1952 is comprised of a chairperson and a minimum of 12 and maximum non official members. The members are appointed officially. The headquarters of the Board is located at Bombay. There are nine regional offices under it: Bangaluru, Mumbai, Kolkata, Hyderabad, Chennai, Tiruanantapuram, New Delhi, Kolkata and Guwahati. The Indian films made in approximately languages that are certified by these regional offices.

There are advisory panels, which assist these regional offices in examining the films. These panels are comprised of educationists, critics, journalissts, social workers, etc. The board examines the films before issuing categories, under the provisions of the Cinematography Act, 1952 Films (Certification) Rules 1983 and various guidance issued by the government in this context. If an appeal is made any certification it is listened by the Films Certification act in tribunal.

FILMS DIVISION

The films Division of India was established in 1948 for making the achievements of independent India in films and problem and preservation of these records. It is an effective document for interaction between the public and the government. This diversion is the largest national agency for the production and distribution of newsreels and documentaries, and 16 MM short tale in the regional languages for the rural audience. This diversion is foremost in the world in the production of documentaries. It also produces educational and cartoon films for the various ministries and departments of the Government of India. The National Films Archive of India, under the Films Division, has in its store 8000 documentaries short length films and animation films, etc. The division is assisted by its 10 branches in the distribution of documentaries and newsreels for exhibition through the cinema houses spread all over India. These branches are located Bangaluru, Mumbai, Kolkata, Hyderabad, Lucknow, Chennai, Madurai, Nagpur,

Tiruanantapuram and Vijaywada. The Films Division also organizes films festivals at various places in the country.

NATIONAL FILMS DEVELOPMENT CORPORATION LIMITED

This organization was established in 1975. It was reorganized in 1980 after the amalgamation of the Indian Films Export Corporation and Films Finance Corporation. The main objective of this organization is to bring improvement in the quality of the Indian Cinema and Development of Modern Technology in the field of films. The Corporation provides financial help, patronage and help in the production, distribution and publicity of the socially useful, positive art films and other films on the practically useful subject, etc., through various mediums and means.

In coordination with various film committees, National Film Circles and various other agencies representation the foreign films, etc; this Corporation also organizes film weeks, glimpses of the Indian films and film festival etc as a measure to spread and develop film culture and understanding.

The Corporation patronizes the production of low-budget quality films on socially useful subjects. The Cine-Artists Welfare Fund is the largest Trust of the Indian Films Industry; it was established by the Corporation with an initial investment of 4.16 crore rupees.

DIRECTORATE OF FILM FESTIVALS

The Directorate of Film Festivals was established in 1973 under the Ministry of Information and Broadcasting of the Government of India. Its main objective was to give patronage to good cinema. It provides a pedestal for the better quality Indian films by organizing national film festival every year. The directorate has also played an important rule for the development of cultural goodwill and friendship at the international level. Within the country, the directorate strives for making available the latest technological development in cinema for the benefit of the public.

Under the cultural exchange programmes, the directorate organized the film festivals exhibiting the films of European

Union, North Korea, Poland, Ireland, Japan and Greece, etc. The Indian films were also sent for screening in the Film Festivals organized in China, France, North Koria, Brazil, Sri Lanka, Chicago. A film week was also sent to the SAARC film festivals organized in France and Egypt. The directorates have taken part in 51 film festivals organized in the foreign countries.

THE NATIONAL FILMS ARCHIVE OF INDIA

The National Films Archive of India was established in 1964 under the Ministry of Information and Broadcasting with the following three main objectives:

1. Research and preservation of the Indian Heritage Cinema.
2. Classification of the documents and statistics and research work related to films.
3. To work as the centre for publication of film culture.

The headquarters of this organization is located at Pune with its regional offices at Bangalore, Tiruanatapuram and Kolkata. This organization also organizes joint shows of films in Mumbai, Kolkata, Bangaluru, Chennai, Hyderabad, Tiruanantapuram, Kochchi, Jamshedpur and Pune.

Aided by the films and television organization, the National Films Archive of India also organizes short term and long-term courses on film reviews.

Unveiling the Physical Self through the Eyes of Pooja Bhatt

27

Sonia Hooda

Exposure means wearing some clothes or no clothes. Exposure literally means how much percentage of male and female bodies is going to be exposed in the movie. Wearing of clothes is a human characteristic. The amount of clothing depends on functional considerations and social considerations. Sometimes minimum amount of clothing can be accepted by society but in reality more clothing can be accepted. When minimum amount of clothing is accepted by society, we called it exposure. Today, in Bollywood movies exposure is on higher position. Without bikini scene most of the audience says movie was boring or there was no masala in the movie, because their first priority is to see exposure whether it is minimum or maximum. This type of audience would not like to see Hum Sath Sath Hai or Hum Apke Hai Kaun kind of movies but they would like to prefer Jism or Raaz like movies. Now-a-day's item song or we can say item number also resemble exposure in Indian cinema. This is a musical performance that has little to do with the film in which it appears, but it presented to showcase beautiful dancing women in revealing clothes, to give support to the market of the film. This term is commonly used in connection with Hindi, Tamil and Telugu cinema to describe a catchy, upbeat often sexually provocative dance sequence for a song in a movie. Item numbers are usually added to Indian movies in order to generate publicity by featuring them in trailers. Item numbers have been criticized for their gratuitous objectification of the female body. Item numbers have also been imitated in Mumbai's bar dancers. In respect of the ban on bar dancers in Mumbai, it has even been argued that the morality of bar dancer's imitation of item numbers cannot be questioned without questioning the morality of screening of item numbers in a film in public theatres.

The chapter means "unveiling the physical self through the eyes of Pooja Bhatt" it will measure how a body of male and female can be represented in female directed movies like Dhokha, Holiday, Kajrare, Paap, Jism-2, etc. To show how exposure and male/female bodies is represented in following movies is the main motive of this research. Pooja Bhatt made her acting debut at age 17 in 1989 with Daddy a television Film directed by her father Mahesh Bhatt. In that film she portrayed a soul searching teenage girl in an estranged relationship with her alcoholic father played by actor Anupam Kher. After some time Pooja Bhatt worked as a director in some movies.

EXPOSURE IN FILMS

Exposure in film is any presentation where people wearing less clothing than contemporary norms. In some cases exposure is in itself the object of a film or is used in the development of the character of the subject. Many actors and actresses have appeared nude, or exposing parts of their bodies or dressed in ways considered provocative by contemporary standards at some point in their carriers. Exposure in film should be distinguished from sex in film. Nudity of a sexual nature is common in pornographic films, there are limitations, such as avoiding the depiction of a penis or a vagina.

Exposure in films is controversial in many societies and various cinematic techniques have at times been used to reduce the actual expose of the human body in film, at times to avoid censorship. In film, exposure may be either partial or full. Partial exposure is when a person appears in less than full clothes (For e.g. When a female is topless). Full exposure refers to atleast one person appearing in film who is completely nude.

OPERATIONAL DEFINITION OF EXPOSURE

The depiction of body/body parts by way of dressing/undressing and supplemented/complemented by way of postures/ gestures/body movements rooted in some cultural context (Indian here) so as to create a visual pleasure for viewers.

Objectives

1. To explore the nature of body exposure from the lens of a female director.
2. To find patterns of difference between male and female body exposure in the films.
3. To find out the exposure in romantic scenes.

Research Strategy Paradigm—Interpretive Research Method

Semiotic and Interpretive. Semiotics is the method which emerged from the tradition of literary analysis. The word semiotics is derived from the Greek word Semeion which means sign and the Semiology or Semiotics is thus a science of understanding sign and symbol and their construction of meanings in the interpretant of that sign. Signs have no inherent meanings in them but they acquire meaning in social situations and context. The method focuses on analytical integrity rather than on representativeness of the sample. A semiological analysis entails the deployment of a highly refined set of concepts which produce detailed account of the exact ways the meaning of an image are produced through that image. Semiology very often takes the form of detailed case studies of relatively few images.

Sampling—Purposive.

Nature of Research—Qualitative.

RATIONALE OF THE STUDY

This study is an attempt to explore the body exposure of male and female from the lens of female director.

The study is one of the few studies that tries to decipher the exposure and the construction of male and female bodies.

As we see in our daily lives that movies of present time only represent exposure. There is no movie we can say not present exposure in front of viewers. Infact it says that if there is no exposure in the movie means movie will be totally monotonous and somehow most of the people only because of the less exposure not gone for saw movie. But here the question is how female director can see the exposure and how she represents male or female in intimate or romantic scenes.

Data Interpretation

- Whole story of the all movies moves around near to male and female. No far place shooting has been done. Like all the movies these all five movies are moves around on some theme.
- In the movie Holiday there is a concept of salsa dance which is flowing in the whole movie infact movie is end on salsa dance.
- In the movie Paap there is Nepal's tradition followed by the director. A woman follow her tradition and lives a saint kind of life but when she falls in love with a guy her thinking changed infact her father's thinking is going to be changed. It tells that love can change life infact our narrow minded thinking.
- In the movie Dhokha there is a theme of terror attacks which is prevalent in our country now a days. In this movie the male is ditched by his wife whose main aim is to create peace in her mulch.
- In Kajrare there is a concept of love of laymen towards a prostitute. How he uses his full strength to make her his wife and how at the end of the movie he finally married to her.
- In Jism 2 there is a concept that a girl is fall in true love with the guy but when he ditched her she becomes a porn star after that she got the chance to take revenge. How she take revenge told in the movie.
- In all these movies directed by Pooja Bhatt like Paap, Holiday, Dhokha, Kajrare, and Jism-2 are the movies in which exposure is seen by female.
- If we talked about the bodies of male and female than female is looking slim in all the five movies, on the other side male has muscular 'v' shape body in all four

movies but in Kajrare there is Himesh Reshamia which has no muscular body in there is hardly a scene in the movie in which he removes his shirt otherwise in Paap, Holiday, Dhokha and in Jism-2 hero removes his shirt in the movie and shows his body.

If we talk about apparels worn by male and female in the movie then we can say that there is no expenditure is done on female dresses only Jism-2 is the movie in which heroine is seen in short different western dresses otherwise in rest of the four movies female is in very simple dress. Infact she worn same type of dress in the whole movie. In case of male except Kajrare in all the movies male is seen uncovered from his upper body part in most of the scenes may be to show their muscular body but in Kajrare there is not a only scene in which hero is seen uncovered from his upper body part, he is seen only in deep neck shirt in the whole movie.

- In most of the scenes of all the five movies there is majority of male dialogues than the female dialogues which shows male dominancy over the female.
- Most of the exposure scenes are captured at outdoor in all the movies.
- In Holiday movie most of the exposure exposed by salsa dance in which couple is danced on tropical music. Tropical music represents passion in itself. In this dance both the male and female are very close to each other and dance well. If we talk about Jism-2 there we can see exposure in female short dresses which also help men to came him closer to female and in the whole movie male and female trying to do lip kiss which is also a part of exposure. In Kajrare there is female exposure mainly we can say because only female is seen in western outfit otherwise male is wearing pant and deep neck shirt in the whole movie.
- In the movie "Holiday" there is most of the use of mirror images in which we can see one male/female instead of two which also shows love in between the couple. In most of the scenes of this movie there is use of water on male-female or we can say most of the scenes of this movie are picturised near water. Because

water helps in increasing the romantic mood that's why this uses in the movie. In Kajrare there is only an exposure by female costumes. If we talk about "Paap" there is exposure exposed by male because in it female is very silent, only her expressions are told but in case of male he tells more infact his body says a lot. In most of the scenes he is seeing uncovered from his upper body part.

- In Dhokha there is simplicity shown by the heroine. She is in open hairs and full dressed in the whole movie which increasing her beauty and her this simple beauty helps men to came closer to female but in case of male he is uncovered from his upper body part in most of the scenes. In holiday there is also a lead heroine in tied hairs and in very simple dressed in the whole movie otherwise male is looking uncovered from his upper body and shown his muscular body.
- If we talked about lighting there is mostly used soft lighting in the movies. "Jism-2" is the only movie in which there is maximum use of dim lighting in most of the scenes. Because in this movie maximum number of exposure is done by the female may be this is the reason to use dim lighting.

CONCLUSION

This research work looks at various elements of exposure and male and female bodies in *Paap, Holiday, Dhokha, Kajrare* and *Jism-2* movies directed by Pooja Bhatt. On the basis of related literature and earlier studies all major points are enlisted related to exposure and construction of male and female bodies. From all the movies only those scenes are captured in which male and female are in romance. Each element of exposure on what basis it is measured is explained briefly. Data analysis is done through shots which are captured from the clippings. At first clipping are cut from the movies in which male and female are in romantic mood after this a shot is captured from that clipping so that study of exposure can be done easily. Whole data is presented with the pictures and explanations of it. On the basis of findings following conclusions are derived:

- In maximum number of movies like in *Paap, Holiday, Dhokha* female dressed simply.
- Among five movies except, *Kajrare,* male is showing his muscular body.
- Female is more dominating in the movies like *Dhokha, Kajrare,* and *Jism-2.*
- In most of the shots soft lighting and light colours are used, giving soothing, pleasant and romantic environment to the couple.
- Most of the romantic scenes are captured near the water and green plants which help in increasing romantic mood of male and female.
- Mid-shot is captured in maximum numbers.
- Each movie is based on different themes and there is no link of them with each other infact representation of romantic scenes in all the movies is in different style. For example, in *holiday* most of the romantic scenes are shot at near the water.
- Majority of the romantic scenes are captured from an outdoor.
- Female have slim body in all the movies.
- Among all the movies there are majority of lip kiss scenes.

References

Angela Wadia (2008), Film and television radio production.
Accessed from Annenberg.usc.edu

A research study on Male muscularity in men's and women's magazine accessed from www.sscnet.ucla.edu

A research study on Objectification of male body in popular Hindi cinema accessed from www.academia.edu

An Amitabha Bagchi's article on Women in Indian Cinema accessed from www.cs.jhu.edu

A research thesis on Gender reflections in mainstream Hindi Cinema accessed from www.caluniv.ac.in

A research report on the changing constructions of women characters in popular Hindi-language cinema from 1970-2007 accessed from wiredspace.wits.ac.za

A research study on the impact of media exposure on male's body image accessed from Arapaho.nsuok.edu

A research paper for Global Media Magazine on Portrayal of sexual minorities in Hindi Films accessed from www.caluniv.ac.in

A press release on Exposure to sexual content in popular movies predicts sexual behaviour in adolescence accessed from www.psychologial science.org

A feminine language in Cinema accessed from aut.researchgateway.ac.nz

A research study on blockbuster movies and what they teach us about women in American society accessed from gradsworks.umi.com

A research study of an M.Phil thesis on Redefining gender in 21st century Spanish Cinema accessed from theses.gla.ac.uk

A research study of women's role and star persona's in the film of Frank Capra accessed www.uwlax.edu

A research study on Gender disparity on screen and behind the camera in family films accessed from www.seejane.org

A research paper study on Globalisation and representation of women in Indian Cinema accessed from arika.org.uk

Alex_larg_roger_hicks_frances_schultz

Concept about semiotics accessed from www.semioticmethodology.com

C.R. Kothari (2004). Research Methodology, Methods and Techniques (Second Revised Edition). New Age International Publishers Concept of Nudity and art accessed from www.godartist.com D.K. Bhattacharyya (2003) Research Methodology Film reviews, accessed from www.seejane.org

Feminist film theory accessed from www.annekesmelik.nl

Indian cinema: the world's biggest and most diverse film industry accessed from www.cornerhouse.org

P.K. Majumdar (2005). Social Science Research.Viva Books Private Limited Research paper o'connor *et al.* 2012.

Screen bodies and eating disorders book study accessed from www.suny press.edu

Wimmer Dominick, Wadsworth, Mass Media Research (Indian Edition).

W. Lawrence Neuman (2007). Social Research Methods, Qualitative and Quantitative approaches. Pearson.

Hindi Cinema : A Secular Perspective

28

RAVINDRA KATYAYN

Right from its inception, Hindi Cinema has been a tool to entertain people. This revolutionary medium has affected our lives, our society and our social system a lot. Whether it is on the social front, or economic, political or religious front, it has gained popularity, earned money and influenced people at large. Filmmakers have used the real life experiences as well as imaginary, mythological, fictional or historical imprints to express their ideas and translate them creatively into celluloid. This is the main narrative of Hindi Cinema. It has been depicting the real images of Indian life and life styles in the most creative, imaginary and fashionable manner. Being the entertainment industry, Indian Cinema has always tried to stick to its main goal of entertaining the people in different ways, failing which its second goal of earning profit would be a huge loss. So, creating a film is a razor-sharp fine act, where even the slightest carelessness can be fatal and may cause a huge loss of money, time and labor and create a furor in the society too. Moreover, it is also a crime against the audience, who is wasting its money and time if it is not created with the required level of responsibility, and sincerity. Audiences like to be entertained but not to be fooled. Cinema is the dreams fulfilled for a short time, with a hope of betterment, in a real life situation.

Hindi Cinema enriches these feelings of betterment in the life of common people. Now it's up to filmmakers to make such sensible cinema, which can guide them to a better life. If it is not possible, it can at least entertain in a healthy way. Hindi Cinema intends to do all these things with a high spirit, but docs not always provide a healthy entertainment. This is the point where it has troubles, and problems of various kinds. One of its kinds of problem is the communal shades depicted in Hindi films for whatever reasons. Being a multicultural and plural society, we have always negated communal ideology and aspects and such traits are never welcomed. In this paper, the focus is on the communal problems and the biases related to it in Hindi Cinema. We all are aware that this is the very problem, which has caused sufficient loss to the Indian people. Thankfully, these biases are not many and have never been the main theme of Hindi films. But as a subsidiary theme also, the idea of dividing and distinguishing people on the base of religion, caste, colour, area, language, nationality and community is very dangerous and may cause sufficient loss to the people and society. To evaluate this, first we have to have a glance at the brief history of Hindi Cinema.

HINDI CINEMA—A BRIEF HISTORY

Pre-Independence Era

In order to understand the communal/secular perspective of Hindi Cinema, we have to look back at the time of partition. Before independence, our filmmakers did not show any differentiation particular to various communities. Also, there was a hidden agenda of Hindi films to raise voice against British Empire. Though it was never reflected directly due to fear of ban, but it was strongly flowing as under current. Even after the partition of 1947, there were no communal biases reflected in Hindi films. Or we can say that no filmmaker dared to make a film on this burning topic, as the after effect of the partition was much more on the society, both in India and Pakistan. So-called leaders to get political mileage, spitted a lot of venom, which affected the people of both countries for a long time and still continuing, but no filmmaker came forward to make a film on this greatest accident/event of our country for many years. Issues like exploitations from Zamindaars, Mahajans, Pundits,

Rajas were given top priority in the Hindi films before and after independence. These issues have been haunting Indian society since ever, so they were always a preferred choice for making films. People liked to see all these real situations on real and seeing a hero saving the common person from the atrocities of such traitors have been a big dream of Indian Cinema. But the issue like communalism has not been highlighted in reel life in this era. One more reason for this negligence is that communalism was not present in our society with greater volume. It has emerged in full throttle only in late eighties.

Fifties and Sixties

Way back in fifties and sixties, the main protagonist of Hindi films, who was a worker in a mill or factory, had a tough fight with mill and factory owners. There also filmmakers did not highlight religious or communal sentiments of masses at large, as this was not their aim and at the same time this was not a hot issue in real life of the society. But filmmakers did have a little fear to portray a Muslim protagonist as a hero. As they were afraid that audience may not welcome this step. This myth was broken by "Chaudavin Ka Chaand" (1960) and "Mere Mahboob". Audience liked these films. But the main protagonist of these films was a rich, delicate, well cultured, navab like person, who did not resemble the common Muslim man of the country. He was a romantic young, who liked romancing with rich girls, dancing with her around green trees, making love in remote forest houses in case of rains, watching mujaras, enjoying all types of super comforts. It was like unlimited dreams. This was the depiction of super life, and was superficial for the common mass of the country. People did enjoy these types of themes on the celluloid but only for three hours. They were not made for them, as these did not touch their problems. But, yes these themes were welcomed and the Muslim protagonist was established and accepted by people against the fear of filmmakers. Moreover, it is to be noted that no person from other minorities like Christian or Sikh, was selected as a main hero of Hindi films till then.

In the same year (1960) long awaited historical saga "Mughal-e-Azam" was released. This film was made in 16 years (1944-60) with a very big budget of 1.5 cr. And it has been the greatest hit of Indian Cinema. Though this film was slated on a historical backdrop, it has great shade of secular image of Indian people. We can point out on one issue that most of the crew and technicians were Muslims in this mega blockbuster. Despite this, there were no signs of communal biases in the film and it was K. Asif's magic that created history of film making in India. The script was secular in all aspects. Birthday of Lord Krishna was celebrated in the court of King Akbar, and Madhubala danced like Meera. We will never forget "Mohe panaghat pe Nandlaal chhed gayo re". This is the spirit of secular India that such type of assimilation of Hindu-Muslim culture was not only welcomed but remained an all time hit. Muhgal-e-Azam was a secular film in true sense, which made this a phenomenal film in the history of Indian films. This also showed that the people of India and filmmakers have liked secular traits, not communal. As early in fifties, filmmakers like K. Asif has clearly understood this secular culture—the stream of collective consciousness of Indian society.

Seventies and After

As the society changed and developed, new issues and problems came in the process. Main protagonist and story of the Films started changing to the underworld or dacoits. Underworld dons and dacoits hidden in jungles or forests ruled the celluloid in seventies. Shole was the height of these types of plots. After great success of Shole, many films came on the similar trends like Shaan, Don, etc. These types of films were the result of the changing social system—Naxalite movement and Trade Unions. Naxalite movement was established due to the rising atrocities of the traditional social system, where common people were the ultimate sufferer. The exploitation was heightened to its peak. As a result, real hero raised his voice against it, and became hero for common people. This was a start of angry young man image. But this angry young man portrayed in Hindi films was fighting with evil peoples rather than fighting with evil system. He was a violent character and used all sorts of violence to take personal revenge. Janjeer, Diwaar, Shahanshah, Coolie, Agnipath are the main films which used this angry young man formulae. After this trend, the image of Hindi film hero was shifted to Police or Politicians. They became central theme of the story. Needless to say that they were villains and this trend again was a reflection of the society. During and after the emergency, lot of socio-politico changes took place, and they invariably affected the script of the Hindi cinema. Nineties have witnessed a new shift in the history of Hindi cinema, where Pakistan and Pakistani soldier/terrorist/militant/leader was the real villain. And hero is fighting with him for personal revenge or for country's sake.

In the 21st century, this trend again shifted and no one is the villain. Now films with different plots and stories are successful. Now the role of the story and script is being given very much importance. These are just some footprints of Hindi cinema.

SECULAR APPROACH AND HINDI CINEMA

Dilip Kumar was hero of 1961 hit film "Ganga Jamuna". In the last scene Dilip Kumar died saying "Hey Ram". Some members of censor board were reluctant to this scene, and wanted to cut it. They did not digest a Muslim saying "Hey Ram" like Gandhiji. Luckily the film was shown with the scene and there was no controversy on this very scene. On the contrary the film was a big hit. A person like Dilip Kumar, who has changed his religious identity by changing his name, has fought against communal forces throughout his whole life. Like Dilip Kumar, a number of personalities of Hindi cinema have never bothered to communal thought and always remained with the very side of plurality.

After eighties, the national politics of India has played a vital role changeover. Until emergency, the national politics was not very diverse. But starting eighties has seen the rise of right wing forces on the national map. And these forces have grown to the corridors of Parliament. This is the reality of our country, of our people. This has affected our films as well. This is the era, film industry witnessed realism as an important factor to affect Hindi films. Hindi films have shown the communal biases in the films as a part of the reality, but they have provided their solutions as well. And those are never communal. The main thought of these films is secular in all respect. In real life, common people never like communal controversies as they affect them badly. In reel life also this idea remains the same. No common man wants to be communal and fight for some unfruitful things. And this common man knows that these biases are spread by those who are gaining many things from these—Power, Money, Position and so on. Therefore, films with evil motives are never welcomed and outright rejected by the audience. If some biases are reflected in the films, they are negated at the end of the films.

FILMMAKING—A TEAMWORK

Filmmaking is teamwork. And it depends on the audience. Even if the whole team is fully convinced on a project, the success of the film cannot be guaranteed. It is made for a large and larger reach, so being communal can't help. Communal ideology may give a sensational and controversial opening but it can't deliver a hit film. After all it is a business first and any other thing afterwards. The fact is the basic instinct of India remains intact with the feel of Unity in Diversity. Those who understand this minimal need of filmmaking, never fail in this area and show a great solidarity—no matter they are making a formulae film or a thought provoking or something different. So a secularist approach is always a successful and novel way to present things to a larger audience and greater acceptability and our filmmakers know this very well.

Not only filmmakers, but also all the technicians, actors and background workers perfectly know that even slightest communal thinking or feeling can affect their product and if the end product is not up to the mark, their career is at stake. There is no moving ahead with such type of ideology in this field. Filmmaking is very insecure and volatile sector. Everyone is uncertain of the success of their product. Fate of years of hard work is decided on a Friday. It's not only the product or success. A big number of people survive on this field. If they are part of a good team, their work will continuously grow and all the members will be benefited. No one alone can boast about one's success, but it is the result of combined team efforts. There is no differentiation in cast, class, region or language in this field. All are welcome. Only the person, who has potential, will survive. This is the true spirit of the industry. And not to mention, this spirit is truly a secular spirit, which is a driving force in the film industry.

SECULAR SPIRIT—A DRIVING FORCE

Most of the stories having any shades of communal biases are used for setting the plots. Religious, fundamental, and political thoughts and events are shown in the films in exaggeration, but only to exemplify the events of the plot and story. End result of these types of stories is always shown and finished on a secular node, in the interest of common person.

More than Hindi films, filmy songs have helped develop a better secular world. And most of the lyricists of independent India have followed true Indian culture and its spirit. Sahir Ludhianavi, the greatest lyricist of films, decided not to go to Pakistan at the time of partition, and remain in India. He was a genuinely a secular person. All time favourite bhajan written by Sahir—*'Allah tero naam, Ishwar tero naam'*- is still sung with great love and honour. Another famous song of "Dhool ka Phool" (Film by B.R. Chopra, 1960)—*"Tu Hindu banega na Mussalman banega, insaan ke aulad tu insaan banega"*—was a big hit. Even the audience cheered on the song and the film also succeeded on box office. Since then, most of the secular lyrics have been written by Sahir Ludhianvi or Shakeel Badayuni, music given by Naushad Ali and sung by Mohammad Rafi. Muslim heros sung these bhajans or songs in Hindu Temples. Hindu Muslim bhai-bhai formulae were common and they worked together. Muslim heroes took 'prasaad' from Hindu ladies and Hindu heros celebrated Muslim festivals as well. So are the rituals. Rakhi is tied by the Hindu girls on the wrists of Muslim heroes. Fighting for the sake of country in armed forces, police forces and other places have been a rich idea to portray Hindu Muslim bhai-bhai formulae on the celluloid. In many films, we can see a Hindu friend sacrificing and saving a Muslim friend and *vice versa.* This is not by chance, but by selection. Chetan Anand's *Haqueeqat*, J.P. Dutta's *Border* and John Matthew's *Sarfarosh* are some of the examples. Most of the filmmakers did not name their villains with their proper or family names. They have not been any Khan, Peter, or Chauhan. Instead, they are better known as Mogambo, Shakaal, Tiger, Thakur, etc. This is the symbol that filmmakers don't want to name any evil person in the name of any particular cast or religion or region.

Some of the important Hindi films, which depict true secular image of Bollywood may be named as—*Zakhm* (1998) by Mahesh Bhatt, *'Bombay'* (1995) by Mani Ratnam, *Sarfarosh* by John Matthew Mathan, *Rang De Basanti* by Rakesh Mehra, *Water* by Deepa Mehta, *Parjania* by Homi Adjania, *Dhokha* by Pooja Bhatt and *Rice Plate* (of Das Kahaniyan) by *Rohit Roy*. These films have shown a clearer image of the Muslims in India and also their true Indian spirit of pluralism. Now it is clearly shown that Indian Muslims are responsible citizens of the country and feel threatened if someone attacks or criticizes our identity. It seems like saint Kabir has been a driving force behind the names of truly secular characters in the films. This trend can be seen in Mani Ratnam's *Bombay*, and Shimit Amin's *Chak De India*. *Sarfarosh* has given a detailed dialogue on the status of Inspector Salim, whose sincerity was being questioned since he is a Muslim. The character of Salim played by Mukesh Rishi was very meaningful and real. Aamir Khan playing the role of ACP Rathore did a close discussion with *Inspector Salim*. This scene was very much liked by the audience, as this is the original feel of Indian Muslims. Muslim protagonists played in *Chak De India* and *Dhokha* are more Indian than Muslim and show that they are taking their responsibilities as routine, where there is no room for communal biases. *Zakhm* has played a vital role on this theme. In a scene, the character played by Ajay Devgan slaps his brother who, unaware of his mother's religion, her faith, is about to go and kill a Muslim boy who had burnt his mother alive. Ajay Devgan strikes him and says, "Yeh tere baap ka mulk hai kya?" (Is this your father's land?) And says, "Kisko nikalega? Inko nikalega, kyon? Kyon ke ye Musalman hai?" This film has proved very promising and people liked it very much. Not because it showed a conflict between two religions, but it slated true Indian sentiments beautifully and provided a stage for discourse.

NEGATIVE TRENDS—A PASSING PHASE

But, things have never been black and white. Everything is not so rosy or beautiful as it looks in this industry. The other side of the coin is, therefore, very important too. Not much, but there are several occasions of communal biases depicted in Hindi films. Famous filmmakers have slated films, which have marked communal footprints in Bollywood. Veteran scriptwriter and poet Javed Akhtar says: "I haven't seen a Muslim character play Holi in any film, although millions of them do so in real life." Further, while a goon can hide gold behind a Hindu deity, one can't show a similar situation in a mosque, as filmmakers are afraid of hurting the sentiments of a minority. Deepa Mehta was not allowed to shoot her film Water in Varanasi even for one day, and harassed for making films that targeted aspects of the Hindu religion rather than looking into other religions such as Christianity or Islam. Why were her films saturated with this content? The answer is simple: she is Hindu; she is an Indian woman. She understands the Hindu culture more than any other, Islam or Christianity.

Josh, Phir Bhi Dil Hai Hindustani, Fiza, Gadar, Hero, Jo Bole So Nihal, Mission Kashmir, Jaal are some films, which can't be certified as secular films. But at the same time, except one or two among these films, all are an utter failure. Some of them highlighted a false agenda, which is not true in Indian context. They show the hidden agenda of ISI (Inter-Services Intelligence) the secret service agency of Pakistan in these films. Storyline of these films depict a dormant anti-India message. It looks like these filmmakers did not understand the difference between injustice and anti-national. The film *Josh* depicts Hrithik Roshan as an innocent person who to fight injustice joins the ranks of the terrorists against the Indian nation. In *Phir Bhi Dil Hai Hindustani,* police is framing up an innocent person (Prabodh Rawal) as an enemy (Pakistani) agent. This implicates that Indian Police identifies innocent people as terrorists. This can't be justified in any case. Even a common person understands this phenomenon and differentiates between an innocent and a terrorist. It is surprising that these filmmakers do not understand this simple thing. Can we say that people who kidnapped Rubaiya Sayeed were innocents? This was the start of terrorism in Jammu and Kashmir. Indian Military or Police is deployed there to fight with the terrorists and anti-national elements. If films cited above show the innocents becoming terrorists due to atrocities of the armed forces, this is totally ridiculous. Similarly, *Josh* is set-up with a Hindu-Christian angle in two gangs fighting for their existence. This is a remake of "Westwide Story", and changed enough to the backdrop of Goa and a Hindu-Christian angle.

This is not a true Indian story, as Goa is a place of solidarity more than any place in India, and a plural society exists in original sense. One can find followers of Hindu, Christian and Muslim religion in a single family. Who did give freedom to these filmmakers to portray such a superficial story, which does not exist in our society at all?

In the same way some films like *Jo Bole So Nihal, Hero* and *Gadar* have also used this formula of instigating the sentiments of common people on the basis of communal ideology. *Gadar* was a simple film but it was set in the backdrop of partition of India and Pakistan, with a romantic story of a Sikh man and a Muslim woman. Sunny Deol infiltrates in Pakistani territory and fights with a war with almost an impossible arsenal of his father in law and Pakistani Military to get his wife back with him. What is more important is the dialogue between Sunny Deol and Amrish Puri. A lot of venum is spitted against each other on the name of Hindu and Muslim. Another Sunny Deol starrer film *Hero* is using a Hindu religious hymn—"Om Jai Jagdish..." whenever hero kills any terrorist. The main aim of these films was to fight against Muslim terrorists, or Pakistani peoples, but the hidden focus behind them looks like they are fighting against Indian Muslims. No doubt that these tricks are not welcomed and anti-Muslim dialogues in these films are not praised by the audience. *Hero, Qayamat, Jaal* flopped badly.

Power packed performance by Sunny Deol could not show the doors of success to a successful formulae film— *Jo Bole So Nihal*. It was a big budget Sikh starrer film, who is a pro-Jat community. The Sikhs did not like the idea and film was immediately off the theatres from Punjab and other parts of country. A bomb was exploded in a Delhi theatre, where this film was screening, to draw the attention and protest against this film, which have a slogan—'No if, no but, only Jutt'.

According to producer-director Mahesh Bhatt, films reflect current trends and Muslim baiting is a part of it. This is only a passing trend, and did not reflect the general thinking in the industry.

It seems Hindi cinema has not done due justice to the minorities. Apart from Muslims, Christians and Sikhs are also a deprived lot. Initially, Christian characters were show in smaller roles. Christian women were shown like barmaids, keeps of the gangsters or bearing not so well image. Christian man was not given big roles of hero; he was a drunkard man, who had a good heart. Same is with Sikhs. Whenever hero is in crisis, a Sikh will appear smiling from any corner as a taxi or truck driver and help hero to come out of crisis. Hero of Hindi cinema many times changes his looks as Sikhs to change his identity for some times in some tricky situations. But we have not witnessed a Sikh being a protagonist in a leading Hindi movie, except *Jo Bole So Nihal* in 2005, but this was not welcomed due to pro-Jat community.

HINDI CINEMA—ITS REACH

Our debate will not end without Anand Patwardhan and Rakesh Sharma. Little different from fiction, these are ace documentary filmmakers of India, who have taken Indian pride to the remote corners of the world. Their films have won critical acclaims in international film festivals and national awards and Filmfare awards. Final Solution by Rakesh Sharma is a film on 2002 Gujrat riots and after effects. It won many international awards. But due to the reality shown in this film, censor board did not pass this film without cuts. And it is not previewed to Indian audience. Same is with the films by Anand Patwardhan. Latest of his brilliant works is *Jang aur Aman* ("War and Peace", 2002). This movie explains the political and nuclear issues of India and other countries. Patwardhan says– "My film is based on the Gandhian philosophy of non-violence. It exposes the political hypocrisies of India, Pakistan and the United States regarding the nuclear issue. They have a problem with the way I have put forward my argument. But [they] cannot point a finger at the factual data I have used in the film as it is true." As a result, this film is not open for preview to Indian audience. Other famous films by Patwardhan are *Prisoners of Conscience* (1978), *Bombay Our City* (1985), In *Memory of Friends* (1990), In the *Name of God* [Hindi title: Ram Ke Naam] (1992), *Father, Son,* and *Holy War* [Hindi title: Pitra, Putra, aur Dharamyuddha] (1994) and *Narmada Diary* (1995).

The major flaw with these films is that they do not reach to a wider section of people as feature films. No theatres are showing documentaries. And in case of absence of censor board certification, they cannot be shown to the people, for whom they are being made. So the prime purpose of making these important films gets defeated. They do get critical acclaims and praise world-wide but what is the benefit to the common person if he/ she is not able to view these nerve-breaking films. A soft and tricky approach to the problems may be the real solution, so that their reach gets widened to the common people.

Finally, the reach of Hindi cinema is global. Bollywood is one of the largest filmmaking industries of the world. Indonesia, USA, UK, Africa, Australia, Malaysia, Nigeria, Pakistan, Bangladesh, Sri Lanka are some of the countries where Hindi films have a larger demand and supply. These countries like Hindi films irrespective of cast, class, religion, language, region or race. So it becomes our responsibility to make such films, which are not related to these issues. A truly global film should not have such narrow mindedness or communal tags. Our filmmakers should take utmost care to tackle these issues and deal with such types of subjects carefully. I strongly recommend that, as a governing body, Censor Board should deal with such issues with profound sincerity, rather than to popularize issues like sex and violence. Such issues are also very important but films vomiting communal poison, whether directly or indirectly should be dealt with strong measures. To preserve the true Indian culture in its diverse unity and solidarity this is the least we can do. After all we cannot deny that pluralism is the soul of Indian society and our films can't be away from this very fact at any cost, as they are the replica of our culture and civilization.

Women and Cinema

29

M. Rabindranath and Sujay Kapil

INTRODUCTION

Hindi cinema has been a mirror for India. It has shaped and expressed the changing scenarios of India to an enormous extent. Hindi cinema has influenced the way in which people perceive various aspects of their own lives. Indian cinema since its origin 100 years ago, has been one of the biggest indigenous industries in India and continues to be the same in the post-globalisation and liberalisation era. Issues of community, gender, society, social and economic justice, nation and religion are explored thoroughly in the commercial cinema. It is unrivaled and carved out a proud history for itself. Indian cinema has come a long way since the black and white film era to the colour movies and to the 3D.

However, it continues to retain its basic essence-entertain, entertain and entertain. Even as internet downloads and television continue to encroach into the theatrical revenues of Indian films, the allure of the 35 mm is irresistible. Indian cinema has come a long way and at the same time, has witnessed a sea-change in the presentation of the women character. The journey of Indian cinema from the first film, Raja Harishchandra – which had no female actors – to the present day, has not been a joy ride. One of the reason for this can be the concept of 'beauty' which changed over time in Indian cinema. Actresses like Madhuabala, Meena Kumari, Nargis Dutt, Nutan, Wahida Rehman and

Vaijayantimala were considered the queens of the Indian cinema during their reign. Thereafter, the beauties from southern India like Hema Malini and Rekha ruled Bollywood. Then the period of beauty queens like Zeenat Aman, Poonam Dhillon, Parveen Babi began in the 1970s which has continued till today, with likes of Juhi Chawla, Aishwarya Rai, Sushmita Sen, Priyanka Chopra, Lara Dutta, Diya Mirza who after winning beauty pageants, entered the Hindi film world and registered a formidable presence.

India is a patriarchal society where the cinematic world tries to project women as in factual life. But how much fact and how much fiction is laced into the characterization of women is quite a debatable topic. There is a fairy tale that women are characterized in films to buttress the male rather than characterize them as the one who keeps the storyline supple. Women are shown in films as bearing the load of sexual objectification that males cannot. "Hence, they become the bearer, and not the maker of meaning", says **Mulvey (1988).**

Women in Indian cinema are born with certain hypothesis that carry on from cult movies to celluloid blockbusters like Sholay to more recent Queen that employ themselves as in severe gender issues. They are either depicted as damsels in distress or crazy feminists or belly-shaking, curvaceous, cleavage–exposing glam dolls whose sole ambition is to attract the attention of the male protagonist. Cinema projects her with the sole aim to be the lady love of the male and bear him kids and have a family. In Indian films it is quite common to insert 'item numbers' which bear no rational connection to the film, but the film-makers assume that the film is easily associated with the item song. **As Nair (2009) says**, "Sometimes the one song ends up making the film a hit, such as 'Chamma Chamma' from the film 'China Gate.'"

Sometimes, we see a female being the protagonist of a film than merely being objects of sexual desire. Sometimes there is a clash between 'modern feminism' and 'traditional values'. Indian cinema plays up an emotional harp and the characterization of 'Women' is as per the demands of the market.

CHANGING ROLE OF WOMEN IN INDIAN CINEMA

Just like the Indian society, Indian cinema was also male-dominated for long. Subject matters were viewed and portrayed from the male audiences' point of view and heroine was considered secondary to the hero. Her role was used to aid in the context of any male character that was central to the story line – be it hero, villain, father, brother, boss or an elderly male figure. Independent existence for a woman was a far cry. This kind of embodiment limits the women's role to provide glamour, sex, relief, emotional melodrama and entertainment. And these patriarchal values were shown on the top in films like, *Dahej* (1950), *Gauri* (1968), *Devi* (1970), *Biwi Ho Toh Aisi* (1988) and *Pati Parmeshwar* (1988) where women were shown as passive, submissive wives as perfect figures and martyrs for their families well-being.

Indian film-makers used to portray women as larger than life characters. Instead of being depicted as normal human beings they were elevated to a higher position of being ideal who can't commit even a minute mistake. Their desires, dreams, feelings, perception were nowhere in the script. They were shown above the realities and limitations of the worldly life. **Chatterji (2002)** says "The patriarchy it functions within, insists on placing the mother on a pedestal, which is natural and logical extension of the worship of the Mother Goddess to include the family unit. The pedestal is conveniently used by the patriarchal family to reduce the same mother to silence, absence and marginality, politically constructed to seemingly connote to the woman concerned." *Abhimaan* (1973) directed by Hrishikesh Mukherjee which had Amitabh and Jaya Bachchan in the main lead began with idea of the wife (Jaya) being a more talented singer than the already singing star husband (Amitabh). This in itself is a rebellion against the stereotype. However, as the story of the film moves on, the wife gives up her successful musical career for pleasing the husband's ego leading to a conventional closure that requires adherence to traditional values of marriage and motherhood.

However, Bollywood was invaded by a swarm of new look directors and film-makers in the 21st century. They broke the conventions and norms. This gave a new flip to portrayal of women in Indian cinema. Directors like Anurag Kashyap, Vikramaditya Motwane, Dibakar Bannerjee, Vikas Behl and many others made cinema undergo a positive change. Realism became the flavor coupled with commercial success.

Gone are the times when the real self of Indian women hardly matched with the film plot. Today we see an increasing numbers of movies creating bold and beautiful image of Bollywood. Earlier too, we've had actresses portraying strong characters who fight the shackles of their social situation and Mother India released in 1957 is a classic example. Mehboob Khan directed *Mother India* depicts the struggle of a rural woman in India, who bravely confronts every problem to raise her two sons. The late actress Nargis Dutt is shown as a loving and brave mother, who raises her family alone and in the end, staying true to her moral root, she shoots her evil son dead to save a woman's dignity and honour.

In order to present a new age and modern women, the Indian film makers gave birth to another stereotype. Indian filmmakers have parachuted on an idea that the display of dancing girls in 'minimum' clothes is the real expression of freedom. Smoking, doping and drinking by women is being shown as a symbol of assertiveness and independence. The camera angles as well as the camera movements used by the cinematographer titillates the audience strongly. When a female character is performing an action the camera always has a tendency to creep around her body voyeuristically. The choreography of a song is done in a way to maximize shaking of her body assets with thrust. This adds to the voyeuristic pleasure and gratification of the male audience. This all adds up to turning a woman into an object up for grabs. For example, *Chandni Bar* directed by Madhur Bhandarkar had many scenes set-up in a Mumbai dance bar where women are scanned top to bottom by the men in the bar. The male gaze is an accepted norm. The natural curves of the body are distorted by unnatural ways of dressing to highlight certain body proportions and for this very reason they are shot from a low angle or a high angle to reveal cleavage. Our elder generation, earlier exposed to the "sensuous" Helen, is now face-to-face with the more "sexy" Bipasha Basu. Many are saying that the change is 'luscious for their 'filmy' palate! "One part of a fragmented body destroys the Renaissance space, the illusion of depth demanded by the narrative, it gives flatness, the quality of a cut-out or icon rather than verisimilitude to the screen." **(Mulvey, 1988)**

Things went downhill after the sixties where films like *Sujata* (1959) and *Bandini* (1963) directed by the legendary film-maker Bimal Roy strongly portrayed women. But , in the post 1970s era the image of a larger than life macho hero emerged and female protagonists were relegated to the background. The men in Indian cinema were either projected as 'romantic and righteous heroes' or the 'bad guy' who occupied a lion's share of screen space contrary to the female characters that always tend to lead a surrendered life even on screen. **As Vrinda Mathur (2009)** says, 'The male characters of Indian cinema, i.e. the heroes (those knights in shining armour) and the villains (those over-energetic sharks) move around the space of the movie like players in a deadly choreographed game of chess - with the women characters as sacrificial pawns. This continued in the 21st century as well. However, there are some notable exceptions as well. Like the film *Mirch Masala* made in 1987 by Ketan Mehta where the female protagonist Sonbai (Smita Patil) defies the entire patriarchal set up for protecting her respect and honour. She also makes the villain (Naseerudin Shah) meet with a gruesome fate in the end. Today, Vidya Balan has established herself as an actress known for powerful performances. Her roles in films like *Ishqiya* (2010), *The Dirty Picture* (2011), *Kahaani* (2012) and *No One Killed Jessica* (2011) not only got critical acclaim but tremendous box-office response as well. Similarly, Priyanka Chopra won accolades for her performance in the film *Aitraaz* (2004), *Fashion* (2008), *7 Khoon Maaf* (2011), *Don-2* (2011) and *Barfi* (2013) where the female dominates over the male characters and carves out an identity for herself. Each of her films projected women strongly in terms of characterization and screen space as well. No doubt, these film set the cash registers ringing at the box-office.

THE PRESENT SCENARIO

In the current situation, Indian women, item number and individualism have evolved into a symbiotic relationship. These three elements have become the toast of Indian cinema. Now stories are not about the shy village girls or the ethnic beauty, this is the generation of rebellious lovers and sexy and confident business women who are ready for an eye to eye contest. The portrayal of women has been witnessing a remarkable change—be it the blood thirsty conniving Priyanka Chopra in *7-Khoon Maaf,* or no nonsense journalist Rani Mukherjee in *No One Killed Jessica* or Parineeti Chopra as the rebellious lover in *Ishaqzaade,* each of their characters stood apart from the conformist women and none of them had qualms about it. The change in the social set up also led to change in the film scripts. Today women are educated, working and earning good amount of money so their attitudes have also changed contrary to earlier times.

Women who were either shown in white or black are now being shown in grey shade charters. The film *Fashion,* depicts the inside of the fashion industry however, it primly revolves around the life of Meghan Mathur who is dejected by the society, yet she comes back with new confidence and zeal. Besides Fashion, the female characters in Madhur Bhandarkar's films are usually shown as bold and empowered women who lead life on their own terms, take their own decisions, are 'rebels' who don't conform to social norms and excel in their respective professions like Chandni Bar (2001), *Page 3* (2005), and the latest one being Kangna Ranaut in *'Queen'* (2014). The film *'Queen'* directed by Vikas Behl needs special mention because in this film the female lead (Kangna Ranaut) is ditched by her fiancée (Rajkumar Rao) because she was too simple for a modern man like him. She goes on a Europe tour and explores life. In the end, when the male protagonist approaches her after being lured by her makeover, he is rejected by the female lead.

Actresses like Vidya Balan, Priyanka Chopra and Konkona Sen Sharma (*Page 3, Wake Up Sid, Life in a Metro, Mr. and Mrs. Iyer*) have led these winds of change. They have appeared in strong and independent roles which for the time being shifted the camera's focus from the women's body to her identity as an individual. Moreover, the emergence of the multiplex cinema has given film makers the confidence to discover new realms of cinema. The concept of niche audiences has made its place in India. The risk of losing money is bare minimal for a film producer.

CONCLUSION

It is not necessary that what Bollywood preaches, the nation follows and *vice-versa*. The portrayal of women in cinema is gradually becoming real, no longer a figment of imagination and sensuality. The characters have become close to authenticity, if not totally authentic. We no longer find an alternate reality on 35 mm screen and we no more see a woman who is afraid to speak her mind rather a woman who can maneuver her way through the crowd. Most often women are able to identify with the characters on screen and the reflection of reality is a high point in transformed filmmaking. Today women command an equal position in the flourishing arena of Indian cinema. Indian women have evolved on the screen and off the screen over these 100 years of Indian cinema. We no longer require a macho hero to run a film, actresses can run the show like a queen.

REFERENCES

1. Chatterji, A.S. (2002) *The Cinema of Aparna Sen*, Calcutta: Parumitha Publication.
2. Mathur, V. (2009), 'Women in Indian Cinema: Fictional Constructs', in Jasbir Jain and Sudha Rai (ed.) *Films and Feminism*, Jaipur, Rawat Publication.
3. Mulvey L. (1988), *'Visual Pleasure and Narrative Cinema'*, in Constance Penley, ed, *Feminism and Film Theory*, New York: Routledge, 1988.
4. Nair, B. (2009), 'The Female bodies and the Male Gaze: Laura Mulvey and Indian Cinema' in Jasbir Jain and Sudha Rai (ed.) *Films and Feminism*, Jaipur, Rawat Publication.

30

Construction of Women Characters in Popular Hindi Cinema during the Period of 1970s-80s : Continuity with Cultural Tradition

Balkrishan Shivram

The women characters in Hindi films are often stripped of all realistic human and social complexities, thus ending up on screen as stereotypes. The ideal woman in Bollywood cinema is traditionally referred as a controlled, chaste, surrendering individual, who is not afraid of making a sacrifice. The "bad" woman on the other hand, has been depicted as westernized, blond-haired, individualistic and sexually aggressive, ready to lead men into ruin. Indeed, Hindi-language film industry has repeatedly reinforced the notion that the glory of ideal Indian womanhood lies in the tolerance she shows toward society and men, even when she is unjustly treated and brutally victimised. Three case studies are selected to understand and delineate the construction of women characters during the period under study; *Pakeezah* of Kamal Amrohi (1971), *Umrao Jaan* of Muzaffar Ali (1981) and *Prem Rog* of Raj Kapoor (1982). I'm also intending to specify how the construction of women characters has changed over a period of time in Hindi films. With Muslim protagonists and settings *Pakeezah* and *Umrao Jaan* focus on the courtesan as the ultimate figure of love and sacrifice. While the figure of the courtesan still remains pivotal to the Bollywood conception of the heroine, these film-makers also explore the central tensions prevalent in Indian society between law, justice, cultural norms and love. *Prem Rog* deals with issues of widow re-marriage.

It was so erratic in this period that one hardly finds a heroine keen of her own accord to stand up to reputable rituals and traditions. Instead, film-makers reflected upon the sordid aspects of women's lives in movies. They explored the subtle nuances and outwardly impenetrable aspects of women, thereby underscoring their struggles with trials and tribulations. As a result that phase saw a considerable acceleration in the type of films with themes that explored the oppression and exploitation of women. The women characters were depicted as passive and subservient, powerless to articulate their needs even in the façade of subjugation, or as liberated but unkind or hard-hearted; more explicitly, they were portrayed as saviours of tradition. However, 1980s began to witness a shift in the essence of women characters, who displayed a need to break free of their environments, thereby rising above what is traditionally expected of Indian women, namely to show tolerance toward society and men, even when treated irrationally .

Ever since the birth of Indian cinema in 1913, women characters in Hindi-films were portrayed as devoted housewives, sacrificing mothers and dutiful daughter-in-laws. "*Pakeezah*" and "*Umrao Jaan*" tell the story of the courtesans that are portrayed as female protagonists within a patriarchal society. Umrao Jaan's character undergoes tragedies such as being kidnapped, then forced into a life of prostitution and ultimately being rejected by the only man that she loved. "Umrao Jaan's" reaction (she lashes out at him) to her lover's dismissal of her does not fit in with the acceptable behaviour of a woman, as it is in contrast to the ideology of submissiveness and acceptance without question that is prevalent in Hindi-language cinema and more specifically, the depiction of heroines. *Pakeezah* and *Umrao Jaan* were released a decade apart, but the women are constructed in a very similar way in their mannerisms and in the way that they entertain. The films aim to engage male audiences by plotting the female heroine as a prostitute, evoking what is refer as "scopophilia" (the pleasure of looking). At the same time, female audience members can relate to the heroine in her struggle to break free of her environment, and rising above what is traditionally expected of Indian women, namely to show tolerance toward society and men, even when unjustly treated. The dress of the courtes an remains the same over the years, as does the action of the dance, from the movement of the hands, to the batting of thick, mascara-laden eyelashes. The courtes an plays with the scarf around her head and peeps at the male audience in demure fashion whilst playing with the veil that she tosses open as the dance routine progresses. The seductive style remains the same. However, if a comparison is to be made between the depiction of the individual characters Sahibjaan in "*Pakeezah*" and "*Umrao Jaan*", Sahibjaan is definitely depicted as the more passively constructed woman who lives with and accepts the knowledge of her role in life as a courtesan. It is interesting that Sahibjaan's lover is prepared to marry her and defies all convention when he announces that he will marry her even though he knows that she is a courtesan. "Umrao Jaan", on the other hand, is depicted as desperately in love with the man whom she is convinced will marry her and waits anxiously for him, but he betrays her. Even though she is hurt by his betrayal, she agrees to marry a bandit because her need to escape overpowers her true feelings. At the time, the bandit represents a form of escape from the life that has been imposed upon her.

Women characters from the films of the seventies and eighties were depicted to mirror the pain and suppression of their lives through their eyes. Sahibjaan's eyes reflect defeat from the very onset of the film, and she does not consider herself worthy of being acknowledged as a person with needs and feelings. The film *Umrao Jaan* relies on the use of the camera to bare the undisguised craving in "Umrao Jaan's" eyes. She is depicted as believing that she deserves to be loved and when she falls in love with the wealthy man who claims to love her back, her character is at peace and she accepts that feeling as a part of her right to live. In direct comparison, Sahibjaan is depicted as too deeply embedded in low self-esteem and she is portrayed as a wounded animal, yet she too, yearns for a better life beyond the brothel. While "Umrao Jaan" is depicted as one who loves poetry and is well versed in the art of enticing the most affluent men,

Sahibjaan is unaware of such politics and moves through her world mechanically instead of purposefully as "Umrao Jaan" is trained. Both women do not have a social life except for the time that they are allowed to use to adorn themselves in preparation of their performances. The women who rule them are both big-built and well-rounded and appear to be nurturing in the way that a grandmother would nurture and care for her grandchildren, but they pamper their "girls" for the sake of monetary gain only and of course the title of successfully running the most renowned brothel in town.

It is evident that tradition and rituals contribute towards the challenges faced by the heroine in the films under study. Manorama in *Prem Rog* is treated unjustly because she is a widow. Tradition also silences her to be willing to endure the suffering. Although Dhevdhar her lover tries to speak out against the suffering, the narrative depicts tradition as being too strongly embedded, making it nearly impossible to do otherwise. Tradition and the construction of the woman character also prohibit a character such as Thakur's wife (Manorama's aunt) from voicing her opinion, even though she is aware of her husband's infidelities. On closer inspection, it is evident that *Prem Rog* raises a voice against the abuses perpetuated against widows, but in terms of the changing construction of women, the women are still portrayed as passive and still struggling to be heard. Manorama, being the heroine, is gifted with a man who fights for her rights, and her character accepts his passion gratefully. While the film-maker forces the issue of widow re-marriage as a right for women, the women characters in the film are constructed as subdued, but their inner constructions are desirous of wanting to express themselves, as portrayed through the characters of Manorama's mother and sister-in-law. Even though they mutely accept their own fates respectively, they "dare" to raise a voice against false rituals (shaving of a widow's hair) and evil (the rape of a virgin widow). The film-maker depicts women as less willing to merely succumb to tradition and rituals. For example, Manorama's mother is depicted as being hesitant about this ritual through her body language, but in the end, she cannot stand up to societal pressures and gently coaxes her daughter into following the tradition.

CONCLUSION

We find that as far back as the mid-70s, cinema was founded on "scopophilia" (the pleasure of looking). Cinema therefore constantly devises narrative strategies to solicit the "look" and mobilize the scopic drive. Filmmakers were therefore exposed to commercial and ideological pressures to make a "spectacle" of the woman, but at the same time must deploy strategies and subterfuges in order to legitimise such erotic voyeurism without antagonising the state, civil society, or female members of its spectating public. The most important strategy has been to create an idealised moral universe that upholds the official definition of femininity within the main plot, and then to provide unofficial erotic pleasures to its target audience through song and dance sequences. While it has been ascertained that commercial Hindi-language cinema relies on voyeurism, it creates tension between how women feel and how men react to the way in which women are dressed or presented as sexual objects. In the specific case studies in this report of the films of the 70s and 80s, the camera lens often focused on the bodies of the prostitutes (e.g., *Pakeezah, Umrao Jaan)* and widows (e.g., *Prem Rog*), spotlighting the dress, movements, and eyes of the heroines which playfully teased the audience members. Movements like heaving breasts and gyrating hips inculcated images of lust and passion in the male viewers while unsettling the female viewers who had to watch their counterparts. If we take the years later and more specifically in the new millennium, the same camera lens still focuses on portraying women in part as voyeuristic objects to entertain audiences. In a film such as *Kuch Kuch Hota Hai*, the manner in which the camera focuses on the body of newcomer Tina, is explicitly demeaning for the female spectators. There is no logic in a woman who returns from abroad being dressed with such minimal clothing. This representation of women is becoming a norm in films of the new millennium. Even though women spectators "cringe" when witnessing this portrayal of their gender, representations of women in this sordid manner are increasing and viewers are being allowed to use the cinematic space as an acceptable space in which to "gawk".

The heroines of the new millennium, in direct contrast to the heroines of times before, are depicted as exceptionally vocal in terms of their needs and desires and the choices that they make as to the direction that they envisage their lives moving. Of particular interest, and worth mentioning are the similarities in the way that film-makers portray the male characters to "rescue" the women from a number of different scenarios. From as far back as 1971, the affluent Shahabuddin from the film *Pakeezah* rescues the love of his life Nargis from a brothel. His nephew, almost two decades later, within the narrative of the same film, rescues Sahibjaan. Significantly, both women yearn to be rescued and their spare time is pre-occupied with dreams of being rescued by their "knights in shining armour". In 1981, the character "Umrao Jaan" filters and examines a string of lovers whom she hopes will rescue her from her dreary life at the brothel. Both Nargis and "Umrao Jaan" do not find amity, but Sahibjaan is united with her lover. The film-makers of *Umrao Jaan* are bold in their depiction of the courtesan, whom they construct as having enough self-esteem to consider herself worthy of a life beyond the brothel. However, in the end, the narrative of the film also gives in to the patriarchal societies and ideologies of the times and as a result, "Umrao Jaan" is forced to suffer defeat at the end.

When Women Learn to Speak : Inching Towards a New Language

31

KAMAYANI BISHT

To begin with, we must recognize and accept the fact that social systems are constructions and that they are not static. Since this paper hopes to deal with women and language in Hindi cinema, the two social systems that will be in spotlight are, gender and language. Going by Judith Butler's theory of performativity, gender is something we "do" and by extension, it may not be unsafe to say that language is one of the tools that are applied for the maintenance of the system of gender in day-to-day activity. Performance of gender and the use of language are mutually complementary and they also change mutually—when they do. The shift in gender performance and linguistic conventions has been evident in recent years and our cultural products, of which cinema is the most popular, have begun to mirror this epistemological transition. Woman has a way of speaking that differs significantly from the male speech and this difference reflects her subordinate place in social hierarchy.[1] Her speech is characteristically tentative, quite like her own position. She has learnt this as a part of the process of her socialization and linguistic difference essentially cohabits contentions of power. If, as Foucault claims, power is nothing but a mere linguistic construct, then, those who get to use language, also get to wield power.

Language is not only an integral tool of socialization, it is also the result of socialization, and a potent mode of communication and representation of cultural and individual identity. The same language has the power to divide the world differently; in this case, male and female. In any interaction, the contribution, a person makes to it, may be seen as a social "move"[2] and this move is decided by the person's perception of the self and the others. Behind any linguistic act, is a plan—and this plan may change from time to time, place to place. Most female linguistic acts, at least in patriarchal cultures like ours, are a response to male initiation of a conversation. Male speech acts are social moves to establish initiative and social dominance while female speech acts reflect social moves of acceptance of male superiority and female subordination.

Speech may be an absence of silence but silence is not necessarily the absence of speech. Significantly, silence has been a major part of female speech. She has either been silenced, through glorification of silence as virtue, or she has learnt to use silence for added weight to what she must say. She is given lesser "air-time" as compared to her male counterparts, both, in reel and real life. Women in our films, (and here I talk of commercial Hindi cinema), are most often objects or audience of male speech acts. If they must speak, not in response to male speech, their speech falls in the stereotypical categories of tantrums, histrionics or gossip. Their speech amounts to caricature that yields little consequence. Women are shown to speak in a highly sing-song manner, with enormous emotional fluctuation for added impact but dramatically reduced effect. When men speak to their company, their conversation is competitive banter[3], anecdotal, narrating their own achievements or random incidents. When women speak, especially to women, they speak to express emotion, to create personal bonds through self-revelation.[4] When men are the audience of such female speech acts, they are impatient listeners who either interrupt or dismiss these conversations as trash. When men speak, women not only listen patiently, but also reinforce male ego through admiration.

While men establish their worth on the basis of their financial, institutional or social status, women stand to be defined on the basis of their "moral" character, their ability to maintain relationships and commitment to societal norms. In this entire design, they are expected to make little or at least judicious use of language. If this design has proven to render women in a position of reduced power, then we may assume that women can, and do, become more powerful by altering their modes of speech; by accessing more assertive positions as speakers. With evolving matrices of gender systems, linguistic patterns have seen a gradual yet definite shift in our social space. This shift has found representation in some of the recent Bollywood films.

A very apt example of how language is an index and vehicle of power is Gauri Shinde's film *English Vinglish.* Shashi Godbole, the protagonist, is the regular Indian housewife, who sells home-made *laddoos.* A good wife, mother, daughter-in-law and home-maker, who enjoys being all of these and gets her share of public adoration through the *laddoos* she sells, she is the woman any Indian household recognizes. Her moment of crisis arises in her daughter's ridicule of her linguistic limitation. Her daughter's class teacher, who is only patronizingly apologetic of being Hindi-challenged, is a contrast to Godbole's feeling of utter humiliation at being only as challenged in English. She is made to become acutely aware of her handicap regarding her ability to converse in English by her daughter's repeated dismissal of her capabilities. Her own language is no more sufficient to even play out the role of a mother. All attempts at communication are silenced, either by the daughter who is growing up in a linguistic environment, not native to Shashi, or by the husband who does not have the time and patience for emotionally loaded dialogue. Thus Godbole, who likes to interact and is otherwise confident, is either silenced or goes silent. Her silence is variously employed—communication of her disagreement, relinquishing of the speech act to others or as a surrender to disapproval.

Her first step out of the four walls that define her limited identity, into a world away from the one that cramped her, takes her on a journey to America, the land of the language she must learn. The money that her *laddoos* have earned her will enroll her in an English Speaking class to salvage her self-respect from the debris of linguistic disaster. It is in this group of equally English-challenged pupils that she regains her comfort and confidence. This motley collection, most of who can't understand each other's language, develops camaraderie of the dispossessed. It is with the French class-mate Laurent, in moments of emotional, linguistically non comprehensible communication that she feels truly admired and reinforced in her being. In transcending meaning that is constricted in oral and verbal acts, do the two have some very poignant sharing and bonding.

Her most liberating moment is the one when she realizes that she has placed an order at a restaurant in a complete sentence in English. As she walks away from the coffee shop, her new-found joy translates into the spring in her gait that oozes confidence. Her act of learning this new language is not one of defiance, or of transgression of her sense of tradition. She must learn this language so that she discovers herself, the self she has forgotten to love, the self that must learn this new language in order to speak to others and to herself. If English is the language of the patriarchal colonizer, she must annex a small part of the space that defines identity and power in linguistic terms.

In her speech at her niece's the wedding, her transformation from someone, reluctant to speak to the world, if not through her husband, into a confident woman who can not only think clearly but can articulate well what she thinks, surprises everyone. Her metamorphosis comes full circle when we see her in a new light through the unbelieving yet admiring gaze of her husband, children and friends. It is now that her *laddoos* are not mere *laddoos*, and she can, without any sense of deficiency and embarrassment, ask for a Hindi newspaper on her flight back to India. She obviously does not intend to intimidate her family with the pocketful of power that she has managed to excavate. Like Prometheus who struggled to steal the light for humanity's good, the little lamp that she will light through a newfound sense of *being* will make her own life, and by default, that of those around her, a little happier.

As demonstrated in the film, the sharing of power, aka "respect", is possible despite the constraints of language as demonstrated in Godbole's social experiences in the alien land of English speakers. However, the fact that this sharing is absent within her indigenous environment, underlines the usurping of power through dispossession of self belief. The female dispossession of speech is thereby not merely a function of language. The dispossession is effected by the patriarchal abuse of power of which language becomes one of the several instruments.

If feminist discourse seeks to establish a new social order in a more equal social reality, easing linguistic gender difference may be an effort at shaping and re-shaping power structures in a way that they become less disempowering for one half of a masculine world. Society is already witnessing a silent transition in gender interactions. Linguistic boundaries between men and women, are becoming more blurred. If, it is power in question, and if language is power, then it is only natural that the new woman will speak a new lexicon.

WORKS CONSULTED

- Aries, Elizabeth. *Small Group Behavior*, 1976, 7-18.
- Eckert Penelope and Sally McConnell-Ginet. Language and Gender. New York, Cambridge University Press, 2003, 129-30.
- Kiesling, Scott Fabius. Power and the Language of Men. In Johnson and Meinhof 1997, 65-85.
- Lakoff, Robin. *Language and Woman's Place*. New York: Harper and Row, 1972.
- McConnell-Ginet, Sally; Borker, Ruth A. and Furman, Nelly (eds.) *Women and Language in Literature and Society*. New York: Praeger, 1980.

NOTES AND REFERENCES

1. Lakoff, Robin, 1972. Language in context. Language, 48:907-924. 1975. Language and Woman's Place. New York: Harper and Row.
2. According to Eckert Penelope and Sally McConnell-Ginet, in *Language and Gender* (2003), "A speech act is a move in a continuing discourse among interactants...A move can be a compliment, a complaint, an insult, a request, a command, a criticism, a question, a one-up, an exclamation, a promise".
3. Kiesling, Scott Fabius. 1997. Power and the language of men. In Johnson and Meinhof 1997, 65-85.
4. Aries, Elizabeth, 1976. Interaction patterns and themes of male, female, and mixed groups. Small Group Behavior, 7: 7-18.

Role of Cinema in Women Empowerment

32

RAMESH KUMAR RAWAT

Cinema plays an important role in women empowerment. From 1930 to 2010 various movies release on various social issues and social status of women in India. In "mother India" a woman can run a family all by herself, face all possible adversities and still continue living without giving up hope is what Mother India is all about. From sacrificing her needs for her family to shooting her own son when he is at fault, Nargis had had to take all the difficult decisions in this movie. Her strength and her morals help her make the right decision. She stands up for what is right and does the needful without a second thought. In "Lajja"Madhuri Dixit who played the role of Janki, a theatre artist who can't tolerate the double standards adopted by men, or Rekha who plays the role of a lady from a village who believes in women empowerment. Lajja brings out the fact that all our society does with regards to gender equality, is talk and preach. However, when it comes to implementation, it fails. In "Dor" Ayesha Takia portrayal of a young widow who has the zest to lead her life despite losing her partner at an early age was appreciated by all. In "Astitva" Tabu's play a role of a wife who always complied to her male chauvinist husband's demands, feeling guilty about her accidental sexual encounter with her singing teacher to making her husband realize that men are nothing but hypocrites when it comes to morals and ethics, Tabu's power packed performance captured the hearts of both the masses and critics. In "Chak De India"a team of girls bring home the Hockey World Cup, one cannot help but shout Chak De. This movie saw the women's hockey team giving the male hockey team a tough fight and then saw them accomplishing a task that was considered to be impossible by everybody (including themselves), except their coach Kabir Khan. This movie surely inspired more girls to step into the world of sports and make their mark there. In all these movies film actress play a role as a empowered wife, mother, professional, player, theatre artist and a social worker. So finally we can say cinema play an important role in women empowerment.

Keyword: Cinema, Women, Empowerment.

INTRODUCTION

In the beginning of film industry, women were not allowed or don't have interest to play roles in the theatres, plays and movies. After two three decades women's are allow and they play an positive role in movies like a mother, wife, sister, daughter, friends, professional, social worker, policemanand many more. All these role show to her in empowered form. In *Mother India, Lajja, Dor, Chak De India, Gulab Gang, AchhutKanya, Madhumati, Jai Santoshimaa, Ramayan, No one kills jaisikalal and Pratighat* movies women play an important role in form of women empowerment to words society. In these movies we can see positive image of women. Through movies film maker, producer and director create respect for women. We can see some following movies play an important role in women empowerment.

MOTHER INDIA

Mehboob Khan's *Mother India* (1957) is Hindi cinema's seminal epic about a grassroots-level Indian family whose fate forever hangs on the caprice of several obdurate forces. *Mother India* (played with incredible warmth by Nargis) is an allegory for Mother Earth who gives endlessly of herself yet demands obeisance to certain laws. Mother India metaphorically represents India as a nation in the aftermath of independence, and alludes to a strong sense of nationalism and nation-building. While some authors treat Radha as the symbol of women empowerment, others see her cast in female stereotypes. Its central character is a peasant woman. The movie materializes the idea of portraying greater patriotism, struggle, social accomplishment and advancement of woman's role in the society in through theatrical gesture.

Nargis Dutt the protagonist of *Mother India,* portrayed a role of a Mother (Radha) in both metaphor and metamorphic manner. She bears a patriotic emblem of her nation. Her righteous deeds throughout the span of movie; raising children during difficult times, disapproving of selling herself off for money and the ultimate decision of taking life of her beloved son to protect women's chastity and values, makes her an ultimate Hero, a figurine of bravado.

The character of Mother India also represents the changing role of the mother in Indian cinema and society in that the mother is not always subservient or dependent on her husband, refining the relationship to the male gender or patriarchal social structures.

Astitva

The movie revolves around a happily married wife who suddenly inherits a large fortune and her puzzled husband who questions its source.This film is about the issues like male chauvinist protagonism, extramarital affairs, and spousal abuse. It is about a woman trying to find a separate identity outside her marriage. It is the unusual story that makes this bold film a unique analysis of the marital relationship.

Manjrekar's critique of the selfish system that reduces a woman to a mere giver is quite understated. Equally impressive is Sachin Khedekar who convincingly portrays the husband who takes his wife for granted and never bothers to look into his heart. Namrata acts out her small role of a modern girl passionate about her ability to prove her excellence in her chosen field, who can understand and empathize with the pain of the older woman.

An extra-marital relationship has been witnessed umpteen times on the Indian screen before. But there have been a handful of films that have captured the relationship between man and woman with the sensitivity it deserves.

Dor

Dor is a realistic and qualitative film that deals with touching emotions like love, betrayal, friendship, forgiveness and redemption. The film deals with an extremely touching and sensitive subject of two women whose lives are inextricably entwined through circumstances. The strength of these women to overcome the harsh realities in their path forms the crux of the story. The subject matter rests solely on emotions that these women go through and like many realistic films this one is devoid of any unnecessary commercial trappings. *Dor* belongs to the social genre of films and explores situations that have a parallel to reality.

Lajja

The film narrates the story of four women who have either been tormented or exploited by men for their selfish gains. It begins from the opulent city of New York and ends at a remote village in Uttar Pradesh. Rekha plays Ramdulari, who tries to make her village women self-sufficient. This progressive woman becomes a victim of the most regressive and darkest side of humanity, in death, that is. Madhuri Dixit is Janaki, who dares to live by her own unconventional rules. Then there is Vaidehi played by Manisha Koirala, who walks out on her husband and sets out on a significant journey. It is through her agonized eyes that the film is seen. No, we are not through yet. There is Mahima Chaudhary too. She is Maithili, who is a bride-to-be. Her helpless father bows to the demands and humiliation of the groom's parents. Maithili the daughter takes it all, until the woman in her takes over.

Chak De India

'Chak De India' is not just a sports film. It is replete with myriad emotions. And the best part is that Shimit Amin tells the story very realistically, making it all the more believable. He also doesn't bring any unnecessary dramatization into the story.The movie has a number of intelligently conceived sequences. For instance, a sequence when the girl's hockey team has to prove their mettle against the men's team. The girls lose by a narrow margin, but they get an applause and salutation from male players. Or another sequence when the girls bash up a bunch of eve teasers. These sequences and the last portions of the second half—when the crucial matches are played—evoke a flood of emotions inside a viewer. Finally, this movie give a message to us, women is not less empower comparative man.

CONCLUSION

Conclude that the movie play an important role of in women empowerment. In "Mother India" the role of Radha (Nargis) in form of empowerment and portraying greater patriotism, struggle, social accomplishment and advancement of woman's role in the society. The character of Mother India also represents the changing role of the mother in Indian cinema and society in that the mother is not always subservient or dependent on her husband, refining the relationship to the male gender or patriarchal social structures. In movie of ASTITVA Mrs. AditiShrikantPandit (Tabu) fight for the existence of women in Indian society and she do it and get existence. In this movie husband learns from his wife and its show equality of man and women. In Dor movie base on two women'sstragal life and its give message to women she can survive alone in Indian society. Tthe story of Lajja movie of four women who have either been tormented or exploited by men for their selfish gains. In this movie they fight for their strong existence. In Chak De India movie number of scene are related from women empowerment like in hockey match women performance was not less man. In another scene in a hotel women not afraid from unsocial elements and fight with them and win.

References

http://www.mapsofindia.com/my-india/movies/mother-india-1957-movie-review

http://www.apunkachoice.com/titles/mot/mother-india/mid_531/reviews-editor/

http://filmkahani.com/50-decade-movie-reviews/mother-india-movie-review.html

http://sillyfunda.wordpress.com/2012/08/31/mother-india-importance-of-the-film-analysis-of-the-characters/

http://www.bollywoodmantra.com/movie-review/dor/

http://www.apunkachoice.com/titles/laj/lajja/mid_168/reviews-editor/

http://movies.fullhyderabad.com/astitva/hindi/astitva-movie-reviews-45-2.html

http://www.apunkachoice.com/dyn/movies/hindi/chak_de_india/chak_de_india-review.html

Deconstructing Tradition : A Study of Women in Satyajit Ray's Cinema

33

Gaurav Sood

The predominant concern in Satyajit Ray's cinema of 1960s and 1970s is the degraded status of Indian women in Indian society. In the 19th century new awakening amongst the Bengali women created a neo social reformation. This reformation was tried in the first part of the 19th century but the actual upliftment of women started from the second half of the century. Being surrounded with the prevalent superstitions in the society women felt that their destiny was to accept these conditions without any protest and they failed to deconstruct the social conditions of the society. The social conditions of women transformed during the second half of the 19th century and the reason was opening up in the field of education. With this women established strongly their positions strongly in the family and tried to establish their social existence by transgressing the traditional boundaries. Satyajit Ray's cinema highlights the changing circumstances of the society through his women oriented cinema. The present study determines to explore the condition of Bengali women through the cinema of Satyajit Ray. The women in the films of Satyajit Ray represent a society where they are silenced, marginalized, undermined and relegated into the social backdrops of home and society. Satyajit Ray harboured deep respect for women and portrayed them morally and emotionally stronger than men in various roles. Interestingly, Satyajit Ray does not project his male characters as negative or hollow to show his women strong and powerful. Ray structures the script to give equal democratic space to male and female in a cinematic and narrative sense.

Satyajit Ray and Rabindranath Tagore are two of the Bengali artists and intellectuals who are seriously concerned with the marginalized position of Indian women in the Indian society. They have with extraordinary clarity depicted women's secluded status in the patriarchal system. In this context social theorist Ashis Nandy claims.

Atleast from Ram Mohan Roy to Ishwar Chandra Vidya Saghar in the area of social reform, from Bankim Chandra Chatterjee through Sarat Chandra Chaterjee to Satyajit Ray in literature and art, from Vivekananda to Aurobindo in religion, womanhood as a symbol and womanliness as a subject of study have been center pieces of creative consciousness in different sectors of Bengali life. (79)

Satyajit Ray's woman-oriented triad is an adaptation from the works of Rabindranath Tagore. His films *The Postmaster* (*1961*) is adapted from the short story "The Postmaster" (*1891*), *Charulata* (*1964*) is based on Bengali novella "The Broken Nest" (*1901*) and *Ghaire-Bhaire* (*1985*) is based on the novel *Ghare-Baire* (1919). Satyajit Ray in these adaptations from the works of Tagore depicts The Indian woman as active, radical, willful and ready to participate in the revolution for her emancipation in the patriarchal society. Satyajit Ray in these films focuses on women making Indian men acknowledge their position in the society and to view her femininity as an essential part of her personal identity. *The Postmaster* (*1961*) is based on an urbanite postmaster who takes up his duties in a small Indian village. In this short film, Satyajit Ray sketches the postmaster as a confirmed representative of the insensitive, middle class Bengali Bhadralok. The postmaster Nandlal, cut-off from all his friends, family members, and the metropolitan city of Calcutta, is presented by Ray as an orphan person in the isolated village. He doesn't interact with the villagers and stays at a distance with everyone. Ratan, the illiterate twelve year old girl, is an orphan who works as a housekeeper at his place. The postmaster is a deterritorialized personality and is away from his family, place and love. Bored by the village, he decides to teach Ratan the Bengali alphabets. This teaching sequence is pivotal in the film as the patriarchal culture operates the postmaster. In spite of the sophisticated, literary education it imparts to the young men, the education system interpellates the young men to stay at a distance and isolated towards the feelings of other people, in this case, the little girl Ratan.

The scene opens with Nandlal lying on the bed and his face towards the camera, gazing at the postcard in an open book. The *mise en scene* of the scene describes his lonely existence as there is large photograph of his mother and sister hanging on the wall. However, the one person who is close to him physically is Ratan, he clearly ignores. Ray captures Ratan wearing freshly washed clothes and positions her in a way that everybody can notice her appearance. Nandlal is too engrossed in the postcard he has received from home. Throughout the sequence, Ratan makes an effort to get her noticed; she desperately wants to be a part of his family. Ray further indicates this through minute gestures and carefully articulated movement of both characters. Ratan initiates this process by pointing towards the photograph of his mother, but Nandlal offers no sign of approval. Instead he hurts the little girl by pointing his sisters' superiority over her. He further emphasizes over his sisters singing talents. Ratan finally grasps that she cannot compete with his sister; she is far too superior in her talent and beauty.

There is a significant difference between the film and the short story of Tagore. Tagore ends the story on a melodramatic note and overstates Ratan's second orphaning once the postmaster leves back for Calcutta. Ray on the other hand, avoids falling into this trap and his ending is desentimentalized and stoic. In the film, Ratan is orphaned and ill treated at an early age, especially by Nandlal's predecessor. She is already an adult by her experiences when we first meet her. This is the reason she acts out of her age, at the end of the film. Tagore's drama sentimentalizes the denouement by an excess of emotion, thereby distancing the spectators from the little girl. Satyajit Ray maintains Ratan's dignity by making her deliberately ignore the postmaster during his departing time. She does not run away from the postmaster, but remains under conspicuous gaze of the postmaster. In the film's final scene, she walks past the postmaster and haughtily ignores the money that he wants to offer her. The second film *Charulata* (*1964*) is directly adapted from Tagore's novella "The Broken Nest" (*1901*). Satyajit Ray in the film attempts to formulate a feminist perspective and also serves as a powerful study of transforming nineteenth century Bengali society. The film set in Calcutta, focuses on the historic moment when the adversarial forces, the Christian and the Hindu engage in a clumsy embrace that generate Bengali renaissance. Although the story takes place in 1879, the film looks back to 1835 when the British government introduced Westrn education into India. Since the country could not be ruled until the ruler could efficiently communicate with the subjects, schools and colleges were set up in which English was taught as a subject and used as a medium for communication.

In *Charulata* film, Ray describes the paradoxes within the divided culture built on the assimilation and borrowings of ideologies. The film concentrates on how culture as an independent, purist entity is no longer sustainable in the changing world. The old traditions and authenticities collapse and the age old principles of trust honesty and work are thrown into jeopardy. *Charulata* is deeply reflexive film and through special strategies it enforces the thematic concern with artifice and illusion. The film constantly alludes to reading and writing, newspaper, journals, novels, weaving and embroidery. Ray creates a highly complex system of correspondences with details of camera movement and set-up. In the film Charu is married to the affluent Bhadralok, Bhupati, who runs an English language newspaper, *The Sentinel.* Sensing her loneliness, he invites her brother, Umapada and his wife, Manda to live with them. He also invites Amal, who is of Charu's age and places him in charge of the education. Finiding no joy in the company of Manda, Charu turns more and more towards Amal until her feelings ripen into love. Amal quietly eggs on her but lacks the courage to reciprocate her incestuous overtures. Amal afraid of being the source of betrayal, leaves one night before informing the hosts and Charu restrains her emotions but cannot hold them back when his letter arrives. Bhupati cates her sobbing and guesses the reason. The film ends with a freeze of their hands. Satyajit Ray in the film takes the position that Bengali Renaissance was essentially a patriarchal fantasy state backed by capitalism, idealism and Anglophilia. People lacked practical wisdom and became a victim of high minded idealism. For the high minded bhadralok, the society was another space, mismanaged by their lack of experience. Bhupati, in his western clothes, represents the new liberal rhetoric but ignores his wife who remains within the *andermahal* or the inner section of the house. As a typical nineteenth century aristocratic Bengali housewife, Charu is forced to function within the traditional boundaries of the extended patriarchal structure. She is expected to supervise all the domestic works and cultivate her idle moments in the practice of feminine pastimes like playing cards, embroidery, playing the piano etc. It is a very daring act on Charu's part to signal her emancipation from the daily household routine and by boldly expressing her attraction towards her husband's younger cousin, Amal. Ray makes this explicit in the scene between Charu and Amal in the garden, overflowing with poetry, passion, recitation under the bright sunshine.

The garden space becomes pertinent where Charu for the first time articulates the feelings not only to the audiences, but also to herself. The half inch gap between the outstretched hands, on which the film ends, becomes the silence that will remain between the couple. Bhupati finally realizes to the crucial reality around him that he had abandoned and neglected in his overriding passion for journalism and politics. At one level, this ignorance acts as a defence for Charu and her husband recognizes her as a vital emotional being. Satyajit Ray ends the film different from Tagore's pessimistic conclusion. In Tagore's novella Bhupati and Charu are unable to reconcile. Satyajit Ray brings Charu at the centre and finally shows husband the way by which their broken nest can be built again. Charu achieves the reconciliation is noteworthy since she finds a viable place in the male dominated culture of nineteenth century India. The third film *Ghaire-Baire* is set against the stormy period of the freedom movement of India. The film presents the central film character Bimala as a woman confronted by the seduction of two distinct worlds that her husband Nikhil and her lover Sandip want to impose. When we first meet Bimala, she has been happily married to Nikhil for nine years. Nikhil is sensitive and highly educated Bengali zamindar. He wishes to emancipate his wife from the strictness of his aristocratic Hindu family and wants Bimala to have an English education. He also wants his wife to use utilize this knowledge and explore her identity. He endorses this idea as an expression of true love towards Bimala. History provides Ray's heroine with another emancipatory alternative through *Swadeshi* movement. Bimala feels the repercussion of *Swadeshi* not as an idea but passion. At this juncture Sandip enters into Bimala's life. She is captivated by the rhetoric and falls victim to his clever flattery. Sandip constantly makes her feel that her beauty, passion and sacrifice is required in fighting for the new cause. Ray captures the unique position of Bimala in the film. She is constantly attracted towards Sandip and this further erodes her loyalty towards her husband. From Bimala's point of view Nikihil appears to be noble but unapproachable, whereas Sandip emerges as potentially threatening and satisfies a lot of her repressed desires. At the end of the film, Bimala repents and weeps uncontrollably before her bedroom mirror. Nikhil embraces her but refuses to block her tear stained image in the mirror. He wants that image to show Bimala her fallen purity and grace, not only in his eyes but in her own. It is only that then he offers forgiveness to her. Ray in the film reinstates the privileged position of male. In the film he reduces, Bimala to a position of widow through three major dissolves. Ray's filmic presentation makes Bimala to follow Hindu tradition and strips her of her womanhood. From a rich wife of a zamindar, she is reduced to a weeping widow with a shaven hair. Bimala in the final scene is turned into an inevitable victim of a history that finally forces her to occupy a position neither at home nor in the contemporary world.

The nineteenth century Bengal, like every other age was incomplete in achieving certain goals within the idealistic domain of free woman. The male of the first half of the nineteenth century made efforts and progress for the social and educational upliftment of women. As portrayed in the films of Satyajit Ray and the real life, the movement of women's freedom in Bengal was guided and dominated by males. The women suppressed under the patriarchal home were again covertly dominated by patriarchy during these social emancipatory movements. Naturally, it was impossible to eradicate the structures of patriarchy from the roots of society. Therefore,

Satyajit Ray rescues his women by providing an authentic feeling by keeping them at the centre of action. They are solely responsible for their subjectivity and actions. Simone de Beauvoir in her text addresses women by claiming that "one is not born a woman; one becomes one" (1). Therefore Satyajit Ray provides the women protagonists a distinct, unique and a generous personality.

References

Beauvoir de Simone. *The Second Sex*. France: Vintage, 1949. Web.

Biswas, Moinak, ed. Apu and After: Re-visiting Ray's Cinema. Calcutta: Seagull Books, 2006. Print.

Cooper, Darius. *The Cinema of Satyajit Ray: Between Tradition and Modernity*. USA: Cambridge, 2000. Print.

Rajadhyaksha, Ashish. "Satyajit Ray, Ray Films and Ray Movie." *Journal of Arts and Ideas*. 23.24 (1993): 9-10. 18 April 2012. Web.

Robinson, Andrew. *The Apu Trilogy: Satyajit Ray and the Making of an Epic*. New York: I.B. Tauris, 2011. Print.

Ray, Satyajit. *Our Films, Their Films*. Bombay: Orient Longman, 1979. Print.

Computerised Coloring of Mughal-e-Azam : Bringing Back the Colors in Indian Classical Cinema

34

NISHCHAL SHARMA

"Clouds come floating into my life, no longer to carry rain or usher storm, but to add color to my sunset sky."

—Rabindranath Tagore, *Stray Birds*

Colors represent many things, from deep thoughts to endless emotions. Color represents celebrations, joy, beauty and vividness. Although cinema had a long history of colored and black and white emotions, the effect of color can't be ignored in mankind history.

Indian cinema is a mirror that reflects the very emotions of Indian culture. The rise of cinema in India was like a miracle. Led by the likes of *Dadasaheb Phalke*, the cinema in india started to spread its wings. Indian society has always adored cinema. In villages, *Naatak, Nukkad* and *puppet shows* were early forms of cinema which were absorbed by the masses.

Slowly, Indian cinema started advancing to new heights. Many cinema potentials like *Ashok Kumar, Raj Kumar, Dilip Kumar, Madhubala* and *Dev Anand* gave cinema a whole new dimension. Although cinema was still very slow in adopting technology at that time, many great Films like *Shri 420, Do Bigha*

Zameen, Payasa, Paying Guest, Mughal-e-Azam and Mother India made whole world recognize the true talents present in India.

Today's Indian cinema is far more vivid. Indian cinema has adopted every single bit of technology they can carry to reach the masses. This includes satellite technology, Internet, computerized video and sound editing, 3D modeling and animations. Use of Computers in cinema has become a great source of efficiency and power. Marketing , promotions and TV-Show hypes has reached a new height, where everything is done to insure a loud presence among the media.

Although we have adopted the technology but Indian cinema has slowly started to loose its charm in terms of originality and quality. May be this is the reason that new director has moved to a *masala formula* in Indian cinema rather than having a concrete storyline. Instead of engaging people in new story platforms, Indian cinema slowly started to use *sequels* or *remakes,* in a wasted attempt to justify its fake talent.

Computer colorisation of an old black and white movie was a very odd idea. The digital coloring of classic black-and-white films has been criticized by contemporary filmmakers and critics because it destroys the lighting and color values of those films. We have seen recreated *Don or Sholay,* but to colorize a classic film and to bring about this idea to life was a difficult job. This idea also points out the lack of true talent in indian cinema in terms of creativity. Yet this idea also shows the motivation of skilled people to bring about this impossible task.

Mughal-e-Azam was a perfect candidate for a colorized version of a film. Since it had a great storyline and was filmed on a modern hardware in late 60's. The original Film had already been a box office hit with great people like *Prithviraj Kapoor, Dilip Kumar and Madhubala*. Since a remake would have never recreated the emotions created by these great people, a colorized version was prefered.

Coloring with Computers is not easy. A major problem with this process is its labor-intensity. In order to colorize an image an artist usually starts by dividing the image into portions, and then assigns a color to each portion. This approach, also known as the segmentation method, is time consuming, as the process of dividing the picture into correct segments is cumbersome. Lack of fully automatic algorithms to identify distorted or complex region boundaries, such as between a subject's hair and face makes this process very painful. Colorization of moving images also requires tracking of moving regions in each frame (also called as motion compensation). But Under *Deepesh Salgia* as project manager, The *Sterling Investment Corporation* took the challenge of colorizing the film. The whole task of restoring negatives to digital forms, colorization and recreating the sound tracks with team of *Naushad* resurrected *Mughal-e- Azam* once again in front of indian people. The response was huge, with many theaters running over 80% occupancy, Making colored *Mughal-e-Azam* the 19th Highest grossing film of 2004 behind *Aitraaz* and *Veer-Zaara.*

Has coloring truly recreated *Mughal-e-Azam* or it just was a reflection of hard work of original *Mughal-e-Azam*? We can't really tell, but its sure that Indian society still accepts black and white cinema with love. Coloring *Mughal-e-Azam* may have not made any difference but one thing is clear that old memory of cinema is still very well celebrated in indian society.

Modern society treats black and white as unprogressive, old, backward and blunt. Many films used black and white effects to show such emotions like in *Three Idiots* to represent Raju Rastogi's Home or to represent *Bhagat Singh* and his comrades in *Rang de Basanti.* Black and white is also used to mimic fear or desperation like in *Bhag Milkha Bhag.* The Film *Black* also reflects the use of color in a negative emotion. May be this shows the reason why colored films were more popular in Indian cinema.

Color is just a perspective, other dimensions of Indian Cinema is how it attaches to masses and reflects their emotions. Bringing back the colors in Indian cinema also creates the sense of respect for classical cinema. Although looking back at the old times, we feel that there were less resources, but still Indian cinema was bright and truthful. Today, even though we have technology and skills, Indian cinema is lacking in originality and truthfulness.

References

Vijayakar, Rajiv (6 August 2010). "Celluloid Monument". *The Indian Express.* Archived from the original on 30 March 2013.

The colour of profit". *The Hindu.* 21 October 2013.

"Box Office 2004". Box Office India. Archived from the original on 14 October 2013.

Dadasaheb Phalke, the father of Indian cinema – Bâpû Vâ?ave, National Book Trust

"First Color Film Made in India". colorsofindia.com.

Colorization, Museum of Broadcast Communications

Bollywood: A Guidebook to Popular Hindi Cinema. Routledge, p. 208. ISBN 0415288533.

Burman, Jivraj (7 August 2008). "*Mughal-e-Azam*: reliving the making of an epic". *Hindustan Times*.

Indian Cinema and Women 35

POOJA MISHRA

Entertainment and cinema are synonyms with each other. Cinema clearly opens a most useful window on to a culture and by studying a culture one acquires deeper understanding of the customs, behaviour patterns, values, arts and crafts and also the practices of everyday life of the people inhabiting that culture. The world of Indian cinema is very fascinating one that has mesmerized every person on a global platform

Cinema plays a very important role in India. Indian cinema not only plays a significant role in integrating society but also imparts human values on people such as honesty, hard work, sympathy, charity, brotherhood. Almost all movies have stories in which goodness is rewarded and wickedness is punished.

Indian women have excelled in every field and have engraved their names in many parts of the universe, but there still seems to be a long route ahead before she attains equal status in the minds of Indian menin a well-defined patriarchal society like India, even the cinematic world deems to project women as in factual life. This is a good thing as films have mass appeal and at least some if not all carry out a message to the public and try to create awareness. There is a myth that women are characterized in films to prop up the male role rather than characterize them as the one who keeps the narrative structure sinuous. Women are insinuated in films as bearing the burden of sexual objectification that male roles cannot. Hence, they become the bearer, and not the maker of meaning says Laura Mulvey.

Most Indian women live a silent life with enormous amount of sacrifices and retain their frustration within themselves for the sake of societal pressure.

"When Dadasaheb Phalke, the Father of Indian Cinema, released his "Raja Harischandra" in 1913, women used to shun movies and it was left to male artists to play female characters.

Times changed by the 1930s. Devika Rani, Zubeidaa, Mehtab, Shobhana Samarth—all women from affluent families—entered the movie business and changed the face of Indian cinema by redefining the importance of women in films. They were followed by Suraiya, Meena Kumari, Madhubala and Waheeda Rehman, stars who brought about a sea change in attitudes as leading ladies.

"AchhutKanya", "Jeevan Prabhat", "Nirmala", "Alam Ara", "Zarina", "Chitralekha", "Parineeta", among others, are some of the movies with woman-centric themes of that era.

In terms of remuneration, status and roles, the leading ladies of that time were at par with their male counterparts.But are women enjoying the same status in the 21st century?"[1] Commercial Hindi cinema has had musical content from its very inception. Often enough extremely popular songs have caused otherwise mediocre movies to achieve superhit status. Mohra packed the theatres because of one of its songs: " Tu cheez badi hai mast mast" (roughly translated this means you are a very intoxicating thing.) Months before the actual release of the film this song was at the top of the various top ten or top twenty countdowns which have become an integral part of TV and radio programming in India in the '90s. Millions of Indian's saw fragments of this song every week. It is the security of this knowledge, gained before entering the theatre, which allows the audience (or at least the male component of the audience) to accept Roma's sexuality and even revel in it. Divested of all politically unsettling possibilities Roma can relax into "... [the] traditional exhibitionist role [in which] women are simultaneously looked at and displayed, with their appearances coded for strong visual and erotic impact so that they can be said to connote to-be-looked-at-ness."[2] This fragment of Laura Mulvey's analysis (from her essay "Visual Pleasure and Narrative Cinema") is not the only relevant one in the context of the two song sequences that we are discussing ("Tip Tip ..." and "Tu Cheez ..."). In both these sequences the woman serves as an erotic object for Amar Saxena on screen and the male audience in the theatre which is expected to identify with him. In "Tip Tip ..." we see Raveena Tandon in the distance as he approaches her. Her features are indistinct as she wriggles and squirms. As soon as we come within proper sight of her the camera preserves the two dimensional nature of her image by rushing in and showing us parts of her body.

"One part of a fragmented body destroys the Renaissance space, the illusion of depth demanded by the narrative, it gives flatness, the quality of a cut-out or icon rather than verisimilitude to the screen." Writing in G, an Indian film magazine, Monica Motwani states, "The heroine may have metamorphised (sic) over the years, but she still cannot break away from the shackles of certain norms set by Hindi cinema years ago."[3] On the other hand there are some who posit a major progressiveness in attitudes towards women. In an article in the Hindu Bhawna Somaya writes "In the process of performing her roles as a mother, sister, wife, daughter or girl friend, the woman of today most often, no longer forgets the importance of her most vital role... as herself."[4]

While this may be an extremely optimistic point of view as the analysis of certain aspects of Mohra here shows, the doom saying that Motwani articulates may not be warranted either.

Women in Indian cinema are born with certain assumptions ranging from cult movies to celluloid blockbusters like Sholay to more recent Fashion that employ themselves as in severe gender issues. They are portrayed either as damsels in distress or demented feminists or simple belly-shaking glam dolls whose sole ambition is to attract the attention of the male gender. In many Indian films it is a common trend to insert 'item numbers' which bear no rational connection to the film in anyways but with an assumption that the film is easily associated. As Bindu Nair (2009:53) says, 'sometimes the one song ends up making the film a hit, such as 'chamma chamma' from the film China Gate.'

Occasionally, do we see a female being the protagonist of a film than merely being objects of sexual desire. In some cases there appears to be a clash between 'modern feminism' and 'traditional values'. Indian cinema often acts like an emotional register and is very resourceful while reading the characterization of 'Women'.

Mainstream Hindi cinema, pretends to establish the autonomy of women through its narrative, but the image it depicts is far from the reality. The model of the Goddess in Indian mythology always remains present very subtly to create this image. The Mother Goddess "Durga" and her counterparts "Radha" and "Sita" are the most popular icons from the Indian (Hindu) mythology to construct the image of woman in Hindi cinema. Though the Hindu Goddesses do not necessarily serve as paradigms for present social values, they do demonstrate certain suppositions about female behaviors, powers, desires and characters.

Whatever may be the icon "Durga", "Sita" or "Radha", each and every one is also the object of sexual pleasure. The details of their physical charm and their sexual encounter depicted in the mythology prove that these power-women are there to please the sexual desire of patriarchy. Portrayals of women in Indian cinema are also constructed in this frame. The male icon could transfer itself from 'Devdas' (1955) to 'Deewar' (1973) to adjust with contemporary social and political perspective but the female characters are never spared. In 'Awara' (1951), Raj Kapoor portrays the typical urban dream-woman of the Nehru-era as a traditional motif. In the form of a beloved "Radha" and "Sita" combined, she excites and inspires at the same time. Nargis's role in 'Mother India' (1957) celebrates the traditional motif of womanhood in a different context. As the narrative expands, she metamorphoses into a strange blend of Mother Goddess "Durga". The most exploited image of womanhood in Hindi cinema is based on the mythological icon "Sita" from the great Hindu epic the "Ramayana". "Sita" is the eternal favourite to the Indian mass because of her sheer power of tolerance and acceptance of all types of humiliation from the patriarchy. "Sita", the neglected wife of "Rama" is the inspiration for building the perfect image of womanhood of Indian cinema from its very beginning.

Following are the socially accepted roles of Hindi cinema actresses which are constructed and supported by the Hindu mythology and the epics like "Ramayana" and "Mahabharata":

Love affairs of "Radha" and "Krishna" provided by the Hindu mythology have got a wide mass support. "Radha" is the illegitimate beloved of "Lord Krishna". She is passionate, intense, possessive, emotional, physical and sensuous. Their love affairs, though child-like playful on the surface level, but in depth it's the story of erotic passion. On the contrary, "Meera" the other icon in love with "Lord Krishna" is based on a real life story from the Royal family of Rajasthan, who was devoted to "Krishna" with spiritual love. "Radha-Krishna" love story has been depicted in hundreds of films, in some of which even the characters are also named as "Radha" and "Krishna". In Prakash Mehra's 'Mukaddar ka Sikandar' (1978), Rekha's unrequitted love with Amitabh Bachchan is a good example of "Meera"-image.

'Marriage' is an institution, which enforces the patriarchal values on women. Before marriage she could expose her body and seduce with sensual body language, but after marriage she is preferred to wrap herself in costly and colorful 'Sari'. The ideal wife as played by the famous actress Nutan in the films 'Gauri' (1968); 'Devi' (1970) and 'Karma' (1986) is still popular. Song in the lips of Nutan "tum hi meri mandir, tum hi meri puja, tum hi devta ho, tum hi devta ho.." is still very popular.

CONCLUSION

Although, woman in the mainstream Indian cinema has undergone so many changes in respect of dress code, body language, moral values, style in song and dance sequences, romantic scenes, but all are at in surface level only. There is no particular way of portraying the Indian woman onscreen in Indian cinema; it is very evident that their roles run parallel to the roles women get to play in the society at particular points in time. Therefore, if we compare andanalyse the journey of women in Indian cinema today, there is no doubt that the Indian woman" has come a long way not only in real life, but also in real life.

REFERENCES

Zee News (zeenews.india.com/entertainment changing-role-of-women-in-indian-cinema

Monica Motwani, The Changing Face of the Hindi Film Heroine, G. Magazine Online, 1996.

Laura Mulvey, Visual Pleasure and Narrative Cinema in Constance Penley, ed, Feminism and Film Theory, New York: Routledge, 1988.

Bhawna Somaya, The Timid and the Assertive, The Hindu Online, March 8, 1996.

Changing Dynamics of Female Character in Indian Cinema 36

Leena Vaidya

Change is an inevitable and inescapable aspect of human life. As civilization progresses it witnesses changes both evolutionary and revolutionary. The role of women, in real life as well as in reel life too, adapts and remoulds itself in response to the turning tides in the ebb and flow of human relationships. Fed by the varied waters of the streams of social interaction, cultural involvement, individual development and many more, women have continuously re-invented themselves and their roles.

In the long journey of more than 100 years, Indian cinema has come a long way and so have the women characters. The varied portrayal of women in Indian cinema has touched the lives of the audiences with their beauty, capability, strength and complexities which is the essence of a true woman.

When Dada Saheb Phalke, the father of Indian cinema, released his *Raja Harishchandra* in 1913, women used to be away from the celluloid and it was left to male actors to play the female characters. But as the wheel of time kept on spinning, the women of the time made their inevitable presence felt in the reel life as they were making it in other fields. Women like Devika Rani, Zubeida, Mehtab and Shobhna Samarth who belonged to the affluent families of the time entered this glamorous world of movies and changed the face of Indian cinema forever.

It is said that cinema is a reflection of the ethos and ideology of any society at a given point of time. It holds a mirror to the society. So, in that sense we can say that to some extent the roles of women in movies run parallel to the roles women get to play in the society at a particular point in time. We all are aware that Indian women have evolved over a period of time and thus have come a long way both in real as well as in reel life.

If we rewind the cassette of 100 years of Indian cinema, we will witness the period when women were portrayed as docile, meek, vulnerable and ideal home-makers. This was the time when certain women had dared to venture into this unconventional profession; which was actually thought to be a male forte. But nevertheless, women like Durga Khote, breaking the shackles of an orthodox Brahmin family entered the big bad world of cinema. Devika Rani with her chiseled, elegant looks was already enchanting viewers, including the Russian artist, Svetsolov Roreich. These were the times when Mary Ivans, popularly known as Fearless Nadiya came on the silver screen in movies like *Diamond Queen* and *Hunterwali;* and made her presence felt as a feminist, much before the term became familier to masses. Thus, the period of late thirties and forties can be seen as a progressive era as far as women were concerned; with the movies like *Aflatoon, Aurat, Anuradh; Chiterlekha , Mumtaz Mahal , Zeenat , Badi Ma and Gaon Ki Gori,* etc. with 40s coming to an end cinema changed from mythological and social forum to a thriving industry where women were depicted just the way they would appeal to the male audience, still having miniscule role on the celluloid and were mere objects of beauty and compassion.

1950s being the era of iconic actor Dilip Kumar, still saw women in the Kaliedoscope of roles creating a niche for themselves. Meena Kumari was introduced in *Baiju Bawra* who continued to enthrall the viewers with films like *Anarkali* and *Parineeta* and further went on to become the "tragedy queen" of Indian cinema. This decade also pushed performing arts in the world of cinema, like Indian classical dance through stars like Sandhya as she performed in V. Shantaram's *Jhanak-Jhanak Payal Baje* in 1955.

Nutan, beautifully portrayed 'Sujata' in the same film by Bimal Roy as a low caste woman and won accolades for the powerful role she undertook. Then, *Mother India* happened in

1957; which not only became the highest grosser of the decade but turned out to be an iconic film appreciated till date. Nargis portraying the role of an ideal, glorified mother appealed to million and reflected the male dominated society during that period as they appreciated women who found their fulfillment only in forfeiting their happiness for the men around whom their lives revolved.

Women shot into limelight in the 60s due to their beauty and big films that launched them. *"Mughal-e-Azam"* in 1960 had Prithviraj Kapoor and Dilip Kumar in the lead and Madhubala as "Anarkali" who ended up stealing the show with her enchanting smile and courtesan dances. In the same decade came Bimla Roy's *Bandini* with Nutan in the lead taking up an unconventional and women centric theme in which the sacrifice made by rural women for the independence of the country was depicted piognantly.

Sharmila Tagore at a young age of 16 was launched in *Kashmir Ki Kali* in 1964 and made many a tongue wag. But women were arriving on the scene and when a film required a young girl, a young girl it would be. *Do Kaliyan* in 1968 launched baby Neetu Singh barely 10 years of age as the protagonist in a double role and the film turned out to be a huge success only on the shoulders of young girl. The late sixties also witnessed bold statements by actresses such as Sharmila Tagore who had temperatures soaring with her bikini scene in *An Evening In Paris* in 1967. To add variety to women characters, the sixties also saw women in negative roles as Shashikala and Lalita Pawar portrayed the epitomes of evil mother in laws and nagging wives.

The seventies was kind of a roller-coaster ride for Indian cinema and for women characters *per se*. The majority of roles offered to women were non-challenging and show-piece roles; quite perfunctory as it involved actresses like Rekha, Parveen Babi, Hema Malini, Rakhi and many more just to run around trees, singing songs and looking pretty and attracting the hero's attention. However, if we dwell deep into seventies, we also come across films like *Hare Rama Hare Krishna* (1971) in which Zeenat Amaan played a rebel girl out of a broken home, who follows the hippy culture into drugs. It was an eye-opener seeing a young girl get into drugs and drift away.

Seeta aur Geeta (1972) catapulted Hema Malini to heavy duty stardom with her double role performance in the film. Meena Kumari of the fifties was reinvented by Kamaal Amrohi in *Pakeezah* where she played an opulent courtesan with panache. The song "Chalte-Chalte" still reminds one, of the subtle eye-movements and dances executed by the actress. *Abhimaan* in 1973 highlighted a man's ego *vis-a-vis* a successful woman. Jaya Bhaduri played the role to the hilt as a successful singer who ends up a demure person to please her man's ego. *Aandhi* in 1975 came in as a storm in connection with women-centric roles. Suchitra Sen effortlessly portrayed an ambitious politician. Although the film during that period could not be filmed in theatre due to controversy regarding the story-line as it apparently hinted slyly towards then Prime-Minister Mrs. Indira Gandhi.

The 80s no different from its predecessor decade in main-stream cinema, however, gave us an exceptionally viberant parallel cinema which made the select audiences introspect on issues pertaining to those times. Directors like Govind Nihlani , Shyam Benegal, Mahesh Bhutt and Ketan Mehta churned out art-films and ruling the rooster were female actors like Smita Patil, Shabana Azami and Deepti Naval who repeatedly outshown in films like *Bhumika, Bazar, Mandi, Mirch-Masala, Arth , Sath-Sath,* in which certain burning issues of the time were taken and brought in front of the public.

Muzaffer Ali's *Umraojaan* in 1981 and Shyam Benegals *Sardari Begum* in 1996 showcased the past era beautifully from a woman's perspective. Rekha was par excellence in her role and Kiron Kher quite convincingly played the erstwhile court singer Sardari Begum. Yash Chopra in eighties merits a mention, the way he portrayed women on screen. His quintessential chiffon clad women, be it Rakhi in *Kabhi-Kabhi*, Rekha in *Silsila* or Sridevi in *Chandani,* have left an imprint on the viewers mind.

Female roles during this era were also tailor made for "vamps" like Bindu, Helen and Aruna Irani, who with their bold dances and costumes cut through the archetype "Hindustani Nari" mould and made a special place for themselves. They were the ones who dared to smoke, drink or engage in premarital sex on serene, unlike other actresses.

The nineties and later years till date amalgamate into a plethora of variety when it comes to the dynamics of female characters in Indian cinema. In 1993, Raj Kumar Santoshi's *Damini* was released and Meenakshi Sheshadri powerfully played the role of woman who is witness to a rape and she goes all out, inspite of life threats, to bring the culprits to book and ultimately get them punished. Previously rape was a hush-hush affair about which one was never supposed to talk but this film gave a clear message of strength and conviction to bring the henious crime for punishment. Shekhar Kapur's *Bandit Queen* also came in 90s and was screened at the Cannes film festival, although it ran into troubled waters back home with the sensors where its release was delayed. Seema Biswas breathed life into Phoolan Devi's character in which complete frontal nudity was shown but not a single lurid remark or cat call was heard in the cinemas as the spellbound audience watched the horrorified, simple, village woman transform into Phoolan Devi.

Indian cinema had now come along way and commercial films were made on serious subjects involing women. Deepa Methta's *Fire* showcased lesbianism in a typical Indian society; A subject very few people would talk about. Social issues like widowhood surfaced well in films like "Water" and much recently *Dor.* The big bad world of fashion was an eyeopener in Madhur Bhandarkar's *Fashion* in which today's modern independent woman and her lonliness, which comes with abundance of money and fame is shown quite skillfully. Vidya Balan in *The Dirty Picture* boldly and proudly reminds us of Silk Smita, the South Indian siren and her roller-coaster life. Vidya Balan once again in *Kahaani* takes the entire film on her shoulders as the main lead with male characters as side tools. Similarly, Sridevi in her comeback film *English-Vinglish* plays an ordinary Indian wife who proves a point to herself. This film too was all and all a female character film with male characters scattered here and there for extra flavour.

In this long journey of Indian cinema, the social attitude towards films and film stars, has changed dramatically. Over the years, there has been a tremendous shift in the portrayal of women on screen. Women characters have evolved from 1930's meek docile, mute housewifes to brave, strong and bold characters as in films like. *Damini, Dushman , No one Killed Jessika* and *Queen* of 2014. Todays women command an equal position in the flourishing arena of Indian cinema. They do have the capabilities of running the entire show on their own. They have shown through certain remarkable films that they are not merely eye-candies or supporting characters but the main protagonist that drives the story. Inspite of all this, the majority of mainstream cinema continue to brandish an image of women which is largely decorative and secondary; it is mainly the parallel cinema, which catering to a select audience, projects women in an entirely different, more equal and more realistic light.

It is high time that mainstream cinema as well as the society that undermines the inner strength of women should acknowledge the dignity and grit of women. We do need a realistic portrayal of characters like Aliya Bhatt in *Highway* , who unlike the past idealized and glorified female characters decides to break away from the pseudo civilized society and lives life to the fullest on her own terms and conditions. Finally, I would like to put an end to my views by quoting Mahesh Bhatt:

> "In India, we can't make sweeping statements claiming that the portrayal of women in Bollywood has progressed or regressed. As director I have always made films giving the women centre stage ... the women in my films have been in charge of their own destiny. Now women can live with dignity without relying on a man for support."[1]

Note and Reference

1. D'Costa, Melissa, "International Women's Day: Bollywood and its bold women characters." *Times of India*; web. 18 August 2014.

37

Depiction of Woman in Indian Cinema : Thematic Analysis of Queen

BANINDER RAHI

To study the representation of woman in Indian cinema has always been a concern for academic fraternity. A lot of research has been done and inferences of many scholars are still pending. Women play a pre-eminent role in a family so as in a society. Attributing values, morality and dignity to a woman is as old as human existence. Our history holds an account of women reflecting the image of the society. She was considered as merely a caretaker, but now her role has been reviewed in the wake of social change. Media, especially films, portray diverse characters of women. Women remain an integral part of the central theme in Indian cinema. Audiences, all age groups, consume content delivered by directors and producers. They comprehend those messages depending upon their cognitive level. There exists probability wherein audiences misinterpret the media messages and draw their own conclusions. Films have diverse audience and young generation is vulnerable. The movie *Queen* was a success. While debunking all women empowerment theories, the movie depicted that if woman unchain herself from old cliché of marriage and discover herself she can live happily. The movie also tried to justify the assertion that you need to violate norms to gain confidence. This research paper attempts to explore such aspects through thematic analysis. Coding would help us to understand how movie equated the happiness and confidence quotients with breaking of norms and values.

Keywords: Social change, media messages, movie Queen and thematic analysis.

INTRODUCTION

Cinema is a reflection of ethos that a society believes in. Cinema has an immense potential to provide its audiences a frame of reference to interpret and analyze things they are surrounded with. No other medium enjoy this power of influence, persuasion and motivation. "Hindi cinema has been a major point of reference for Indian culture in this century. It has shaped and expressed the changing scenarios of modern India to an extent that no preceding art form could ever achieve". (Bagchi Amitabha, 1996) To study the representation of woman in Indian cinema has always been a concern for academic fraternity. Women play a preeminent role in a family so as in a society. Attributing values, morality and dignity to a woman is as old as human existence. Our history holds an account of women reflecting the image of the society. She was considered as merely a caretaker, but now her role has been reviewed in the wake of social change. Media, especially films, portray diverse characters of women. It won't be wrong to say that Woman as a 'subject' shares a long history with Indian Cinema. It started in 1957 with the movie *Mother India*. This movie showcased the problems being faced by the people, especially women, after the Independence. However, with the passage of time the issues and subjects got changed. We had many bold movies like *Corporate* (2006), *Fashion* (2008), *Dirty Picture* (2011), *English Vinglish* (2012), *Bobby Jasoos* (2014) and *Queen* (2014). However, the commercial movies are depiction of stereotypical women. "Historical and recent literature on the subject of the representation of women in Indian cinema suggest that in commercial (blockbuster) Indian films, grossing the highest at the Indian box office, the roles of actresses are stereotypical in nature". (Nandakumar, 2011) For the purpose of this research paper, the film *Queen* is taken for the study as the movie focused on breaking the triteness and clichés drafted by Indian society. The movie star cast Kangna Ranaut (as Rani), Lisa Haydon (as Vijay Lakshmi), and Rajkummar Rao (as Vijay). While debunking all women empowerment theories, the movie depicted that if woman unchain herself from old cliché of marriage and discover her inner self she can live happily. The movie also tried to justify the assertion that you need to violate norms to gain confidence. Rani is dumped just a day before her wedding by her fiancé Vijay. Devastated, she decides to flee, because staying home to lick her wounds is not an option. So, she finds herself in Paris, and the journey she embarks on makes 'Queen' the kind of coming-of-age, discovery-of-self tale that Bollywood usually doesn't touch with a bargepole. (Gupta Shubhra, 2014)

OBJECTIVES

This paper tries to understand and interpret:

1. The definition of freedom as given in the *Queen.*
2. To take a deeper look at breaking norms and values to attain happiness quotient.
3. To conduct a qualitative thematic analysis of the movie through emerging codes.

METHODOLOGY

For the purpose of this research paper, a thematic analysis of the movie is done. This is a common general approach to analyzing qualitative data that does not rely on the specialized procedures of other means of analysis. In this exploratory approach, the analyst codes (marks or indexes) sections of a text according to whether they appear to contribute to emerging themes. (Schwandt A. 2007). A deductive way of thematic analysis is used. Visual data has been qualitatively analyzed with the help of drawn codes or themes.

DATA ANALYSIS AND CODES

The way Rani (protagonist) conducts herself in different set-ups (or situation) and convictions she used. Operational definitions of the themes are defined below:

1. Stereotypical/Modern: The set-up of the film
2. Coward/Bold: The change in the protagonist
3. Physical Strength: Fighting spirit of the protagonist
4. Ethical/Unrighteous: Decision protagonist makes

STEREOTYPICAL/MODERN

The film begins with a wedding scene which turns tragic when Vijay denies tying knot with Rani, which in Indian society is considered as a taboo. A wave of shock grips the family. Rani locks herself and family fears of suicide attempt. Also, Rani uses words like *Mummyji, Daddyji, and Dadiji*. Rani's *Chota Bhai* accompany her everywhere. Her dressing sense, hairstyle and preferences typify the stereotypical nature. Then she decides to proceed to honeymoon alone. Later part of the movie shows a transition in her character. Preferences get changes. She moves around Paris without *Chota bhai*.

COWARD/BOLD

The protagonist, after facing a couple of problematic situations in Paris, decides to return to India. However, Vijay Lakshmi instills confidence in her and she stays back. Vijay Lakshmi and Rani both visit a bar and Rani first time drinks. She feels great and finds herself happy. She also remembers how Vijay used to forbid her to drink. In Amsterdam, Rani refuses to share a room with three strangers, all males. Afterward, she does become a friend to them. In the end she rejects Vijay, makes her account on Social Networking Site-Facebook-uploads photos of her one sided honeymoon.

PHYSICAL STRENGTH

Though sounds unusual, Rani fights with a robber in Paris and emerge as winner. The sources of discrimination against women are most commonly associated with their biological nature. For example, they are devalued for being more emotional than men, less rational and physically weaker…(Goldenberg and Roberts, 2013).

UNRIGHTEOUS

The Protagonist drinks (booze) and smokes. She says, "*Mera haal na Gupta Uncle jaise ho gaya hai. Gupta Uncle ko na cancer ho gaya hai.Unho ne to kabi sharab nai pi, cigarette nai pi, phir be cancer ho gaya. Isse accha toh pi lete.*" How many buyers are there for such convictions? Does our society endorse such behaviour? Research has documented that consumption of tobacco products lead to health ailments.

CONCLUSION

Is such kind of transition in a woman is acceptable in Indian society? How many of us are ready to accept a bride who smokes and consume alcohol? How many of us believe in the kind of freedom shown in the movie? 'Queen' has cinematically debunked all women empowerment theories. It says that there is no need of laws to protect women from ills of society and parents need not to provide moral lessons to girls. Rather losing virginity and boozing are steps to empowerment. Success of the movie lies in the proof of people stamp on it. Indian movie makers, more often, forget that their prospects are still immature Indians, whose society is still bound by certain societal norms. On the contrary, Western societies prove the threshold idea of 'Queen'. Their men and women divorce and re-marry anytime at the drop of a hat and marry anybody anytime.

Situating Gender in Indian Cinema 38

SANDEEP SINGH RAGHAV

Gender issue is one of the most significant component of Indian Cinema. Cinema is purely the mirror of society. It is a most commonly held notion that division of society based upon gender differences comprises the largest heterogeneous group of the society. The notion or phenomenon of gender differences arise from the social construct of the society that is inherent in its history. Most often the word gender is used as synonymous to sex. But they both have separate connotative meanings. Sex is a more scientific term that explains physical traits and sexual preferences, whereas gender describes the characteristics and role that a society or culture delineates as masculine and feminine.

Gender role therefore refers to characteristics and behaviour that different cultures attribute to the sexes. Therefore in a culture man is male sex plus masculine social role whereas woman is female sex plus feminine social role.

It is the differences in social and cultural defined role that results in the heterogeneous growth of the society. The woman of feminist section of the society remained deprived and less empowered than their man or masculine counterpart.

Cinema is one tool by which the status of woman in Indian society has been shown. The history of Indian Cinema is not much old. Dadasaheb Phalke is popularly known as the father of

Indian cinema. He produced first full length motion picture in India in 1913 named as *Raja Harishchandra.* Dadasaheb is the pioneer of Indian film industry a scholar on India's languages and culture, who brought together elements from *sanskrit* epics to produce his *Raja Harishchandra* 1913, a silent film in Marathi. The female roles in the film were played by male actors. The film marked a historic benchmark in the film industry in India. It was a commercial success and paved the way for more such films. The first talking Indian film was *Alam Ara* which was released in 1931 by A. Irani. After this there were so many talkie films that were produced in different Indian languages. The chain of films and their subject matters increases day-by-day. In independent India the film industries flourish and the theme of films based on different religious, political and social issues. The issue related to the gender gives a new strength to the films. In few films, the status of women is presented in an impressive manner.

Cinema is one better option to highlight women issues in her family as well as society. The emotions and feelings of women are easily expressed through cinema. Indian cinema has been a major point of reference for Indian culture in present century. It has shaped and expressed the changing scenarios of modern India to an extent that no preceding art form could ever achieve. Indian cinema has influenced the way in which people perceive various aspects of their own lives. The movie *Mother India* that we have discussed here clarifies the status of women in Indian Society. To some extent this movie identifies areas where "modern feminism" comes into contact with "traditional values". But before the analysis given, we summarize the plot of this film.

The artist who played a significant role in the film were Raj Kumar and Nargis. This is the story of Radha (Nargis) who marries Shamoo (Raj Kumar) and comes to his village. There she discovers that Shamoo's mother, Sunder Chachi, has pawned their family land to pay for the wedding. The village usurer, Sukhilala, takes three-fourths of their produce as interest on the loan of 500 rupees that he gave her. Every year they give most of their produce of Sukhilala but they are unable to pay off the loan because all they give to him is counted as interest. Sukhilala is able to get this deal through because Sunder Chachi is illiterate and has put her thumb imprint on a contract she cannot read. In an effort to clear an arid piece of land which they own, Radha and Shamoo try to move some big boulders. In this process one of the boulders roll on to Shamoo's arms and he has to have them amputated. He is unable to come to terms with his helpless condition and runs away leaving Radha alone. Soon after this Sunder Chachi dies. This is her sexual favours. She resists for a long time but is unable to bear the fact that her children are starving. So she goes to his place. Just as she is about to submit to him she gets a divine singal that her husband is still alive. She leaves Sukhilala's house and confronts her problems with new hope. Next we see her as an old woman and her two sons Birjoo (Sunil Dutt) and Ramoo (Rajender Kumar) as grown men. Ramoo is a responsible type but Birjoo is a ne'er-do-well who resents the fact that Sukhilala continues to take three-fourths of their produce. Birjoo's inability to control his aggression makes him a nuisance to the villagers and finally, despite Radha's pleas, he is thrown out of the village and becomes a dacoit. When Sukhilala's daughter is getting married he threatens to come and abduct her. Radha assures Sukhilala that she will protect his daughter's honor and, when Birjoo comes and tries to abduct her, Radha shoots him dead.

STATUS OF WOMEN IN THE MOVIE MOTHER INDIA

Mother India was made exactly ten years after India became independent of British rule. The socialist experiment initiated by Nehru was in its early years. In this film the director, Mehboob, tried to combine together the socialistic ideals and "traditional values". The film begins with Radha as an old woman being asked to inaugurate a new canal which has been constructed through her village. The men who preside over the function are dressed in simple and ordinary dresses and are all wearing Gandhi caps. They keep referring to her as the mother of the village and refuse to let anyone but her inaugurate the canal. This initial sequence with its plethora of contemporary images is an important device for establishing the context within which the rest of the film is to be viewed. Even before we get to know her story we are informed of one certain incontrovertible fact: Radha is a survivor, she is the woman who will usher in the new period of prosperity and development that stretches ahead.

That a woman should be identified with India is not surprising. The term "*Bharat Mata*" is a part of the Indian psyche. *Mother India* starting the way it does may makes it seem like another feel good melodrama bout invincible motherhood with its inevitably reductive reading of women. As the film proceeds with scenes of Radha and Shamoo's marriage we are put in the familiar position of indentifying the rhetoric of patriarchy. There is a song accompanying the bridal procession which proclaims that the woman's fate is to leave home. There is the scene in the bridal chamber where Radha coyly awaits her groom. As he approaches her the voice singing in the background tells us how Radha is not special in any way and her fulfillment lies in gaining the acceptance of her husband. She falls to his feet and he picks her up and admires her.

These scenes and her subsequent submissive behaviour towards her husband and her mother-in-law serve an important function in Mehboob's scheme of things. Radha is portrayed as every woman. She is a normal ideal wife and daughter-in-law. Her love for her husband is equated to divine love. She is responsible and full of common sense. Essentially the women in the audience are expected to identify fully with her and the men are invited to look at her in a non-sexual light and identify her as their own wives or mothers or neighbours. This initial process of forming a bond with the audience by making a direct connection with perceived notions of the woman in the street is an important strategy. At various points in the movie this connection is re-emphasized. An example is the scene in which Radha decides to give herself to Sukhilala in exchange for food for her starving children. She tears her *mangalsutra* and throws it to the floor. In a scene which never becomes voyeuristic, Sukhilala chases her around the room showering her with things. Finally, just as he is about to be grab her she falls to the floor and discovers her *mangalsutra* lying right there. She immediately attributes this to the goddess whose statue Sukhilala keeps in his room. She picks up her *mangalsutra* and leaves. The goddess has protected her chastity. In another direct evocation of "Indian Values" she is shown covered in mud when she goes to Sukhilala's home. The dirt covered woman Sukhilala lusts after is the point of coincidence of motherhood and wealth.

This is not the only aspect of the portrayal that may be seen as politically incorrect by feminists. Radha has three sons while Shamoo ridicules Sukhilala for having a daughter. Her sons are shown leading her by the hand even when they are very small. But even in the beginning when Radha is a submissive bride the counterpoints is playing along. Shamoo's ony parent, Sunder Chachi, is a woman who has raised her only son alone and got him married off in style. She is a strong woman who is good to her fact that she is a woman. Her illiteracy is shared by all the men in the village as well. In fact she puts up a spirited show at the village council meeting where her case comes for hearing. Sunder Chachi's independence continually offsets any negative impact that Radha's initial submissiveness causes. It is significant that Radha comes into her own only after the old woman finally passes away.

With three-fourths of the produce going to Sukhilala. Shamoo and Radha have to work hard just to make ends meet. There are numerous images of Radha and Shamoo sickle in hand, harvesting the grain. In fact, we are even shown silhouettes of the two of them, sickle in hand' with their heads tilted up looking into distance; a typically socialist image. She is alongside him always, the perfect comrade, unhindered by her gender. There is no contradiction between this role and the traditional wife's role. The effective interleaving of the shoulder-to-shoulder images with the silent housewife images makes their coexistence credible.

When Shamoo leaves her and goes away because of his inability to deal with his own inadequacy the stage is set for her to come into her own. The real break with the melodramatic is the fact that Shamoo never comes back although she never loses hope. This hope is shown to be the source of her strength as things go from bad to worse. But the strength is undoubtedly her own. She takes on to herself the responsibility for raising her children. Since her bullocks have been taken by Sukhilala, she has to pull the plow herself. The close-up of Nargis Dutt as Radha with a plow on her shoulder pulling at it with an expression of pain and concentration is an image which is burned into the mind of every Indian.

The song which accompanies this scene typifies the nullification of the seeming dichotomy between the socialist working woman and the traditional Indian woman. The lyrics are fatalistic in the extreme, *"Duniya mein aaye hain to jeena hi padega, jivan hai zehar to peena hi padega"* i.e. If we have come to this world then we have to live. If life is poison then we have to drink this poison. It goes on further to declare that in this life only *laaj* is a woman's *dharma*. Both of these words have a number of meanings but the intended meaning of *laaj* seems to be honor and that of *dharma* seems to be somewhere between duty and religion. The point being that a woman can carry these fatalistic beliefs which are part of her conditioning and use them in the service of the positive ethic of struggling against the odds.

Circumstances deteriorate till the scene in Sukhilala house which has been discussed above. Her womanhood and faith in the continuing wellbeing of her husband is renewed by means of a deus ex machina which could really have been no more than a coincidence. She can now go it alone and is shown doing so. The film now moves forward in time and shifts its emphasis slightly. This second half of the film follows the scheme of the first half. Radha is shown to be a typically doting mother who revels in the love and affection of her grown sons. Again there is a safeguard which prevents us from thinking of her as a stereotypical wet-eyed powerless dependant mother. This safeguard is the knowledge of the sacrifices she has made for them and the fact that they owe their existence to her. But the process of identification is encouraged as she goes through all the motions that would not be out of place in any of the numerous mother-glorifying films that are turned out all the time.

Her son Birjoo turns into a dacoit. She tries to protect him from the villagers who want to kill him. She runs after him and pleads with the villagers to forgive him. But when he abducts a woman from her marriage Radha takes a stand and tells him to return the girl or she will shoot him. Birjoo scoffs at this saying that she is his mother and can never do something like that. At this point she says, "I may be your mother, but I am also a woman" and she shoots him dead as he gallops away. The lyrics that Radha had sung earlier, "In life *laaj* is a woman's only *dharma*" becomes more significant now with the only becoming emphasized. Radha's act of solidarity with the girl being abducted is not because of any particular attachment with that particular girl in fact the girl is the daughter of her old enemy,

Sukhilala. It is an act of solidarity with the whole of womanhood. And in putting this above Radha's love for her son. Mehboob makes a really daring and progressive statement. The gender issues raised by this movie are wide and varied.

Beside *Mother India,* another films like *Phool Bane Angare, Sholey, Sarak, Rudaali, Lajja,* etc. touch upon many socially significant issues like disputes between mother-in-law and daughter-in-law, troubles and sorrows of newly married women, relationships of a woman with her brothers and sisters, husband, family, in-laws and co-wives. The beautiful description of the female as a sister in her own home has been presented in the few films like *Bhai-Behan, Chhoti Behan, Sacha-Jhutta, Josh,* etc. These films focus on the love and affection of a sister towards her brother and also of the affection a woman has towards her father and mother. These films touch upon the familial relationships that women considered most important. Films like *Sau Din Saas Ke, Gharana, Ghar-Ghar Ki Kahani,* describe the frequent quarrels that the daughter-in-law has with her mother-in-law. She often complains about being ill-treated by her mother-in-law. These films are the effective, description of how a newlywed was subjected to unreasonable demands imposed by her mother-in-law. She was subjected to the demands and wishes of her husband's family.

Love is, quite clearly, the most popular subject of many films such as *Ek Duje Ke Liye, Sohani Mahival, Love Story, Gadder Ek Prem Katha.* The lovers could be of any caste or section of society. These films focus more specifically on love affairs. These films show that how women are treated in different ways by their lover. Sometimes her lover loves her a lot and sometimes he uses her for his own pleasure. In the many films, it is shown the attitude and mindset of a man towards a woman who first loved her, used her for his pleasure and then left her crying and forgot all about her. The best examples of this kind of films are *Suhaag* and *Lavaris.* In some films the social evil of bride price has been picturized. It is shown that poor or sometime the drinker father or guardian of a girl used to sold her to a rich or a powerful man in the lieu of some money and the result of this sinful act is that she became a pleasure thing for the male section shown in the film or sometime she chooses death. Some films also describe the rituals of marriage and female beauty.

These films refer to the perspectives on social relations that frequently go against the grain of representations originating from dominant groups. Some films tend to express social distance: not just the distance between a woman and her husband, but also between kin groups linked through marriage and between men and women generally. Sometime the theme of film that focuses on the women issues generally-stake out an arena of cultural representation from gendered, female perspective.

The cinema actually mirrors enforced separation through migrant labor that the political economy has tied into women's lives. As we can see from the texts of particular film songs as well as women's commentaries about them, shown in pictures like *Ganga Jamuna, Ram Teri Ganga Maili,* men's expected absence is the basic theme. It can be used to indicate the lack of worldly success of men who stay at home, as a counterpoint to the joys of being together and as an index of beloved or married women's alienation within the joint family. These films can dramatize the emotional distance between men and women, where men simply do not sympathize with women's concerns. It can speak to the pain of man's preoccupation with other women. Also, it can evoke the sorrow of abiding separation through death.

The separation experienced in a fresh infatuation, the separation of misunderstanding through pride or jealousy, the separation of absence in a distant land, and also the separation caused by death shown in the films. Women are not singing just about migrant labor but rather using this reality to describe their problems dealing with relations between the genders.

An effort has been made in this presentation to explore the issues regarding the position of women in Indian Cinema. It is evident that changes may possibly have been experienced with the passage of time. The study has been done through an examination medium of different films of Indian Cinema.

References

Desai, Jigna, Beyond Bollywood, The Cultural politics of South Asian Diasporic Film, Phychology Press, 2004, ISBAN 978-0-415-96684-9.

Guljar, Govin Nihalanni, and Saibel Chatterjee, Encyclopaedia of Hindi Cinema, Encyclopaedia Britannica, New Delhi, 2003, ISBAN 8179910660.

Khanna, Amit, The Business of Hindi Films, Encyclopaedia of Hindi Cinema: Historical record the business and its future narrative forms, analysis of the medium, Encyclopaedia Britannica, India, 2003, ISBN 978-81-7991-066-5.

K. Moti Gokulsing, Wimal Dissanyake, Indian Popular Cinema: A Narrative of Cultural Change, Trentham Books Limited, 2004, ISBAN 978-1-85856-329-9.

Rajadhyaksha, Ashish, Willemen, Paul, Encyclopedia of Indian Cinema, Routledge, 1999, ISBAN 978-0-684-31351-1.

Casting Women in Stereotypical Moulds in Indian Media 39

RAVINDER CHAUHAN AND ANITA RATHOUR

How women are depicted in popular media has a deep impact on the public, both men and women.

Woman in the Indian society is a symbol of motherhood, embodiment of virtue as a wife, exhibiting qualities of service and self-restraint. She has down the ages remained a social entity and not an individual economic being. We have had successful women in the pages of our history but not many. Being a patriarchal and conservative society men have normally played a more dominant role. Women are challenging the old social structure and writing success stories in professional fields.

Gender stereotyping continues to be reinforced, thanks to the popular culture generated by Indian television, Bollywood, radio and print media. As per an advertisement of a fairness cream, a young girls, who is dark and average looking, fails to attract a good bridegroom, thus causing frustration to her father. And one fine day she finds herself fair and lovely and within 15 days she succeeds in getting handsome groom. Her father, who initially cursed his destiny, now feel proud of his daughter (because she has fetched a match). Thus, empowerment has to come to women from outside, even a fairness cream.

Similarly, in another advertisement of an eye hospital on radio a girl narrates: "So many boys rejected me because of my spectacles and then I went to an eye institute which cured me and then I was selected, and now I am happy and married." It is strange that the so-called empowered woman still continues to be selected or rejected like a commodity. It would be incorrect to presume that messages sent through the media are meaningless. In fact, they have a deep impact upon the public, both men and women. There are numerous ads which lure women into buying expensive jewellery, sarees and cosmetics. Women are thus often projected like fools who can be easily manipulated and befooled.

Our films and television serials always depict the images of women that are either too bold or too weak. Where are the ordinary looking women? Actually a majority of women are average, neither too weak nor too strong, just like their male counterparts, struggling to survive in private and public spaces. We hardly find such women in films, serial or advertisements. The popular media often depicts gender violence in extremely strong incidents such as rape, molestation or murder. But in reality, these are not the most frequent and scary crimes committed against urban middle class women. More frightening are the mundane humiliations that a woman in employment has to face while travelling, marketing, working or simply surviving silently. In fact, a persistent show of extreme forms of violence against women on television, in the name of news has rendered the viewers immune. It hardly pricks the viewers, unless one has a personal connection with the incident.

Bollywood too persistently depicts a popular culture that reinforces the conventional image of women as beautiful, submissive and ultra-feminine. The eulogising of the wedding ceremonies in some Hindi movies has played havoc with the whole project of women's empowerment. These messages have percolated down right to the bottom of social hierarchy, enhancing the desires of even the poorest of the poor to marry of their sons lavishly, especially in the north India. Despite the law against dowry, it has assumed monstrous proportions in the country. The way violence is depicted on television and films, especially against women, it titillates the audience. Over-made up women shown in television serials have more or less ruined the project of women's empowerment in India. The negative depiction of women sarpanches and panches shown as dummies, the depiction of heroines in Hindi films resembling yesteryears' vamps and the macho image of male heroes strongly reinforce gender stereotypes. But the most disturbing fact in this context is an absolute non-resistance from the civil society, especially women to such media messages.

Instead, as per media reports, young girls in many South Asian countries are starving themselves to a zero figure, many of them are getting their thighs surgically thinned down, where not only the fat but even their muscles are removed, making them handicapped for life and many of them are reported to be swallowing worms in order to lose appetite and remain thin. Why so? One major reason is that it is television/films, which is educating our young and not so young women on the definition of empowerment. Films like "Main Hoon Naa" project the image of an ideal teacher through Sushmita Sen, who more than teaching, is able to arouse the sensuality of her male students. So much premium has been attached with physical appearance and femininity, courtesy films and television that aging women struggle hard to stay young, dreading age more than death. Intensive consumerism has indeed resulted in a trivialization of gender issues, even on the part of women themselves. It has trapped not only the young women but even small kids who are seeking empowerment in consumerism.

In an advertisement by a garment store, a small girl child says: "Whatsoever I wear, people tell me that I look beautiful". Such marketing uses children ruthlessly, killing their childhood and pushing them into youth immediately after infancy. Such is the impact of the mass media that parents compete with each other to make their little daughters look sensuous and pretty. Popular culture should have worked towards a liberating, and empowering experience. But in reality it has not only been reinforcing the traditional notions of masculinity and femininity, it has seriously impaired gender empowerment by trivializing the whole issue for vested commercial interests.

However, our society is evolving. Positive indicators can be seen. There is a change in the woman's attitude supported by valid statistics. The fertility rate has declined, indicating the acceptance of family planning and late marriage norms. Today, many women are economically independent, have job satisfaction and play a decision-making role at workplace and home. Certainly, society is changing its mindset. Women are proving their worth not only in the urban areas but in rural India also. They are leading rural movements. Still a lot needs to be done in order to give them confidence to carry on their struggle further and empower them in real sense.

Education can bring a qualitative change in the life of a woman and really empower her by making her economically self-reliant and socially aware of her own dignified existence. Women must be encouraged to learn the martial art of judo and karate to defend themselves effectively against anti-social elements and "social wolves" of all hues within and outside the four walls of their houses. But, this is not, 'just a self-defence look issue.' The educated women must beyond making themselves physically strong and come together in large numbers on a single platform to wage a consistent war against the practice of dowry, helpless condition of widows, childhood marriages, domestic violence and sexual abuse at work places.

The middle-class Indian woman has come a long way from the time her role was confined to home and hearth. However, mindsets have remained caught in a time warp. She might have traversed a long distance but societal and cultural expectations are still to catch up.

They must try to fathom the game being played by the commercial cinema and TV channels with their degenerate "reality shows" that project the female body as a commodity in countless advertisements which certainly make many of our youth ethically depraved and insensitive to the problems of girls and women. Many of our urban women happen to be highly educated and they lead different women's organizations also. Still they fail to sympathize with the sufferings of their sisters belonging to the lower middle class and rural families because of their own elitist prejudices. In Delhi, Haryana, Punjab, Rajasthan and Uttar Pradesh, several women have become victims of "Honour Killing" at the hands of their own family members. We find even highly educated women helplessly tied down to tribal beliefs and prejudices. We can never become cultured and civilized without respecting the individual freedom, choice and dignity of our womenfolk.

The gender equation is in transition and here we are talking of the urban, educated, middle-class women who is professionally accomplished. There is a distinct change in motherhood from being a measure of womanhood earlier to now a matter of choice, where one can even postpone having children. The quality of parenting has changed because earlier a woman was only an emotional leader and father was the instrumental leader who was a disciplinarian. She has also become the disciplining parent and is also focusing on the child's career. The cultural expectations of the men are not undergoing corresponding changes and this has created an overload for women.

Today's mothers have to raise children being mums as well as women in their own right. Going beyond boundaries of child-rearing and homemaking, comes with a price tag of a guilt: "Am I putting my needs before the family?" These are challenging times for mother and child, whether from behind the kitchen counter or office desk she is less clear about where to draw the line. She has doubts about boundaries she has to set for children. What with such a deluge of information on the subject of "child rearing" by "experts". Breakup of traditional family structure and myriad temptations and pressures on the child of today all add up to her dismay.

Due to the "unchanged" and multiplied expectations, motherhood has become tougher for the middle class women. The dual role of balancing home and work requires her to possess additional skills viz. cooking (multi-cuisine), washing, driving, shopping, attending parent-teacher meetings, and doing bank-related tasks. She has to excel in her profession, meet social obligations, monitor her children's career and peer group. Tasks traditionally performed by the father have shifted to the mother, courtesy her ability to drive and her efficient multitasking. A large number of women are opting for one child only since they feel completely drained out in their experience of motherhood. While at work, especially when she is in a non-conventional profession, she is expected to exude professional commitment, but the moment she comes home, she is expected to take off that robe of a professional and get quietly into that of motherhood, giving out her hundred per cent to children. Incase of a lapse, viz. academic failure or erratic behaviour or ill health of the child, she has to bear severe criticism. Can society, which constantly celebrates human rights and freedom, be more kind towards women?

Persistence of patriarchy manifested through the continued violation of women's human rights notwithstanding, the state interventions along with the emergence of women's movement at the grassroots have placed the contemporary Indian woman in an extremely advantageous position as compared to her mother and grandmother, irrespective of religion, caste and region. While the Constitution granted her equal rights with men in arenas of employment, education, freedom of speech, personal liberty and so on, later constitutional amendments have further consolidated her human rights. While issues of imperfect and half-hearted implementation, along with politicization of gender issues in a populist democracy have frequently been highlighted in various discourses, the fact remains that women in this country have already made their visibility felt in local, regional and national political bodies, sports, bureaucracy, academics, art and literature, science and technology, defence services, corporate sector and so on. But the question is: can the state alone empower women?

The state and the laws alone cannot empower women. Gender quality and justice will remain a mirage till women learn to stand up for themselves, even struggle more than their male counterparts and endeavour to break the glass ceiling.

To conclude, although the country has done a good job, its role in gender equality must not be overestimated. Since it is the women who are to catch up with men in societies that are not used to such equations, be it at home or workplace, in Europe or in Asia, it is the women who shall have to struggle more. Yes, they will have to exert much more than men in the same positions in order to sustain whatever they have achieved. It is women who shall have to break through the glass ceiling and reach the spaces where decisions are made.

I do not believe that once women reach there automatically gender equality shall be achieved. Women in decision making position shall have to remember lakhs of other women who have not yet tasted empowerment either economic or political or individual. It is painful to see women members of Sexual Harassment committees on the universities ridicule women victims of sexual harassment and siding with men, for small political benefits. If women are not prepared to stand for themselves, no one else would, neither the state, nor men, nor the civil society. While there are a handful of successful women enjoying freedom at par with men, there is a huge majority who have not yet even learnt to dream of possessing such freedom either at home or outside. It is only as a pressure group and in sisterhood that the state and society will be forced to sit up and look at them seriously.

References

Altekar, A.S., 1966, The Position of Women in Hindu Civilization, Motilal Banarasidas, Delhi.

Basu, Aparna, 1984, Gujarat Women's Response to Gandhi, *Sama Shaki*, Vol. 1, No. 2.

Connell, James, 1966, She Who Rides a Peacock, Indian Students and Social Change, Asian Publishing House, Bombay.

Darwin, E., 1797, A Plan for the Conduct of Female Education in Boarding School. Derby Dreway.

Desai, Neera, 1977, Women in Modern India, Vora and Co. Publisher Private Ltd., Bombay.

D' Souza, A., 1975, Women in Contemporary India, Manohar, Delhi.

Dube, S.C., 1963, "Men's and Women's Role in India: A Sociological Review", Women in New Asia, (ed.), Barbara E. Ward, UNESCO.

Dube, S.C., 1976, Modernisation and Education, in Tradition and Modernisation, (ed.) S.K. Srivastava Indian International Publications, Allahabad (India).

Foster, George, M., 1963, Traditional Cultures and the Impact of Technological Change, Harper and Row, New York.

Hate, C.A., 1969, Changing Status of Indian Women in Post-Independent India, Allied Publishers Pvt. Ltd., Bombay.

Horowitz, Irving, 1966, Three Worlds of Development, Oxford Press, New York.

Indra, M.A., 1955, The Status of Women in Ancient India, Oriental Publishers, Benaras.

Kapur, Promila, 1974, The Changing Status of the Working Women in India, Vikas Publishing House Pvt. Ltd., Delhi.

Kaur, Inderjeet, 1983, Status of Hindu Women in India, Chugh Publication, Delhi.

Learner, Danial, 1966, The Passing of Traditional Society: Modernising the Middle East, The Free Press, New York.

More, W.E., 1963, Social Change, Prentice-Hall Inc., Englewood Cliffs.

Pannikar, K.M., 1955, Hindu Society at Cross Roads, Asia Publishing House, Bombay.

Contribution of Female Singers in Indian Cinema

40

Arati Mishra

India is the largest film-producing country in the world; pro-ducing over 900 films annually. Indian cinema, thus, are gaining popularity like never before. Bollywood is the nerve of Hindi Film Industry and Actors here have god like status in the eyes of the people. For example (Rajnikant in South and Amitabh Bachchan in Hindi Film).

Even before the Film is released is songs are splashed across all the music channels so as to enthrall the audience and get their attention to the up coming Movie. Often movies are dependent on their musical score for its box office successes. Hence, Playback singers are as significant to the Movie as the Actors themselves.

Today's women are handling production direction, choreography, and of course play back singing which goes way back to 40 and 50 era. "The first female singer in Hindi Cinema was Rajkumari Dubey. She started her singing career in 1940's and became famous with her songs with Mukesh in movie Bawre Nain and song from Pakeeza Najriya ki mari mari more saiyan. Female singers were very rare in that Era."

Coming back to our female playback singers with 40-50's era came Nurjahan with a number like *lari lappa,* Suraiya with a song *tu mera chand mai teri chandani,* Shamsaad Begum with *Leke pahela pahela pyar* and *kajra muhobbat wala ankhiyone me aise dala.*

How can we forget those sweet, evergreen and unforgetable melodious songs. Geeta Dutt too joined the bandwagon with her songs like *Waqt ne kiya kaya haseen situm* and *mera sundar sapna tut gaya, babuji dheere chalna,* etc.

How can we ever forget Lata Mangeshkar who started her career copying Shamshaad Begum with a song like *Hawa me udta jaye mera laal dupatta malmalka ho ji ho ji*. She is called and awarded Nitingale of India in singing even today in her 80's. Sister Asha joined playback singing copying Geeta Dutt with the song like Bhanwara Bada Nadan hai. Where will our heroines like Helen and Bindu, Padma Khanna, Aruna Irani be without Ashaji? It is hard to say which made them more popular her singing or their dancing.

Then came singers like Suman Kalyanpur, Kamal Barot, Meena Mangeshkar and others. There contribution was not much though. The Lata-Asha duo ruled over Hindi Cinema playback singing for years to come.

Then with late 70's came whole new group of singers like Alka Yagnik with hits *mere angne me, Ek do teen char panch,* Sadhna Sargam with hits like *pahela nasha, saat smundar parse tere* and *chupke se* . Anuradha Paudwal with hits like *Nazar ke samne zigar ke pass. dhak dhak karne laga* and her devotional songs, Kavita Krishnamurty with song like *hawa hawai hawa hawai, pyar huva chupkese ye kya huva chupkese* and many other melodius songs.

But today we have all the shows like, Sa Re Ga Ma Pa, Amul Voice, Fame Gurukul, Indian Idiol, Voice of India, Recently India's Raw Star and so many others which encourages girls from early age to start training for playback singing. Many parents dream and be proud of their daughters if they ever became successful. Singing has become a profession for women and talent is being searched and recognized. Parents are proud unlike old times when it was considered that women are to stay home and take care of house and kids.

Joined them in 90's and at the turn of new century are Sunidhi Chahuan with song *Mast mai Mast, Bhage re man, Shreya Ghosal* with hits like *Bairy piya bada bedardi, Jaadu hai nasha hai* and today we have so many new female playback singers joining us.

Every Hindi movie has, on average six to ten songs sung by versatile male or female singers. The lyrics of these songs are written by well-established poets and lyricists. Famous music directors prepare tunes and background music of these songs.

These songs become very popular among people. They like to listen to these songs again and again on radio, TV, CD player, etc. Millions of cassettes/CDs are sold every month. Cinema, thus, is rendering a great service to the cause of music. India has a great tradition of classical, folk and general music. All these types of music are promoted by films. Cinema, therefore, serves our tradition of music.

FEMALE PLAYBACK SINGERS

India is a country of religions, different regions with different languages so are the interests of people. Although every audience has its popular singers but most Indian female singers are versatile enough to match expectation of their audience nationally and internationally right from writing, composing, singing and performing.

A number of talented Indian female playback singers, who have sung in various national or international languages;

Name	*Languages*
Alisha Chinai	Hindi, Telugu, Kannada
Alka Yagnik	Hindi, Bengali, Punjabi, Malayalam, Tamil, Oriya, Gujarati, Nepali, Assamese, Marathi, Telugu, Kannada, Urdu, Bhojpuri, English
Anuradha Sriram	Hindi, Telugu, Tamil, Kannada, Malayalam
Anushka Manchanda	Hindi, Telugu, Tamil
Aarti Mukherji	Benagli, Hindi etc.
Asha Bhosle	Telugu, Hindi, Marathi, Assamese, Bengali, Gujarati, Punjabi, Tamil, English, Russian, Czech, Nepali, Malay, Malayalam, Konkani, Oriya and other languages
Banumathi	Telugu, Tamil, Hindi, Kannada
Bhavatharini	Tamil, Telugu, Hindi, Kannada
B.R. Chaya	Kannada
Bela Shende	Marathi, Hindi, Tamil and Urdu

Name	*Languages*
Bombay Jayashri	Tamil, Telugu, Hindi, Kannada
Chaitra H.G.	Kannada, Telugu, Tamil, Malayalam, Bengali, Konkani, English
Chinmayi	Telugu, Tamil, Hindi
Chitra Singh	Hindustani, Bengali
Falguni Pathak	Hindustani, Gujarati
Geeta Dutt	Hindi, Bengali
Harshdeep Kaur	Hindi, Punjabi, English
Hard Kaur	Hindi
Hema Sardesai	Hindi
Hemlata	Bengali, Bhojpuri, Punjabi, Haryanvi, Rajasthani, Marwari, Brij Bhasha, Gujarati, Marathi, Sindhi, Oriya, Assamese, Tamil, Telugu, Malayalam, Kannada, Konkani, Dogri, Multani, Saraiki, Garhwali, Bundeli, Nepali, Arabi, Farsi, Urdu, Sanskrit, Prakrit, English, French, Mauritius, African, Italian, Zulu, Dutch, Hindi
Ila Arun	Hindi, Tamil, Telugu
Jaspinder Narula	Hindi, Punjabi
Kavita Krishnamurthy	Hindi, Punjabi, Telugu, Tamil, Malayalam, Kannada, Oriya, Nepali, Gujarati
K. S. Chithra	Malayalam, Telugu, Tamil, Kannada, Oriya, Hindi, Bengali, English, Russian, German, Arabic, Tulu, Sinhalese, Assamese, Punjabi, Nepali
Lata Mangeshkar	Hindi, Marathi, Assamese, Bengali, Oriya, Malayalam, Telugu, Tamil, Kannada, Gujarati, Punjabi, Assamese, Konkani, Urdu, Sanskrit, Rajsthani, Bhojpuri, English, Nepali
Madhushree	Hindi, Tamil, Telugu, Kannada, Bengali
Mahalaxmi Iyer	Hindi, Telugu, Tamil, English, Assamese, French, Marathi and other languages
Malgudi Subha	Telugu, Tamil, Kannada, Malayalam, Hindi

Name	*Languages*
Mamta Sharma	Hindi
Minmini	Malayalam, Tamil, Hindi
Monali Thakur	Hindi, Tamil, Bengali
Mubarak Begum	Hindi, Urdu
Nandita Das	Kannada, Oriya, Hindi
Neha Kakkar	Hindi, Marathi, Telugu, Kannada
Nihira Joshi	Hindi, Marathi
Nithyasree Mahadevan	Telugu, Tamil, Kannada, Hindi, Sinhalese, Punjabi, Bengali, Urdu, Marathi
Noor Jehan	Hindi, Urdu, Punjabi, Sindhi
P. Susheela	Telugu, Tamil, Malayalam, Kannada, Hindi, Bengali, Oriya, Marathi, Sinhalese, Tulu, Sanskrit
Palak Muchhal	Hindi and other 16 Indian languages
Shalini Singh	Tamil, Telugu, Kannada, Hindi
Priya Himesh	Tamil, Telugu, Kannada
Priyadarshini	Kannada, Telugu, Tamil, Malayalam, Hindi, Sanskrit
Rajkumari	Hindi, Gujarati, Punjabi
Reena Bhardwaj	Tamil, Telugu, Hindi
Rekha Bhardwaj	Hindi
Richa Sharma	Hindi
Ruma Guha Thakurta	Bengali, Hindi
S. Janaki	Kannada, Telugu, Tamil, Malayalam, Kannada, Hindi, Oriya, Tulu, Saurashtra, English, Japanese, Baduga, German, Simhala, Bengali, Sanskrit, others
S.P. Sailaja	Telugu, Tamil, Kannada, Malayalam
Sadhana Sargam	Hindi, Marathi, Telugu, Tamil, Kannada, Malyalam, Gujrathi, Sanskrit, Punjabi, Bhojpuri, Ahirani, Assamassi, Kumaowni, Sindhi, Marwadi, Dogri, Bodo, Kashmiri, Manipuri, Sandhali, English, Oriya, Tulu, Konkani, Gharwali, Maithili, Bengali, Punjabi, Oriya, Urdu, Nepali
Sandhya Mukherjee	Bengali, Hindi, Urdu, etc.

Name	*Languages*
Sanjivani (Sanjeevani Bhelande)	Hindi, Marathi, Nepali, Gujarati, Telugu, Bengali, English
Shamshad Begum	Hindi, Urdu, Panjabi
Sapna Mukherjee	Hindi
Shalmali Kholgade	Hindi, Marathi, Tamil, Telugu, Bengali
Shamshad Begum	Hindi, Urdu, Panjabi
Sharda Rajan Iyengar	Hindi, Telugu, Marathi, Gujarathi
Shilpa Rao	Hindi, Tamil
Sharda Sinha	Hindi, Bhojpuri, Maithili, Angika
Shreya Ghoshal	Hindi, Angika, Bengali, Marathi, Telugu, Tamil, Malayalam, Kannada, Urdu, Oriya, Punjabi, Bhojpuri, Assamese, Nepali, Gujarati, Konkani
Shruti Pathak	Hindi, Urdu
Shubha Mudgal	Hindi, Tamil
Shweta Pandit	Hindi
Sona Mohapatra	Hindi, Oriya
Sonu Kakkar	Hindi, Punjabi, Kannada, Tamil, Telugu,
Sowmya Raoh	Kannada, Tamil, Telugu, Hindi
Sudha Malhotra	Hindi
Sujatha	Malayalam, Hindi, Telugu, Tamil, Kannada
Sulakshana Pandit	Hindi
Suman Kalyanpur	Hindi, Marathi, Assamese, Gujarati, Kannada, Bhojpuri, Rajasthani, Bengali, Oriya, Punjabi, Urdu
Sushma Shrestha	Hindi, Nepali, Marathi
Sunitha Sarathy	Tamil, Telugu, Hindi
Sunidhi Chauhan	Hindi, Telugu, Tamil, Kannada, Urdu, Punjabi, Marathi, Bengali, Oriya
Suraiya	Hindi, Urdu
Suvi Suresh	Tamil, Hindi, Kannada
Suzanne D"Mello	Tamil, Telugu, Hindi
Swarnalatha	Telugu, Tamil, Malayalam, Kannada, Hindi, Urdu, Punjabi, Badaga, Bengali, Oriya, Nepali, Marathi
Tanvi Shah	Tamil, Telugu, Hindi
Tulsi Kumar	Hindi

Name	Languages
Usha Khanna	Hindi, Urdu, Oriya
Usha Mangeshkar	Marathi, Hindi, Assamese, Gujarati, Bengali, Nepali, Oriya
Usha Uthup	Hindi, Telugu, Tamil, Assamese, Marathi, Bengali, Gujarati, Punjabi, English, Russian, Czech, Nepali, Malay, Malayalam, Kannada, Oriya
Vaishali Samant	Marathi, Hindi
Vani Jairam	Hindustani, Marathi, Gujarati, Bhojpuri, Hariyanvi, Oriya, Bengali, Telugu, Tamil, Malayalam, Kannada

Role of Cinema in Nation-Building

41

Pankaj Dodh and Himani Thakur

INTRODUCTION

A nation refers to a geographically intertwined arrangement which has a common culture, history, race, ethnicity and national symbol. In the sense a nation comes to existence when an association of the people unites in a specific geographical region to preserve, nurture and spread some generally acceptable shared values, preferences and identities. If we gaze back in the history of human associationship the primitive organisation that exists in Greece, Athens and Sparta were known as ancient city state.

The Roman, Ottoman Empire and at latter the European imperialism tried to demonstrate their respective racial hegemony over relatively fragmented and weak nationalities in various parts of the world. However, the treaty of Westphalia, (1648) was a landmark in the growth and development of the nation-state system in Europe and subsequently in other parts of the worlds.

Various factors, such as political ideas of Machiavelli, Jean Bodin, Thomas Hobbes, Hegel, etc., spread of mass communication technology and democratization of modern political culture have contributed to the emergence of powerful nationalities in to a more united and coherent nations in various parts of the world in the nineteenth and twentieth century world affairs. Present chapter seeks to highlight the importance of cinema in nation building in India.

NATION AND NATION-BUILDING

A nation refers to a large body of people united by common descent, history, culture, or language, inhabiting a particular state or territory. It is therefore clear that the feeling of commonality is at the root to form a nation. Now to focus on the more substantive issue, the nation-building. Nation building is a continuous and complex process in which various elements plays a dominant role in the national building process. After the formation of a nation, the first important need to consolidate and nurture the foundations of a nation is the formation of a political organisation called state. In deed the major task of nation building is done by the state. Cinema as a tool of mass communication has played a significant role in nation-building. With its wide reach, cinema is among the most effective portrayers of the evolution of nation and the transformation of its society. The maturing of a nation-state into a national society is reflected through the cinema and just like the other tools of socio-cultural dissemination including the media and theatre, cinema can also manifest the strategic thinking of a nation (A. Vinod Kumar, 2013).

ROLE OF CINEMA IN NATION-BUILDING IN INDIA

Cinema as a new medium of entertainment started in the early 20th century. This was the time when Indian national movement was in its climax so it was quite natural and equally needful that cinema and nationalism had to join hands for mutual benefits and national reconstruction (Shyam Bengal). Cinema is one of the important ingredients of nation-building in India. India is a country of magnificent diversities and heterogeneity. There have been a wide range of diversities based on caste, class, language, religion and region which sometimes have seriously threatened the unity and integrity of the nation.

Cinema has played a vital role in nation-building through instilling the feeling of nationalism by producing movies like: Swadesh (2004), Lagaan (2001), Bombay (1995), Rang De Basanti (2006), Chakde India (2007), Hinustani, (1996), the Legend of Bhagat Singh (2002), Border (1997) etc. have played a dominant role in exhorting the people of various faiths and convictions to unite for the cause of national-building.

In the Nehruvian era the Indian movies made substantial contributions in shaping the national culture and raising nationalistic passion especially during the years of conflict with China and Pakistan. A few movies like *Haqeeqat, Prem Pujari* and *Hum Dono* have used war and conflict, or trans-border relations as the central plot and thus provoked the nationalistic fervor among the masses. The movies in the post-1990s notably, *Border, LoC* and Superlative productions like *Tango Charlie, Terrorist, Kannathil Mutthamital* and*A Wednesday* have also touched upon the theme of nationalism (A. Vinod Kumar, 2013).

One important dimension of cinema as an important factor of national building is the economic contribution of it to the nation. The Indian film and television industry has to play an important role in nation- building. In calendar year 2008, the combined revenues of the Indian film and television industry were over Rs. 35,000 crores (USD 7.7 billion) which approximately constitutes 0.532% of the Gross Domestic Product ("GDP") of India (Motion Picture Distributors Association, 2010). In the sense, cinema plays a vital role in consolidating the economy of the nation. Cinema and television provide employment to a large numbers of people in the society. The growing unrest among the unemployed youth is a serious problem and is a threat to the nation-building in India. Cinema and television could help to solve this problem in a considerable measure.

Similarly, could better help to solve many evils that are continue to pull the nation backward even today. The problem of untouchability, racial discrimination, communalism and crimes against women are some of the challenges before the nation building today. Movies and television episode can be a major catalyst in the respect. For instance, the movie, Black Friday, (2004) highlighted the need to fight against religious fundamentalism which is one of the most serious challenge to the national security today.

A large number of movies have sent a strong message of communal harmony and religious tolerance among various religious groups in the country. Several movies in the pre-independence and post independence era presented a great harmony in both Hindu and Muslim social practices. 'Hindu family social' formed the twin of 'Muslim family social'. Hindu and Muslim as brothers became a dominant motif in several Hindi movies in India. Movies like 'Hamrahi' (1944) and 'Parosi' (1946) have presented a vivid picture of social harmony between Hindu- Muslim communities. Similarly many well known artists, such as Manto, Ali Sardar Jaffri, Kaifi Azami, Abbas and many others portrayed and projected a secular outlook of Hindi cinema.

Similarly, in the late 1950s many movies written by the progressive writers had focused on the need of communal harmony between the two dominant communities in India. For instance, in 'Dhool Ka Phool' (1959) an elderly Muslim adopts an abandoned child whose religious antecedents and not known. He sings a song, "you would not be either a Muslim or a Hindu, you are a son of a man and shall be a human" (Tu Hindu Bane ga, na Musalman Banega; Insan Ki Aulad Hai, Insan Bane ga) (Shyam Bengal) as we all know, religious fundamentalism and communalism are the most serious threat to unity and integrity of the nation. Hindi cinema could play a leading role in creating an ambiance of religious tolerance and harmony among various religious groups in India.

More importantly, cinema could play a dominant role in social reform and the modernization of the nation. In spite of increased percentage of education a large number of people are still lost in alien faith and traditional obscurantism which is a serious challenge to the modernization of the nation. Cinema could play a dominant role in making a strong public opinion against harmful social practices in the country.

Many Hindi movies have highlighted the issue of economic reforms in India. These movies have brought out the exploitative nature of traditional economic practices in various parts of the country. The movies like Mother India, Kissan, Peepli Life have focused on the measurable conditions of the poor people. Such movies have given a strong message to the policy makers, social reformers and civil society organizations to work towards a society based upon more just, fair and equitable distribution of earth's resources. Many movies based on the problem of peasant, farmer and workers movement in India have inspired the policy makers in India to initiate land reform in various parts of the nation.

Hindi cinema has also contributed toward inspiring the citizen to have a strong feeling of patriotism and sacrifice toward the nation. Bollywood has shown its sense of patriotism very often. It has made several films based on India's independence, its struggle, freedom fighters like "Anand Math" (1952), which included the song "Vande Mataram" and most of the legend actor Manoj Kumar's films (Sushmita Sen, 2014). For instance, Ramesh Sehgal directed movie, "Shaheed" (1948) was based on the freedom movement and struggle of the nation. In addition, the movies like, Purab Aur Paschim (1970), Kranti (1981), Krantiveer (1994), The Legend of Bhagat Singh (2002), Rang De Basanti (2006), A Wednesday! (2008) have deeply exhorted the minds and hearts of the Indian youth to work toward the unity, integrity and development of the nation.

CONCLUSION

On the basis of above explanation, it is clear that cinema has played an important role in the shaping up of national identities and ethos in the both pre-independence and post-independence era. A large number of movies have contributed towards instilling the urge of national unity within the framework of unity in diversity. Cinema has immensely contributed towards secularization of Indian culture and thus enabled us to live in harmony with diverse faiths in the countries. Cinema has played a dominant role in mobilizing the common masses to stood against all social evils such as, dowry, child labor, untouchability, caste-class based exploitation and crimes against women.

Cinema has also contributed towards economic growth, political socialization and socio-cultural modernization in the country. However, cinema has some negative dimensions also. Excessive violence, communal motif and too much commercialization, and hollowness have added to a lot of negativity and deconstruction in Indian society and public domain. It is therefore important to carefully filter the ideas, values and identities that cinema inculcates among the people and society at large.

References

A. Vinod Kumar (2013) "Cinema and Strategic Culture", Online Web: http://www.idsa.in/idsacomments/CinemaandStrategicCulture_VinodKumar_120213.html, Accessed on 15 March, 2015.

Motion Picture Distributors Association (2010), Online Web: http://www.tisf.org.tw/newsletter/2010/India_film__TV.pdf Accessed on 14 March, 2015.

Shyam Bengal "Secularism in Indian Cinema" Online Web: http://www.jnu.ac.in/SSS/Archive/P.C.JOSHI%20Lectures/Shyam%20Bengal.pdf, Accessed on 15 March, 2015.

Sushmita Sen (2014), " Independence Day Special: 10 Best Patriotic Films—'Mother India', 'Rang De Basanti', 'Border' and Others", Online Web: http://www.ibtimes.co.in/independence-day-special-10-best-patriotic-films-mother-india-rang-de-basanti-border-606841, Accessed on 15 March, 2015.

Index